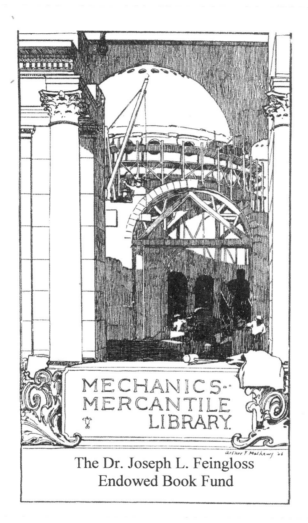

America Abroad

America Abroad

The United States' Global Role in the 21st Century

STEPHEN G. BROOKS

WILLIAM C. WOHLFORTH

OXFORD
UNIVERSITY PRESS

Oxford University Press is a department of the University of Oxford. It furthers
the University's objective of excellence in research, scholarship, and education
by publishing worldwide. Oxford is a registered trade mark of Oxford University
Press in the UK and certain other countries.

Published in the United States of America by Oxford University Press
198 Madison Avenue, New York, NY 10016, United States of America.

© Oxford University Press 2016

CIP data is on file at the Library of Congress
ISBN 978–0–19–046425–7

1 3 5 7 9 8 6 4 2
Printed by Sheridan Books, Inc., United States of America

To Avery Brooks, Charlie Wohlforth, and Owen Wohlforth.

Contents

Preface

WHEN WE FINISHED our last book on America's role in the world in 2007, we hardly thought we would write another on the same general subject. In *World Out of Balance* we probed the main scholarly traditions in international relations for insights about how the world works when one state dramatically outweighs all others on the scales of power. But almost as soon as it hit the shelves, its underlying premise, that the United States would long occupy a singular position at the top of the international system—until then almost universally taken for granted—came under strong challenge. In his 2002 *Financial Times* article, historian Paul Kennedy—by far the world's most widely read expert on the rise and fall of great powers—stated flatly, "Nothing has ever existed like this disparity of power; nothing." By 2010 he was reasserting for readers of the *New Republic* his more familiar theme, that the United States, overburdened and confronting fast rising rivals, was "naturally losing its abnormal status in the international system and returning to being one of the most prominent players in the small club of great powers."

Had the world really shifted so fast as to warrant this new focus on a coming "post-American" world? To answer that question, we would need to do something we had not done in our previous book: carefully measure how the distribution of power was changing and do so in a way that was sensitive to the changing nature of power in the 21st century. The distribution of capabilities among states is a moving target—it never stands still—and the first part of this book represents a years-long effort on our part to comprehend the changes afoot and project their likely trajectory. Our answer is revealed in chapters 2 and 3, which show that, although the world is changing, America's role within it is not shifting nearly as much or as quickly as is commonly believed.

It was not just perceptions of power that shifted quickly. The scholarly conventional wisdom about what the United States should do with its power also underwent a sea change. What had been a handful of scholars calling for America to pull back from its overseas commitments in the early 2000s became a cacophonous crowd by the decade's end. This newfound popularity of a grand strategic approach that is alternatively called offshore balancing, retrenchment, disengagement, or restraint tracked shifts in US public opinion toward increasing weariness with America taking on a leadership role globally.

Had the benefits of America's long-standing effort to shape the global environment really declined so dramatically that it no longer made sense? We did not have an answer to this question. In our previous research we thought it best to concentrate on evaluating the strategic setting the United States faced; we did not ignore arguments about grand strategic choices, but they were limited to short concluding sections of the type academics write to draw out various policy implications of their work. In a 2002 article in *Foreign Affairs* that was mainly about the United States' unprecedented power primacy, we wrote a section at the end enjoining Washington to be multilateral and magnanimous and, above all, to avoid the temptation to overuse its awesome capabilities. In *World Out of Balance*, we devoted just a few pages in our concluding chapter to the idea that the United States could and should use its outsized position of influence to reform and revitalize key international institutions and rules.

To address the question of grand strategic choice in a systematic way—that is, to try to get to the normative choice of what to do on the basis of positive inquiry about how the world works—would demand intense research on a complex counterfactual question: What would the world be like if the United States retrenched? The result is the analysis that appears in chapters 4–10 of this book. No certain answer is possible, but if you wait for certainty you can never make a choice. After years of study we satisfied ourselves that the best available knowledge supports a choice to sustain the basic "deep engagement" grand strategy. Were we in charge of US foreign policy, that's what we'd do. We would, however, implement deep engagement in a more restrained manner than has often been adopted—one which focuses on achieving a small set of core objectives. What those key objectives are, why pursuing them is valuable, and why expanding beyond them is counterproductive is explained herein.

Acknowledgments

OUR EXPERIENCE WRITING this book gives the lie to the claim that location no longer matters in a globalized world. The fact that Dartmouth College is home to a large group of international relations scholars whose research intersects with US foreign policy in various ways made a huge difference. Jeff Friedman, Mike Mastanduno, and Brian Greenhill all offered invaluable feedback to us over the years as we worked on this book. In addition, we were particularly fortunate that some of the most intellectually forceful and persuasive critics of deep engagement anywhere are based at Dartmouth. From the very beginning to almost the last day we worked on this book, their generous "deep engagement" with our project made it much stronger. Over the years we got to debate Daryl Press—a very early, prolific, and forceful proponent of pulling back—in the hallway, by the watercooler in the faculty lounge, and even before a crowd of students and community members at Dartmouth's Dickey Center for International Understanding. It's hard to count the number of ways in which those interactions shaped our research. Ben Valentino not only engaged with us on sharpening our arguments but also invited Wohlforth to participate in an initiative supported by the Tobin Project on reevaluating US security commitments. And when it came to assessing the benefits and especially the potential risks and downsides of America's Asian alliances, Jennifer Lind was generous with her wisdom and patient with our questions.

We're grateful to Dartmouth's Dickey Center, whose director, Daniel Benjamin, brought high-level policymakers to town who were willing to share their knowledge and experience with us. In particular, we thank Steve Simon, James Mattis, William Fallon, Mara Rudman, and Mike Morrell for helpful discussions about our research. The Dickey Center also plays host to Dartmouth's postdoctoral fellows in US foreign policy and international security, whose presence is a great boost to research of the kind presented in the book. Special mention must go to Jonathan Markowitz, who organized an all-day book manuscript review for us attended by Paul

Avey, Michael Beckley, Alexander Lanoszka, Adam Liff, Rob Reardon, and Josh Shifrinson.

Dartmouth also figures in these acknowledgments because of its out-standing undergraduate students. We are particularly thankful to those who worked with us as research assistants on this project: Joanne Hyun, Holly Jeong, Ming Koh, Gardiner Kreglow, Charlotte Snow, Bryan Thomson, Keshav Poddar, Yerin Yang, and Yannick Yu.

The willingness of scholars, think-tank analysts, and policymakers beyond Hanover to take the time to engage with us was nothing short of astonishing. For their valuable input at various stages of this project, we are grateful to Michael Beckley, Tai Ming Cheung, Thomas Culora, Allan Dafoe, Andrew Erickson, Taylor Fravel, Andrea Gilli, Mauro Gilli, Eugene Gholz, Charles Glaser, Lyle Goldstein, Jim Holmes, Josh Kertzer, Adam Liff, Jon Lindsay, Austin Long, Stephen Macekura, Jonathan Markowitz, Evan Montgomery, William Murray, Carla Norrlof, Keshav Poddar, Barry Posen, Jeremy Shapiro, Joseph Singh, Andrew Winner, Thomas Wright, and Riqiang Wu.

We also benefitted from comments by attendees at seminars at many universities and think tanks: Aberystwyth University, the Brookings Institution, Brown University, the Cato Institute, Columbia University, George Washington University, Georgetown University, Johns Hopkins Applied Physics Laboratory, the London School of Economics, Moscow State Institute of International Relations, the Massachusetts Institute of Technology's Lincoln Laboratory, Northeastern University, Ohio State University, the Tobin Project, the University of Cambridge, the University of Ottawa, the University of Oxford, the University of Southern California, the University of Vermont, and the US Naval War College.

Finally, we are indebted to Dave McBride at Oxford University Press for his interest in our project, for his outstanding line-by-line feedback on the entire manuscript, and for his guidance as we brought it to completion.

Some of the analysis and data presented in chapters 2 and 3 appears in condensed form in two articles: "The Rise and Fall of the Great Powers in the 21st Century: China's Rise and the Fate of America's Global Position," *International Security*, Vol. 40, No. 3 (Winter 2016), pp. 7–53 and "The Once and Future Superpower: Why China Won't Overtake the United States," *Foreign Affairs*, Vol. 95, No. 3 (May/June 2016), pp. 91–104. In a collaborative article with John Ikenberry ("Don't Come Home, America: The Case against Retrenchment," *International Security*, Vol. 37, No. 3 [Winter 2012/13], pp. 7–51) we subjected the case for retrenchment to a critical analysis. Some portions of that analysis appear here, most notably in chapters 7 and 8.

I

Introduction

SINCE THE END of World War II, international politics has been profoundly shaped by two constants: the United States' position as the international system's most powerful state and its strategic choice to be deeply engaged in the world. Although the Soviet Union's massive military capabilities and geopolitical location in the center of Eurasia earned it peer status as a superpower in the Cold War, by most measures and in most observers' eyes, the United States retained overall preeminence.[1] The fall of the Soviet Union in 1991 and contraction of Russia's power to its 17th-century borders transformed the United States' preexisting dominance into a power position without precedent in the history of the modern interstate system.

Though it was a signal event, the Cold War's end did not transform the United States' basic grand strategy. From today's vantage the definitive break remains the close of World War II, when the United States decisively ended the hands-off approach to the world's strategic affairs that it had taken since George Washington's farewell address.[2] The first part of the 20th century witnessed only halting steps away from this course. Although the United States participated in both world wars, it waited on the sidelines long after the conflicts began and decidedly focused inward between them. It was only at the end of World War II that the United States switched to a grand strategy of "deep engagement" with the world—militarily, politically, and economically.[3] During the seven decades since, the United States has sought to advance its interests in security, prosperity, and domestic liberty by pursuing the three overlapping objectives that define its grand strategy: managing the external environment to reduce near- and long-term threats to US national security; promoting a liberal economic order to expand the global economy and maximize domestic prosperity; and creating, sustaining, and revising the global institutional order to secure necessary interstate cooperation on terms favorable to US interests. Even as concerns about other priorities such as democracy promotion, human rights, and humanitarian intervention have waxed and waned between administrations and even sometimes within them, pursuit of these three objectives has been constant since the end of World War II.

The United States' globe-shaping efforts have borne fruit. After 1945, US leaders sought to foster the creation of an interconnected global economy, in part because they recognized that the collapse of global trade in the 1930s had provided fertile ground for political extremism and conflict and that American actions, notably the Smoot-Hawley Tariff, had helped push the world toward economic closure.[4] Not only has trade exploded in value during the post–World War II era, but a larger mosaic of international economic connections—economic globalization—has emerged due to new forms of production and financial linkages. In turn, the United States moved beyond its conflicted interwar posture toward international institutions, becoming history's most active and successful institution builder. All of the principal institutions that the United States pushed for at the end of World War II remain, while the past seventy years have witnessed the emergence of a dense web of new institutional ties. Finally, the United States abandoned its long-standing reluctance to form permanent alliances with other major powers and established a set of alliances and a long-term forward military presence in Western Europe and East Asia. And although the United States did not establish formal alliances or base troops in the Middle East, it did shift to a much more active role in managing security affairs there. These alliances and partnerships have proved remarkably stable over the decades and have helped the United States achieve many desired security objectives, such as containing the Soviet Union, brokering peace between Israel and its Arab neighbors, limiting nuclear proliferation, and fostering cooperation for combatting terrorism after 2001.

Washington has thus been remarkably successful regarding the three constant objectives that have animated it since World War II. Perhaps the best measure of this success is how often it is taken for granted, as American leaders, elites, and the general public focus their attention on triumphs and (more often) disappointments in pursuit of additional objectives beyond the grand strategy's constant core.

For the first time in decades, the two constants that have shaped international politics—the United States' status as the leading state and its role as a globally engaged power—are in doubt. Will the United States long continue to be the only superpower in the international system? And if so, should it maintain its effort to actively shape the global environment by continuing to be deeply engaged in the world? This book answers these two questions in the affirmative.

A New Strategic Landscape for the United States?

Until just a few years ago, our argument would have been seen as conventional. As of the mid-2000s, few questioned that the United States would long maintain its status as the sole superpower and that it should continue to be deeply engaged in the security and economic affairs of key regions. At that time, the question animating scholars was why the United States seemed unable to attain much more grandiose aims in world politics beyond the long-term core objectives of its foreign policy.[5] That debate assumed that "sole superpower" was too tame a word for US preeminence and that the deep engagement grand strategy was the most minimal realistic foreign policy role for Washington. But in recent years assessments of America's international position and preferred global role have undergone a sea change.

The narrative regarding the US international position has clearly shifted: pundits, scholars, and policymakers frequently and prominently argue that the United States has tumbled from its previous global position and that a fundamental, system-altering power shift is underway. The repercussions of the financial crisis of 2008, the military resurgence of Russia, and especially the continued dramatic rise of China have rapidly accelerated expectations of a coming post-American, multipolar world envisioned in bestsellers by the likes of Fareed Zakaria and Parag Khanna, as well as in forecasts by the National Intelligence Council and numerous prominent private sector analysts from Goldman Sachs to the Eurasia Group.[6] The details of the claims and terms used to describe US decline vary, but they add up to the assertion that a fundamental shift is occurring toward a new kind of international system with a very different role for the United States.[i] While most analysts

---

i. Polls show that the public agrees. The Pew Research Center notes: "For the first time in surveys dating back nearly 40 years, a majority (53%) says the United States plays a less important and powerful role as a world leader than it did a decade ago. The share saying the US is less powerful has increased 12 points since 2009 and has more than doubled—from just 20%—since 2004." Pew Research Center, *Public Sees U.S. Power Declining as Support for Global Engagement Slips: America's Place in the World 2013* (Washington, D.C.: Pew Research Center, December 2013), http://www.people-press.org/2013/12/03/public-sees-u-s-power-declining-as-support-for-global-engagement-slips/.

expect America to retain some advantages, they predict sufficient relative decline in enough dimensions of state capability to mark an end to the prolonged period of US centrality of the last seven decades. This is the import of
terms such as "post-American world," claims such as "unipolarity has ended,"
and popular historical analogies such as that between China's rise and the
ascent of Germany before World War I.[7]

Less well known is that the conventional narrative regarding the future
of US grand strategy has also shifted markedly, especially in the academy. In
the 1990s, only a few scholarly voices called for the United States to pull back
from its globally engaged role.[8] However, the chorus grew rapidly in response
to the 2003 Iraq War and reached a crescendo after the post-2008 economic
and budget crisis. By 2010, many of the most prominent security studies
scholars—and indeed the vast majority of scholars who write on the future
of US grand strategy—argued that the time had come for a shift toward disengagement or retrenchment (or "restraint," as many analysts misleadingly
term it).[ii] While there are important differences in the details of their recommended strategies, these scholars are unified in advocating that the United
States should pull back through some combination of: (1) curtailing or eliminating its overseas military presence, (2) eliminating or significantly reducing
its global security commitments, and (3) minimizing or eschewing its efforts
to foster and lead the liberal institutional order.[9] Some of these analysts favor a
decisive pullback and others a more limited one, but the key point is that they
reject the default expectation that has long defined US grand strategy: that

---

ii. For reasons that will become clear below, restraint is a very problematic term. Most
notably, the term implies that the pursuit of deep engagement is, and must be, "unrestrained" regarding the use of force. And yet proponents of deep engagement and retrenchment have expressed differing views on the advisability of different interventions. For
example, prominent advocates of retrenchment voiced support for intervention in Libya. See
Robert A. Pape, "When Duty Calls: A Pragmatic Standard of Humanitarian Intervention,"
International Security, Vol. 37, No. 1 (Summer 2012), pp. 41–80. A number of proponents
of deep engagement opposed the intervention in Iraq; see, for example, G. John Ikenberry,
"America's Imperial Ambition," *Foreign Affairs*, Vol. 81, No. 5 (September/October 2002),
pp. 44–60. In turn, some scholars whose analyses lend support to deep engagement have
consistently opposed forceful democracy promotion; see, for example, Robert J. Art, "A
Defensible Defense: America's Grand Strategy after the Cold War," *International Security*,
Vol. 15, No. 4 (Spring 1991), pp. 5–53; and Robert J. Art, *A Grand Strategy for America* (Ithaca,
N.Y.: Cornell University Press, 2003). "Disengagement" or "retrenchment" are more apt
terms, because they both correctly place the emphasis on the chief area of disagreement in
the grand strategy debate: Should the United States retain its core global commitments and
global role or instead pull back? More precisely, retrenchment is the short-term strategy the
US would have to pursue to reach a new grand strategic posture of disengagement or offshore
balancing.

the United States should retain its existing global commitments and global role. Instead, their default expectation is that Washington should pull back.

Retrenchment proponents argue that the current US grand strategy of deep engagement has high and rising costs that dwarf its benefits. In their view, the United States' deep engagement strategy is excessively costly and is leading to imperial overstretch—all in support of allies who can well afford to defend themselves and thus should no longer be "subsidized." Moreover, they stress that America's intrusive grand strategy generates global pushback and resentment among both governments and foreign publics. Their assessment is that large-scale retrenchment would simultaneously defuse global anti-Americanism and disable free riding by US allies. Furthermore, retrenchment advocates stress that even if allied governments did not step up to fulfill every mission the United States now performs, most of these roles are unrelated to US security and create the risk of entrapping the United States in wars that are not in its national interest. In short, advocates maintain that retrenchment will not only save blood and treasure but also result in a more secure America.

During the 2016 presidential campaign, many of these same arguments were advanced by leading Republican candidates—most notably, Donald Trump.[iii] That followed a startling break from a tradition of stalwart Republican support for Pentagon spending when a number of GOP fiscal hawks in Congress proposed scaling back the US overseas military presence in Asia and Europe as a means of reducing the budget deficit; moreover, the onset of deep defense cuts associated with sequestration in 2013 met with acceptance from Republican lawmakers, again surprising many observers.[10] Significantly, complaints about the current scale of the US overseas role do

---

iii. In extensive interviews with the *Washington Post* and *New York Times*, Trump forcefully articulated most of the arguments that are central to the scholarly case for retrenchment: (1) allies are freeriders who take advantage of the United States, (2) the US runs serious risks of being entrapped in unwanted conflict by allies, (3) the US is declining due to excessive military spending, (4) nuclear proliferation to key allies would not be harmful to US interests, (5) allies will likely step up to contain rivals in the absence of US security guarantees and if not then this is not a US concern, and (6) US security guarantees do not yield net economic benefits to the United States. Needless to say, he also advocated policies—notably, protectionism and severe immigration restrictions—for which academic supporters of retrenchment have not expressed support. See "Transcript: Donald Trump Expounds on His Foreign Policy Views," *New York Times*, March 26, 2016, available at http://www.nytimes.com/2016/03/27/us/politics/donald-trump-transcript.html?_r=0. "A transcript of Donald Trump's meeting with the *Washington Post* editorial board," *Washington Post*, March 21, 2016, available at https://www.washingtonpost.com/blogs/post-partisan/wp/2016/03/21/a-transcript-of-donald-trumps-meeting-with-the-washington-post-editorial-board/.

not only exist on the Republican side: a growing chorus of liberal Democrats have recently argued that US allies should be forced to fully defend themselves so that Washington can reduce military spending and thereby free up resources to boost domestic welfare.[11]

These positions track significant shifts among the American public. For the first time in fifty years of polls asking respondents whether the "US should mind its own business internationally," more than half (52%) of the public now agrees (until a few years ago, the highest level ever recorded had been 43% in 1976).[12] In turn, 51% of the public now feels that the United States does too much to help solve world problems, and 80% agrees with the statement "We should not think so much in international terms but concentrate more on our own national problems and building up our strength and prosperity here at home."[13] The same basic trend shows up among conservative Republicans, who have long been the strongest supporters of an active role in world affairs; their support for this approach has plunged by almost 20% in recent years: 58% favored the United States having an active role in world affairs in 2004, but by 2011, only 39% favored this position.[14]

Moreover, it has become commonplace to argue that changing American public sentiment may someday compel politicians to shift toward retrenchment even if they are not inclined to do so. Randall Schweller, for example, argues that "the ever-widening gap between America's means and ends will, sooner than later, repair the severed connection between reality and U.S. foreign policy. It won't be long before the American people—encumbered by federal debt that will reach 70 percent of GDP in 2012 and a debt-to-revenue ratio approaching 262 percent—demand significant retrenchment from their government's far-flung global commitments."[15] In keeping with Schweller's argument, 65% of the US public now say they favor scaling back military commitments to reduce the debt.[16]

Analysts steeped in the later Cold War and the globalization narrative of its heady aftermath may underestimate the significance of these shifts. After being relegated to the fringes for two generations, the question of whether the United States should "come home" has been decisively put back on the table in US domestic politics. It is important to remember that deep engagement remains the outlier in the larger sweep of American history. Public figures who favor retrenchment are thus in a position to tap into a set of arguments and traditions of disengagement that have deep roots in the American historical experience and political discourse.

Likely in response to this changed public mood and the growing calls from prominent politicians for pursuing some form of retrenchment, US policymakers who favor maintaining a globally engaged role are increasingly feeling the need to argue directly that it would be a mistake for America to turn inward. For example, in his 2014 speech at West Point, Barack Obama maintained that "in the 21st century American isolationism is not an option. We don't have a choice to ignore what happens beyond our borders."[17] Similarly, then–Secretary of State Hillary Clinton argued in a 2011 article:

> With Iraq and Afghanistan still in transition and serious economic challenges in our own country, there are those on the American political scene who are calling for us not to reposition, but to come home. They seek a downsizing of our foreign engagement in favor of our pressing domestic priorities. These impulses are understandable, but they are misguided. . . . For more than six decades, the United States has resisted the gravitational pull of these "come home" debates and the implicit zero-sum logic of these arguments. We must do so again.[18]

Yet perhaps because it has been so long since any significant challenge has existed to the view that the United States should remain globally engaged, the case forwarded by policymakers for why Washington should sustain this role remains embryonic.

In sum, a new skepticism is taking hold about the stability of two long-standing pillars of the post–World War II international system: America's status as a peerless superpower and its pursuit of deep global engagement. This new landscape puts an increased premium on developing a systematic understanding of exactly what underlies America's position of power in the international system and whether a globally engaged role in the world is the most beneficial course for US foreign policy. That is the purpose of our book.

Our analysis provides the foundation for a distinct position in the evolving debate on US grand strategy. It makes clear a crucial distinction between the United States' constant commitment to its deep engagement grand strategy and the many additional strategic moves the United States has made in pursuit of objectives such as democracy promotion, fostering human rights, humanitarian interventions, and the spread of other liberal values. The advisability of such additional missions and commitments is what much of the debate in Washington has long been about, whereas the scholarly grand strategy debate is squarely focused on the sustainability and value of deep engagement itself. America thus stands before three broad grand strategic options: to focus on the core missions of the deep engagement grand strategy, to expand beyond it by adopting a "deep engagement plus" stance that adds new missions and obligations, or to pull back by disengaging from some or all of the key strategic commitments. Our analysis indicates that the wisest course is for America to pursue the first of these three options—a stance that places us in between those who call for an expansive style of global leadership and those who wish for America to pull back from the world.

Why the United States Will Long Remain the Sole Superpower

The two questions we address in this book are linked; it makes little sense to debate the merits of deep engagement if America's position in the international system has declined too much to be able to sustain its long-standing grand strategy. For this reason, the first two chapters of this book examine whether America still occupies a unique position atop the global hierarchy of power that enables a globally engaged grand strategy, and if so how long it will occupy that position.

In chapter 2 we develop a systematic examination of the distribution of capabilities, one tailored to 21st-century global politics and the requisites of superpower status today. As we show, China's rise has put it in a class by itself: it alone has achieved the economic scale to put itself in a position to perhaps someday become a peer of the United States, but it is nowhere near achieving that status yet. The bottom line is that the United States remains the globe's sole superpower, but China's economic ascent is a major change that deserves the intense focus it has attracted.

Chapter 3 then takes on the dynamic aspect, analyzing how long the United States' unique position of power within the system is likely to endure. In assessing the speed with which China might transform it into something other than a one-superpower system, we delineate three key differences from previous eras that invalidate analogies from past power transitions—unlike past rising powers, China is at a very different technological level than the leading state; the distance China must travel to reach peer status is extraordinarily large because the size of the US military advantage is much bigger than the analogous gaps in previous eras; and the very nature of power has changed: transitioning from a great power to a superpower is much harder now than in the past due to the greatly enhanced difficulty of converting economic capacity into military capacity. As we show, to properly capture China's trajectory, it is now crucial to specify a set of distinct stages that a state must pass through to rise from great power to superpower status. The upshot of our analysis is that China's rise along this path will be very slow. We close the chapter by outlining a conceptual framework for assessing and categorizing change in today's international system that, unlike the popular "polarity" framework, does not either exaggerate or downplay the significance of China's rise.

Why the United States Should Continue a Grand Strategy of Deep Engagement

In light of the analysis in chapters 2 and 3, which shows the United States is and will long remain the world's only state in a position to sustain a globally engaged grand strategy, America faces a unique choice: Should it do so? The remainder of this book answers this question. Chapter 4 begins the assessment by identifying the foundational elements of US grand strategy and explaining how and why our treatment differs from others commonly found in the literature. Here we fully develop the argument that the grand strategy is defined by its core, foundational elements. Of course, the United States has made many other additional strategic moves over the seven preceding decades in pursuit of "deep engagement plus" objectives such as the spread of democracy. Many observers highlight that changeable element—seeing shifts from one kind of plus to another as shifts in grand strategy. We contend that the fundamental objectives and the array of tools used to pursue them have remained remarkably consistent and thus that this core is the grand strategy, properly defined.

Our focus on the long sweep of post–World War II US strategic engagement lends the analysis a state-centric cast. The grand strategy is built upon relations with states, and its aims center on preventing conflict and fostering cooperation among states. But our analysis has great relevance for nonstate and transnational issues ranging from the global economy and environment to terrorism that are influenced crucially by the political climate of interstate relations. In particular, we examine how deep engagement may exacerbate or ameliorate the challenge of terrorism, allowing us to assess the overall interaction between the strategy's effect on interstate relations and the severity of that transnational threat.

Like all strategies, deep engagement is an intervention in the social environment to make it more favorable. Unlike almost all other strategies, deep engagement is truly "grand" in scope and temporal scale. Often missed in contemporary discussions is that its main aim is defensive: to prevent a much more dangerous, unstable world from emerging and to forestall the breakdown of cooperation regarding the global economy and other issues of great importance to the United States. To evaluate it demands an answer to a similarly grand counterfactual: What would the world be like if America retrenched? The only way to discipline such an analysis is to undertake a careful analysis that invokes all of the relevant scholarly knowledge about international politics. Chapters 5 and 6 ask: What verdict does international relations scholarship render on the basic precepts of US grand strategy? In chapter 5, we perform two tasks. First, we unpack the theoretical logic of how deep engagement produces security. Second, we evaluate its most important mechanisms for influencing the strategic environment. In chapter 6, we assess patterns of evidence to determine whether America's specific security commitments actually generate enhanced security and advance other US national interests as the strategy intends. Ultimately, chapters 5 and 6 show that the scholarly verdict is positive: deep engagement's basic mechanisms for generating a global security environment favorable to US national interests rest on sound social science.

Much of the case for retrenchment ultimately rests on deep engagement's expected costs and risks. Chapters 7 and 8 assess all the major arguments that retrenchment advocates invoke to reach their assessment. Chapter 7 examines the potential economic costs of deep engagement. Chapter 8 then analyzes the potential security costs: allied free riding, the problem of entrapment in costly wars on behalf of allies, global pushback by state and nonstate actors, and the continuing related risk of temptation and threat inflation. Our analysis in chapters 7 and 8 shows that although advocates of retrenchment do identify important potential costs, overall they radically overestimate their combined magnitude.

But the analysis of grand strategy cannot be limited to security affairs, as is typical in the work of virtually all scholars who advocate retrenchment. Deep engagement also encompasses economic goals (an effort to sustain economic globalization and shape it in ways that advance US economic prosperity) and institutional goals (maintaining the global network of international institutions to foster institutionalized cooperation in ways advantageous to US national interests). Since virtually all analysts who favor retrenchment neglect these nonsecurity goals, they miss many of the benefits of the current grand strategy that would be placed at risk if the United States were to follow their preferred foreign policy course.[19] Chapters 9 and 10 redress this shortcoming, providing a comprehensive analysis of the nonsecurity benefits of deep engagement. Chapter 9 outlines the theoretical logic of hegemonic order that explains why deep engagement can have significant nonsecurity benefits for the United States. Chapter 10 then shows that the United States actually does derive a series of economic gains from its globally engaged security policy.

Our analysis thus yields a favorable net assessment of deep engagement for the United States' basic interests in security, prosperity, and the preservation of its domestic institutions. This is a big claim, but it is limited. It does not mean that the United States never makes strategic or tactical mistakes, or that other countries and foreign publics do not have any cause for resentment of or disappointment with its behavior. It does not mean that the United States is motivated by anything other than pure self-interest, or that it is consistently a force for global good. On the contrary, the United States has its fair share of flaws, and, given its outsized role in the world, those flaws can produce negative global ramifications; the aftermath of the 2003 invasion of Iraq is arguably the most dramatic recent example, but there are obviously many others, including its support of a great many unsavory leaders over the decades and its use of military tactics—such as high-intensity drone strikes—which often result in the death of many civilians.

To be sure, the strategy does contribute to some general goods, such as institutions for addressing global problems, freedom of navigation, and alliances that dampen nascent security competition. And there are many governments around the world that consistently see their interests as more or less congruent with those of the United States even when US policies fail or backfire in ways that are costly or annoying to them. But our analysis is focused not on evaluating what the strategy does for the world but on what we believe is the main desideratum for the United States: what the grand strategy does for US national interests. If the United States does pull back from the world, it will not be because the pursuit of deep engagement is seen as disadvantageous to the world but because it is seen as not serving the foreign policy interests of the United States.

Adding It All Up

The book's two major contributions add up to a distinct position in the sharpening debate about America's global role. By clearing up conceptual confusion and providing a comprehensive assessment of global capabilities, we demonstrate that a foundational material pillar of the post–World War II international system—the United States' unmatched global power position—will long remain in place. By providing the most comprehensive assessment of US grand strategy's grounding in theory and evidence yet attempted, we demonstrate that a foundational policy pillar—a globally engaged America—remains the wisest choice.

Even as our analysis refutes the case for US retrenchment, it also tempers increasingly strident demands that Washington pursue a more ambitious kind of leadership. Ever since the Cold War's end, US presidents and sections of the foreign policy elite have periodically experienced dissatisfaction with America's deep engagement strategy. Often taking for granted the effect that the pursuit of the strategy's core objectives has on world politics, they have defined US aims more expansively: to right humanitarian wrongs where possible, to lead efforts to address every potential threat to regional stability globally, to be seen as spearheading the solution to each major global crisis, to address what are thought to be the root problems in various regions by supporting democratization, and so on. The success of these endeavors has often become the main benchmark for assessing US foreign policy and the utility of deep engagement. And by that measure it is easy to conjure up a major crisis for America's grand strategy and its position in the world. How strong can America really be, so-called declinists wonder, if it so often fails to attain the objectives it sets for itself? And what good are US alliances and commitments, critics reasonably ask, if they do not translate into the ability to achieve these outcomes?

If nothing else, we hope to convince readers of the inadequacy of this popular way of thinking about America's role in the world. While it has the benefit of being grounded in today's crises and policymakers' preoccupations, this approach is based on a profoundly biased view of power in international politics. For power is every bit as much about the ability to prevent unfavorable outcomes as it is about the ability to cause favorable ones. Indeed, if you are basically a status quo actor, and if the way things currently are structured is, overall, to your liking, then having enough "blocking power" to prevent a less congenial order from emerging is more important than the positive power to actively create new outcomes that marginally improve matters. As the country that played the lead in setting up today's order, the United States is in precisely this position.

To assess the United States' power position and the optimality of its strategy, you need to step back from the pressing crises of the day and assess the degree to which its capabilities and strategy are shaping the world in profound ways; although it cannot be seen, preventing other actors from undermining the underlying order is a major way in which the Unites States can and does shape the global system. Policymakers invariably lack the time to think this way, and it is not the job of journalists to do so: they reasonably direct their attention to what is happening now and not toward what would have happened had the United States stepped back from deep engagement. Conducting such an assessment is complex and inevitably must engage deeply with counterfactuals, scholarly theories, and patterns of empirical evidence.

Such an analysis cannot yield answers to every immediate policy challenge the United States faces, which will in any case likely be replaced by a new set of pressing concerns in the interval between our writing and your reading of these lines. But the examination in the pages that follow yields important conclusions of lasting significance: the United States (and, indirectly, many other actors as well) benefits immensely from sustaining deep engagement, and it will long remain the only state in a position to play such a global role.

That being said, the perennial demand to go beyond deep engagement in pursuit of a more expansive foreign policy vision should be tempered. For in a world where the distribution of capabilities is not frozen and other states, most notably Russia and China, are gaining greater ability and periodically showing greater willingness to challenge US positions near their borders, sustaining deep engagement cannot be an afterthought but must be the priority. Indeed, expanding missions over and above the core grand strategy may put it at risk. President Barack Obama took a lot of criticism for making "Don't do stupid shit" a grand strategic maxim. But if doing "stupid shit" threatens the ability of the United States to sustain deep engagement, then he had a point. Missing was a second maxim: "Keep your eye on the ball," which for seven decades has been the core mission of reducing threats to US security in key regions and keeping economic globalization and the institutional order humming. The United States has been strikingly successful in that mission. We show that it can and should continue to pursue it. Once we truly understand its benefits, the wisdom of resisting the temptation to add too many other missions will be more apparent.

2

Assessing America's Global Position

WHAT ARE THE criteria for superpower status, and, more generally, how should the distribution of power in the system be measured? We answer these questions with a comprehensive assessment of the distribution of power that has major implications for current debates about change in the international system. What we seek to gauge are the resources or capacities that governments can draw upon to act in international politics. We recognize that some of these capacities are hard if not impossible to measure before they are used or tested (e.g., the unity or resolve of a population).[i] Even when we focus on measurable aspects, there are always tough trade-offs: whether to use single versus multiple indicators; if multiple, which ones and how many to use; whether to examine them separately or combine them into an index, and, if so, how to weight various elements.[1] We come to these questions after more than a decade of study and research in which we have employed a broad-based conception of measurement that focuses on three key dimensions of state capability to assess the gap between the United States and other powers: military, technological, and economic.[2]

Such a broad-based approach is imperative, in part because no single element of power can capture the full array of resources a state may bring to the pursuit of its goals in international politics. States with skewed portfolios of capabilities are less capable of acting in different arenas and more dependent on a limited policy toolkit. Moreover, each of the core elements of power

i. A basic distinction that is made in the power literature is between power as material resources that governments can draw upon and power as the ability to realize ends; see, in particular, David Baldwin, *Paradoxes of Power* (New York: Basil Blackwell, 1989). Following the practice of many scholars, our measurement efforts use the term "power" in the former sense. In the later chapters of this book, we consider the degree to which the United States can translate these resources into desired outcomes via its grand strategy.

interacts with the others in potent ways. Economic capacity is a necessary condition of military power, but it is insufficient; technological prowess is also vital, especially given the nature of modern weaponry. Technological capacity also magnifies economic capability, and military capability also can have spinoffs in both the economy and technology. Furthermore, military capability can have indirect but important implications for furthering a leading state's economic interests. To highlight any one element at the expense of others is to miss these key interactions.

The wellsprings of national power clearly change over time.[3] To assess today's system, we therefore implement a Goldilocks approach to measurement: one conducted at a sufficient level of generality to answer enduring questions about the nature of the international system but much more detailed and attuned to the requisites of superpower status in the 21st century than popular broad aggregates or single metrics that can be used over long spans of time. This middle-range approach to measuring power is especially important today because, as the next chapter will discuss in depth, key differences from previous eras invalidate analogies with past power transitions. Our investigation shows that the United States indisputably remains the sole superpower, and that the gap between it and the other powers, notably China, remains very large. But although China has not become a superpower, its rise is a notable change that deserves the intense focus it has attracted. Though nowhere near a peer of the United States, China—unlike all the other major powers like Germany, Russia, and Japan—has the overall scale needed to make attaining that position a real possibility someday. This analysis enables us to assess in the next chapter the likely speed of China's ascent in the scales of international power in the upcoming decades.

Military Capacity

The standard approach to measuring the distribution of military power is to compare defense expenditures. Table 2.1 is an updated version of a table from our 2008 book *World Out of Balance* showing the primary military spending figures of interest using the latest available data.[4] Figures 2.1 and 2.2 move beyond a static snapshot and show the data for the key measures that have changed the most since 2000 for China and the United States. They show that although China's military spending is rising and America's is falling in comparison to the 2000s, defense spending and defense research and development (R&D) are still heavily skewed toward the United States. (We lack data on China's military R&D expenditures, but a recent estimate is that

Table 2.1 Defense Expenditures for the Major Powers, 2014

	Defense Expenditures ($ Billion)	% Great Power Defense Expenditures	% World Defense Expenditures	Defense Expenditures % of GDP	Defense R&D Expenditures ($ Billion)
United States	610.0	50.5	34.0	3.5	78.6
China	216.0	17.9	12.0	2.1	n.a.
Japan	45.8	3.8	2.6	1.0	1.0
Germany	46.5	3.9	2.6	1.2	1.2
Russia	84.5	7.0	4.8	4.5	n.a.
France	62.3	5.2	3.5	2.2	1.3
Britain	60.5	5.0	3.4	2.2	2.1
India	50.0	4.1	2.8	2.4	n.a.
Brazil	31.7	2.6	1.8	1.4	n.a.

Notes: Data is estimated for China's and Russia's defense expenditures, as well as for their defense expenditures as percentages of their own GDP. R&D expenditures are for 2012.

Sources: Stockholm International Peace Research Institute, "Trends in World Military Expenditure," 2014, http://books.sipri.org/files/FS/SIPRIFS1504.pdf (consulted August 2, 2015); Organisation for Economic Co-operation and Development, OECD Main Science and Technology Indicators, Volume 2014 (Paris: OECD, 2014), pp. 76–77.

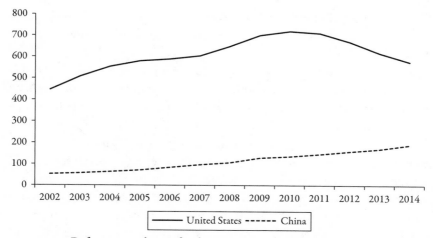

FIGURE 2.1 Defense expenditures for the United States and China, 2000–2014 (in billions of constant 2011 US dollars).

Note: Data is estimated for China.

Source: Stockholm International Peace Research Institute, Military Expenditure Database, http://www.sipri.org/research/armaments/milex (consulted August 2, 2015).

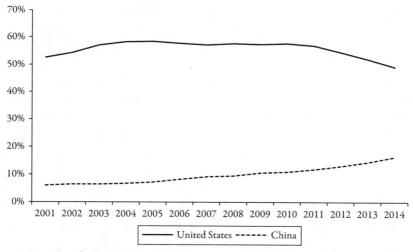

FIGURE 2.2 Defense expenditures for the United States and China as a % of Great Power Defense Expenditures, 2000–2014.

Note: Data is estimated for China.

Source: Stockholm International Peace Research Institute, Military Expenditure Database, http://www.sipri.org/research/armaments/milex (consulted August 2, 2015).

China's spending may approach $6 billion per year, which would make it the second highest spender in the world but which is still only around 7% of the US level.)[5]

Defense expenditures clearly tell us something about states' relative military capabilities, but they are vulnerable to an important objection: how much a state decides to spend on its military is a choice, and it may be misleading to use these numbers to capture something that is supposed to be a constraint on choice.[6] Clearly, something that a state can easily choose to change is not a good yardstick for measuring a property of the international setting that purportedly shapes states' decisions over time.

The degree to which this is a problem depends on the relevant time frame and the speed with which other resources can be converted into military capabilities. No matter what a state decides, its ability to create new military capabilities in the short term—say a year or two—is very limited. As the time horizon stretches to decades and generations, more and more elements of military capability become matters of choice as long as the state has the requisite pool of resources from which to draw. The length of that horizon—the gap between a choice to attain some capability and the creation of that capability—is a function of the technology of production. Key here is that there is variation in how hard it is for states to make things. Nuno Monteiro makes a useful analogy to Alfred Marshal's theory of production in which, "in the short term, price adjustments depend entirely on demand, because supply is fixed. In the medium term, price adjustments can be made by increasing supply, within the limits of firms' productive capacity. Increases in supply beyond this limit require investments in additional productive assets and can therefore only be achieved in the long term." Monteiro stresses that "we must distinguish between a state's present military capabilities, its ability to convert other elements of power into additional military capabilities, and its ability to generate additional elements of power that can then be converted into military capabilities." The latter two—the pool of militarily relevant resources to which a state has access and the state's ability to convert those resources into usable military capabilities—are not simple matters of choice but are powerfully constrained. Analysts of international politics can treat military capability just as economists treat supply in some of their models: as a relatively inflexible external constraint in the short term, and even in the medium and longer term in some situations.

Military spending therefore does reveal something important: long-term investment in the capacity to generate military power. Cumulated over years and decades, military spending can yield capabilities that are very hard to match even for a state with a lot of money to spend. This is especially the case today given the dramatically increased complexity and difficulty of both producing and using advanced weaponry. To capture this, it pays to examine the key military capacity that allows the United States to act as a superpower. We stressed elsewhere that the United States enjoys not just a quantitative edge in defense spending but a "unique capability to project power around the globe" due to the fact that it "leads the world in exploiting the military applications of advanced communications and information technology and it has demonstrated an unrivaled ability to coordinate and process information about the battlefield and destroy targets from afar with extraordinary precision."[7] These are the capabilities we need to assess more thoroughly.

The ideal place to start is Barry Posen's influential study of the "command of the commons," arguably the best overall guide to understanding the nature of military power among the top tier of states today. The command of the global commons—that is, the sea (outside littoral regions), space, and air (above fifteen thousand feet)—is "the key military enabler of the U.S. global power position," Posen argues.[ii] He helpfully provides guidelines for measuring America's command of the commons, identifying four components— command of the sea, command of space, command of the air, and the infrastructure of command—and notes the key elements of military capacity that are relevant for each of them. When Posen wrote his article in the early 2000s, US command of the commons was so self-evident that it was essentially unnecessary to measure the different components of this index. Yet the rise of China has since so altered the conversation that it is important to take a fine-grained look at how the United States matches up with other states using the set of criteria that Posen identifies.

Figure 2.3 shows the full range of relevant indicators as a distribution among the major powers. Regarding America's command of the sea, in addition to the two indictors that Posen highlights—aircraft carriers and nuclear

---

ii. Posen stresses that "command does not mean that other states cannot use the commons in peacetime. Nor does it mean that others cannot acquire military assets that can move through or even exploit them when unhindered by the United States. Command means that the United States gets vastly more military use out of the sea, space, and air than do others; that it can credibly threaten to deny their use to others; and that others would lose a military contest for the commons if they attempted to deny them to the United States. Having lost such a contest, they could not mount another effort for a very long time, and the United States would preserve, restore, and consolidate its hold after such a fight." Barry R. Posen, "Command of the Commons: The Military Foundation of U.S. Hegemony," *International Security*, Vol. 28, No. 1 (2003), p. 8.

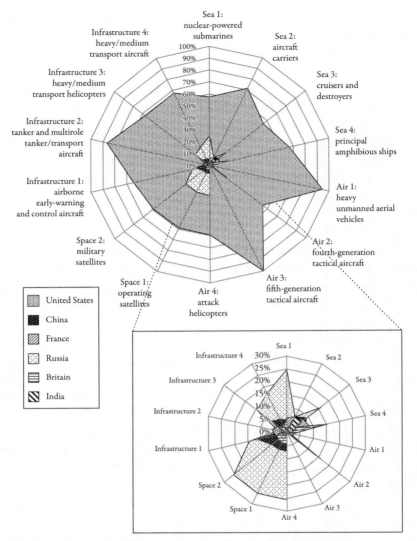

FIGURE 2.3 Command of the commons: distribution of six major powers.
Source: Stephen Brooks and William Wohlforth, "The Rise and Fall of Great Powers in the 21st Century: China's Rise and the Fate of America's Global Position," *International Security*, Vol. 40, No. 3 (Winter 2015/16), pp. 7–48.

attack submarines—two other pertinent indicators of power projection capacity are the number of cruisers and destroyers and the number of amphibious ships. Posen cites two indicators for command of the air: drones and military aircraft that allow for the use of precision-guided munitions. For space, Posen zeroes in on civilian and especially military satellites as providing vital sources of information for conducting military operations throughout the

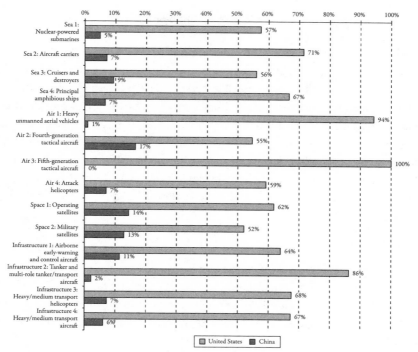

FIGURE 2.4 Command of the commons: US and China as % of six major powers.
Source: Stephen Brooks and William Wohlforth, "The Rise and Fall of Great Powers in the 21st Century: China's Rise and the Fate of America's Global Position," *International Security*, Vol. 40, No. 3 (Winter 2015/16), pp. 7–48.

world.[iii] And regarding the infrastructure of command—a necessary condition of command of the commons—Posen highlights military installations in foreign countries, military transport ships, long-range airlift aircraft, and aerial tankers as basic building blocks of this infrastructure. The United States has a ramified network of military bases throughout the world and is clearly in a league of its own in this regard; Figure 2.3 shows the extent of the gap between the United States and other countries for the other indicators.

The inset of Figure 2.3 also shows the distribution excluding the United States, suggesting how large Russia's military power would loom in a world without the United States. Figure 2.4 then breaks out the US-China comparison. Note that the raw counts in these figures do not account for the United

---

iii. Note that the United States "commands" space in the sense of having a commanding position in exploiting space for military purposes. Unlike the sea and air commons, however, in space the United States is less able to deny entry to others, including Russian and Chinese antisatellite capabilities. And US command of the air is restricted to the air over the commons (more accurately, it excludes airspace over the territory of those few states with top-end air defense).

States' overall qualitative advantage[8] or its qualitative and quantitative advantages in nuclear weaponry.

In sum, compared to any previous era except the years between 1991 and the early 2000s, the overall gap between the United States and other states in the military realm remains unprecedented in modern international relations. Defense spending figures make this look obvious, but scholars caution they may exaggerate the gap's significance because states with growing economies might decide to spend more to close the gap. Although Chinese military expenditures are rapidly increasing, our more finely grained measures of the United States' command of the commons show that, if anything, defense spending understates the extent of the global military gap.

Technological Capacity

Why bother with measuring technological capacity when no one questions the United States' unique combination of large-scale and technological prowess? The answer is essentially the same as in the military realm. Things are changing just enough to prompt some analysts to question the United States' unassailability on this key metric. Journalistic treatments frequently portray China as on course to join the high-technology high table. "It's Official: China Is Becoming a New Innovation Powerhouse," proclaims a prominent recent example.[9] Prognostications like this invite a deeper look at technological capacity. To do this, it is crucial to examine both inputs and outputs—and to keep these two distinct.[10] After all, a country may devote a lot of resources to technology, but for a variety of reasons the resulting output may not be commensurate. And analysts need to be careful when measuring output: in today's global economy some or even much of the high-technology items produced in a country may actually be largely the result of other countries' technological capabilities.

To start with the numbers that drive the narrative about China's technological rise, commentators typically point to three key statistics: "China's high-tech output is nearing that of the United States, China is committing an increasingly large portion of its wealth to R&D, and [there is] a huge jump in the number of Chinese graduates with engineering degrees."[11] High-technology production would seem to be a good measure of technological capacity, but it is not. The high level of geographical dispersion of production by multinational corporations (MNCs)—a trend that has accelerated over the past several decades, especially in technological industries—renders this metric misleading.[12] In many of the more globalized industries it has become increasingly difficult or even irrelevant to make comparisons on the basis of whether something is made in one country or another. This is especially true when the comparison of greatest interest involves China, because of the unique nature of its political economy. Half of all Chinese exports consist of "processing trade" (in which parts and components are imported into China for assembly into finished products and are then exported afterward), and the vast majority of these Chinese exports (84% in 2010) are directed not by Chinese firms but by foreign companies (mostly affiliates of MNCs from Organisation for Economic Co-operation and Development [OECD] countries). In turn, foreign companies are also the source of 29% of Chinese "ordinary exports"—that is, nonprocessing trade.[13]

Using China's high-technology output as a measure of its technological capacity is thus misleading, given the extent to which foreign companies drive Chinese exports. But what about other statistics that analysts typically highlight? As Figure 2.5 shows, Chinese spending on R&D has surged since 2000, from $27.2 billion in 2000 to $208.2 billion in 2011 (US R&D spending has gone up by almost as much during this period in absolute terms but from a much higher initial base—from $269.5 billion in 2000 to $429.1 billion in 2011). Should those trends continue, China's overall R&D spending might surpass that of the United States (and the EU) in a matter of years.[14] In turn,

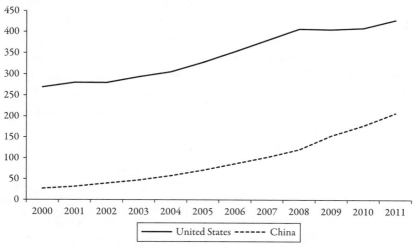

FIGURE 2.5 Gross domestic expenditure on R&D, 2000–2011 (constant US dollars, PPP).

Source: National Science Foundation, "National Patterns of R&D Resources: 2011–2012 Data Update," http://www.nsf.gov/statistics/nsf14304/content.cfm?pub_id=4326&id=2 (consulted August 2, 2015).

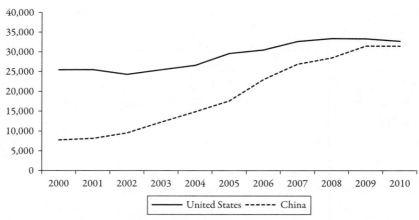

FIGURE 2.6 Number of scientific and engineering doctoral degrees granted per year for the United States and China, 2000–2010.

Source: National Science Board, *Science and Engineering Indicators 2014* (National Science Foundation: 2014) (consulted August 3, 2015).

Figure 2.6 shows that since 2000 China has closed the sizeable gap that had long existed regarding doctorates in science and engineering between the United States and all other countries.

As in the case of defense spending, the significance of these trends depends on how big the existing overall technology gap is and the speed with which increased inputs can be expected to yield sufficiently increased output to begin to place China in the same technological league as the United States. China is certain to reap some rewards from these enhanced technological inputs, but there are natural limits to how fast it, or indeed any country, can ramp up its technological inputs in a productive way.

Inputs can be thought of as a country's material investments in and infrastructure for technological development, as well as its stock of human capital (which reflects the education, skills, tacit knowledge, and health of its populace).[15] Table 2.2 shows an array of technological infrastructure inputs, including gross expenditures on research and development. An additional input is R&D intensity—the R&D/GDP ratio—because it "provides another measure for international R&D performance [and] does not require conversion of a country's currency to a standard international benchmark yet still provides a way to adjust for differences in the sizes of national economies."[16] We also use a very broad information and communication technologies (ICT) infrastructure index constructed by Cornell, INSEAD, and the World Intellectual Property Organization

Table 2.2 Technological Infrastructure

	Gross Expenditure on R&D as a % Share of GDP	Gross Domestic Expenditures on R&D (market exchange rates, in billions)	Gross Domestic Expenditures on R&D (PPP, in billions)	Cornell/INSEAD/WIPO Information and Communication Technologies Index Score for 2014 (out of 100)	Cornell/INSEAD/WIPO Information and Communication Technologies Index Ranking for 2014 (out of 143 countries)
United States	2.85	442.7	429.1	83.0	5
China	1.84	134.7	208.2	36.1	73
Japan	3.39	199.9	146.5	78.1	10
Germany	2.88	104.6	93.1	74.3	15
Russia	1.09	20.7	35.0	60.6	28
France	2.24	62.4	51.9	72.7	17
Britain	1.77	43.6	39.6	86.5	4
India	0.76	14.2	24.3	25.9	99
Brazil	1.16	24.9	25.3	51.6	41

Note: Gross Expenditure on R&D is for 2011 except for Brazil, which is for 2010.

Sources: National Science Board, *Science and Engineering Indicators 2014* (2014), pp. 4–19; International Monetary Fund, *World Economic Outlook Database,* (October 2013), http://www.imf.org/external/pubs/ft/weo/2013/02/weodata/index.aspx (consulted August 3, 2015); Cornell University, INSEAD, and the World Intellectual Property Organization, *The Global Innovation Index 2014: The Human Factor in Innovation* (2014), pp. 135–282 (consulted August 4, 2015).

Table 2.3 Human Capital

	Number of Scientific and Engineering Doctoral Degrees Granted Per Year	Number of People with Tertiary Education, 2012 (in millions)	2010 Human Capital Level (in billions of constant 2005 US$)
United States	32,649	70.2	99,641
China	31,410	31.1	13,447
Japan	7,396	30.9	33,645
Germany	11,989	12.6	24,576
Russia	15,714	44.6	6,391
France	8,220	10.0	19,118
Britain	11,055	13.5	19,079
India	7,982	n.a.	9,355
Brazil	5,470	13.2	8,968

Notes: For doctoral degrees granted per year, data is for 2010, except for Japan, which is from 2009; France, which is from 2009; India, which is from 2006; and Brazil, which is from 2008. For China, percentage of population with tertiary education is from 2010 and number of people with tertiary education is from 2009.

Sources: United Nations University International Human Dimensions Programme on Global Environmental Change and United Nations Environment Programme, *Inclusive Wealth Report 2014: Measuring Progress Toward Sustainability* (Cambridge, UK: Cambridge University Press, 2014); National Science Board, *Science and Engineering Indicators* (National Science Foundation, 2014); Organisation for Co-operation and Economic Development, *Education at a Glance 2014: OECD Indicators* (Paris: OECD, 2014) (consulted August 11, 2015).

(an agency of the UN).[17] These numbers ratify the United States' unique combination of a very large scale (massive gross expenditures) and highly developed technological infrastructure.

The quality of the people (their skills, education, experience, and so on) who actually use a country's resources and infrastructure to generate technological innovation is clearly another key input. Table 2.3 presents data on educational attainment both in science and engineering and more generally. Again, the United States stands out in relative and absolute terms in most categories except for China's eye-catching annual number of science and engineering degrees.

To obtain a reliable assessment of technological capacity, we need to know what all these inputs actually yield as output. Figure 2.7 presents output measures that, unlike high-technology production, are reliably national in origin for all the countries concerned. The number of triadic patent families (which measure a set of patents taken in the United States, Europe, and Japan to protect an invention) is widely accepted as a measure

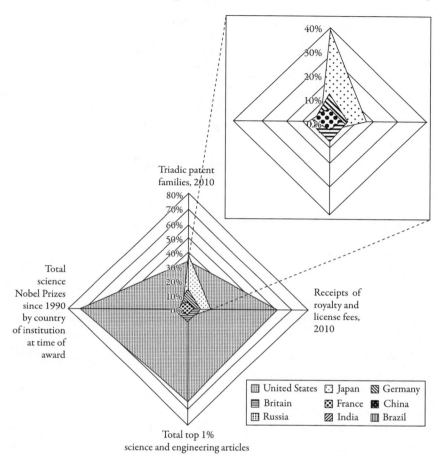

FIGURE 2.7 Technological output and influence indicators: distribution of nine major powers.

Source: Stephen Brooks and William Wohlforth, "The Rise and Fall of Great Powers in the 21st Century: China's Rise and the Fate of America's Global Position," *International Security*, Vol. 40, No. 3 (Winter 2015/16), pp. 7–48.

of technological competitiveness. Even more probative are royalty and license fees, which show that the US is in a league of its own while China has barely begun to register as a source of innovative technologies. The recent geographic distribution of top cited articles in science and engineering tells the same story, as does the recent distribution of Nobel Prizes in science.

The inset of Figure 2.7 also shows the distribution of technological capacity for the other major powers, indicating that Japan is the most significant state in this regard after the United States. Figure 2.8 focuses specifically on

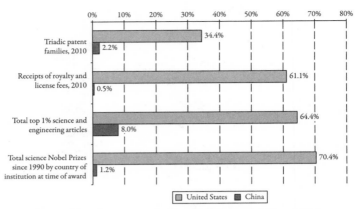

FIGURE 2.8 Technological output and influence indicators: US and China as % of nine major powers.
Source: Stephen Brooks and William Wohlforth, "The Rise and Fall of Great Powers in the 21st Century: China's Rise and the Fate of America's Global Position," *International Security*, Vol. 40, No. 3 (Winter 2015/16), pp. 7–48.

the US-China comparison and reveals the immense technological gap between them.

While these data are informative, they do not provide a synthetic overall ranking of a country's technological competiveness. Fortunately, ranking countries on the basis of technological competitiveness has become something of a cottage industry in recent years. A prominent article by Archibugi, Denni, and Filippetti provides a comprehensive survey of eight different synthetic indexes that have been developed to measure the technological capabilities of countries.[18] Table 2.4 reproduces the table from their article that surveys the country rankings derived from these eight synthetic indexes. The study was published in 2009, and since then some of the indexes have been updated. Table 2.5 shows the updated rankings for these indexes. The gap between the technological ranking of the United States and China is extremely large across all of these indexes.

If one had to translate all of these various numbers into a single phrase, it would clearly be "robust US technological dominance." Of all the figures noted above, this reality is arguably best captured by royalty and license fee data, which reveal that the United States is far and away the leading source of innovative technologies (its $128 billion in receipts of royalty and license fees are four times higher than the next highest state, Japan), whereas China is a huge importer of these technologies while exporting almost nothing (less than $1 billion). As in the military realm, enough is changing to feed a narrative about China closing the gap. But the key point is that the change we see is on the input side—most notably, China's growing R&D expenditures—and

Table 2.4 Synthetic Indicators of Technological Capabilities (2009)

	World Economic Forum, Innovation and Sophistication Indicator Rank 2006–2007	World Economic Forum, Technological Readiness Indicator Rank 2006–2007	World Economic Forum, Innovation Indicator Rank 2006–2007	Global Innovation Index Rank 2006	World Bank, Knowledge Index Rank 2006	Archibugi and Coco (2004)	United Nations Conference on Trade and Development, Technological Activity Index Rank, 2001	United Nations Industrial Development Organization Technological Advance Index Rank, 2002
United States	1	8	3	7	6	5	4	3
China	45	45	35	32	44	44	44	26
Japan	4	17	1	4	13	8	5	2
Germany	17	18	5	8	14	12	9	5
Russia	44	44	41	23	35	28	23	31
France	27	22	13	14	17	19	16	11
Britain	16	6	11	12	9	13	15	4
India	38	39	23	43	45	45	45	37
Brazil	32	33	42	39	30	36	38	44

Source: Daniele Archibugi, Mario Denni, and Andrea Filippetti, "The Technological Capabilities of Nations: The State of the Art of Synthetic Indicators," *Technological Forecasting and Social Change*, Vol. 76, No. 7 (September 2009), p. 925.

Table 2.5 Updated Synthetic Indicators of Technological Capabilities

	World Economic Forum, Innovation and Sophistication Indicator Rank 2014–2015	World Economic Forum, Technological Readiness Indicator Rank 2014–2015	World Economic Forum, Innovation Indicator Rank 2014–2015	Global Innovation Index Rank 2014	World Bank, Knowledge Index Rank 2012
United States	5	16	5	6	9
China	33	83	32	29	93
Japan	2	20	4	21	20
Germany	4	13	6	13	10
Russia	75	59	65	49	46
France	19	17	19	22	22
Britain	8	2	12	2	18
India	52	121	49	76	120
Brazil	56	58	62	61	58

Sources: World Economic Forum, *The Global Competitiveness Report 2014–2015*, http://www.weforum.org/reports/global-competitiveness-report-2014–2015 (consulted August 13, 2015); Cornell University, INSEAD, and the World Intellectual Property Organization, *The Global Innovation Index 2014: The Human Factor in Innovation* (2014); The World Bank, "Knowledge for Development: KEI and KI Indexes" (consulted on August 15, 2015).

not on the output side. Given that the overall technological gap between China and the United States is so massive, the process of closing it will be a lengthy one. America's unique combination of massive scale and technological prowess will be a long-term feature of the distribution of capabilities.

Economic Capacity

No effort to assess the distribution of capabilities is complete without an analysis of how US economic output compares to that of other major powers. A state's economic output is the raw material its government can draw upon as it seeks to create other elements of capability as well as to exercise many other forms of influence over its environment.[19] To be sure, converting economic output into military power and technological capacity is a complex and time-consuming process. But to emphasize that undeniable reality is not to gainsay the importance of raw economic heft in the measurement of state power.

We start with standard measures, notably GDP. When making comparisons about the international power of countries, it is preferable to use GDP data based on market exchange rates rather than purchasing power parity (PPP) estimates.[20] Table 2.6 tells the now well-known story of the United States as the world's biggest, richest, and most productive economy, with fast-rising China just entering the ranks of the middle-income countries. Although the rising level of US public debt has generated worried discussion in policy circles, as a proportion of GDP (70%) it remains lower than all of the other large advanced economies and is only very slightly higher than in the mid-2000s (64.7% in 2006).

Figure 2.9 shows that China is narrowing the gap not only in overall economic size but also in GDP per capita, albeit from a very low starting point. The differential effects of the post-2008 Great Recession, which stalled US growth for many years afterward but hardly affected China's, are particularly noteworthy. From 2007 to 2013, China's economy rocketed from one-quarter to one-half that of the United States. Per capita GDP rose from 6% of the US level ($2,600) to 13% ($7,000).

The USDA's long-term time series on country shares of world GDP provides an excellent means of discerning changes in the economic weight of actors on the global stage over time. As Figure 2.10 shows, after the post-2008 Great Recession, the US share fell roughly half a percent below its lowest previous point, reaching 22.8% in 2014 (compared to 23.4% in 1982). But of the three actors whose relative economic weight the figure tracks over time, the change in the United States' trajectory is by far the least dramatic. As expected, the dramatic upward rise is China's, whose GDP share rose from 4.5%

Table 2.6 Economic Indicators for the Major Powers, 2014

	GDP, Current Prices ($ Billion)	% Great Power GDP, Current Prices	% World GDP, Current Prices	GDP Per Capita, Current Prices	Public Debt (% GDP)	Hours Worked (per person in employment)	Productivity ($ GDP per hour worked)
United States	17,418	36.0	22.5	54,596	71.2	1,789	67.4
China	10,380	21.5	13.4	7,588	15.1	n.a.	n.a.
Japan	4,616	9.6	6.0	36,331	231.9	1,729	41.5
Germany	3,859	8.0	5.0	47,589	74.7	1,371	62.3
Russia	1,857	3.8	2.4	12,925	13.4	1,985	25.9
France	2,846	5.9	3.7	44,538	95.3	1,489	62.7
Britain	2,945	6.1	3.8	45,653	79.1	1,677	50.5
India	2,049	4.2	2.7	1,626	51.3	n.a.	n.a.
Brazil	2,353	4.9	3.0	11,604	59.3	n.a.	n.a.

Notes: GDP for China, Germany, and Russia are IMF staff estimates, and GDP per capita for those countries and India are also IMF staff estimates. Public debt is estimated for 2014. Hours worked are for total employment and are for 2014 except for France, which is for 2013. Productivity for United States, Japan, Russia, and France is estimated.

Sources: International Monetary Fund, *World Economic Outlook Database* (April 2015), http://www.imf.org/external/pubs/ft/weo/2015/01/weodata/index.aspx (consulted August 7, 2015); Central Intelligence Agency, *CIA World Factbook*, https://www.cia.gov/library/publications/the-world-factbook/(consulted August 8, 2015); Organisation for Co-operation and Economic Development, "OECD Employment Outlook 2015, Statistical Annex" (Paris: OECD, 2015); Organisation for Co-operation and Economic Development, *Level of GDP Per Capita and Productivity*, http://stats.oecd.org/Index.aspx?DataSetCode=PDB_LV (consulted August 8, 2015).

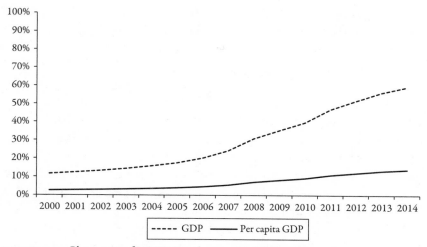

FIGURE 2.9 China as % of US GDP and per capita GDP, current prices.

Source: International Monetary Fund, World Economic Outlook Database (October 2014), http://www.imf.org/external/pubs/ft/weo/2014/02/weodata/index.aspx (consulted January 17, 2015).

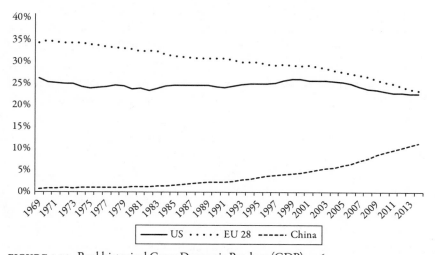

FIGURE 2.10 Real historical Gross Domestic Product (GDP), 1969–2014.

Source: USDA Economic Research Service, http://www.ers.usda.gov/data-products/international-macroeconomic-data-set.aspx (consulted January 17, 2015).

in 2000 to 11.3% in 2014.[21] The most marked decline is that of the combined economies of the EU 28, whose global GDP share has declined steadily since 1969 and sank nearly 20% between 2006 and 2014.

Long-Term Growth Trajectories

Where might these trajectories be headed? Without a crystal ball, no one can know for sure, but a cottage industry has nevertheless emerged to assess the future of what has been the most dynamic part of the picture: China's growth. To help understand what China's economic future may look like, analysts often focus on comparisons to the earlier experience of rising "Asian tigers" like Japan, Taiwan, and South Korea.

Analysts agree that to match the historical growth experience of Taiwan, South Korea, and Japan in the decades ahead Beijing will face much harder challenges than those it has confronted in sustaining rapid growth up to now. China has only recently attained middle-income status. This is a remarkable achievement, but it is much easier than moving from middle-income to high-income status.[22] As a recent World Bank report summarizes: "Growing up is hard to do. In the postwar era, many countries have developed rapidly into middle-income status, but far fewer have gone on to high-income status. Rather, they have become stuck in the so-called middle-income trap. . . . Of 101 middle-income countries in 1960, only 13 became high income by 2008."[23] Analysts also agree that even if China can, in fact, escape the middle-income trap as Japan, South Korea, and Taiwan were able to do, its growth will still be much lower in future decades than in the past (it has averaged around 10% growth for the past three decades).[24] As David Dollar underscores, Japanese, South Korean, and Taiwanese "GDP growth rates averaged close to 10% in the early stages of accumulation, similar to China's performance. Beginning at about the stage of development where China is now, there was a tendency for growth rates to decline."[25]

Although there is agreement that China will grow more slowly in the decades ahead than in the past, analysts differ greatly concerning how much more slowly. A much cited recent estimate on the lower end comes from Harvard economists Larry Summers and Lant Pritchett, who posit that China will grow at an average of 3.9% per year over the next two decades.[26] Justin Lin, a former World Bank senior economist who is now an advisor to the Chinese government, presents a prominent estimate at the higher end, arguing that China can grow between 7.5% and 8% over the next two decades.[27] Most estimates are in between, such as a widely noted recent World Bank forecast which projects that China will grow at 7% from 2016–2020, 6% from 2021–2025, and 5% from 2026–2030.[28]

The degree of China's slowdown is inherently hard to discern because many of the factors affecting China's long-term growth cannot be predicted, in particular whether the Chinese government will have the necessary will and skill to undertake needed reforms.[29] Still, there is widespread agreement concerning one key constraining factor on China's future growth that can be predicted with great precision over the next few decades: demography.[30] China will be "graying at a tremendously rapid, and indeed almost historically unprecedented, pace over the next generation," and analysts agree that this will make it harder for it to break through the middle-income trap than it was for Japan, Korea, and Taiwan and indeed all previous societies that did so, which were demographically much younger when they made this transition.[31] China's population is becoming old much earlier in its development cycle.[32] For example, when they were at China's current level of development, both Korea and Taiwan did not have high old-age dependency ratios, and they both still looked forward to decades of expansion of their working-age populations (that is, people aged twenty to sixty-five). China is in an entirely different situation (see Figure 2.11). As a World Bank report summarizes: "China will grow old before it grows rich. Its low fertility rate

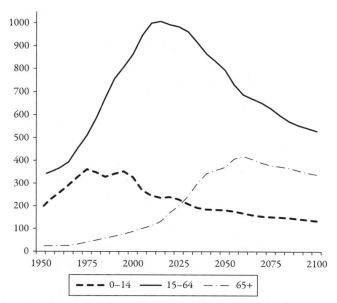

FIGURE 2.11 Population for China by major age group, 1950–2100 (in millions).

Note: All figures are using medium variant.

Source: United Nations Population Division, *World Population Prospects: The 2015 Revision,* http://esa.un.org/unpd/wpp/DVD/ (consulted August 12, 2015).

and consequent low population growth rate will mean a rising share of old people in the economy. The old-age dependency ratio—defined as the ratio of those aged 65 and over to those between the ages of 15 and 64—will double over the next 20 years. By 2030, China's dependency ratio will reach the level of Norway and the Netherlands today. Just as important, China's working-age population will decline after 2015."[33] In contrast, because it is such a significant destination for immigration and has a fertility rate right around replacement level (usually calculated at 2.1 children per couple), the US working-age population will continue to expand in the decades ahead, and it will not face the prospect of a rapidly rising old-age dependency ratio (see Figure 2.12 and Table 2.7).

The United States and China face dramatically differing demographic futures—one comparatively young and growing and the other rapidly aging and shrinking. Needless to say, its relatively rosy demographic future does not free the United States from the need to confront numerous well-identified challenges, including a rapidly declining infrastructure, rising inequality, and

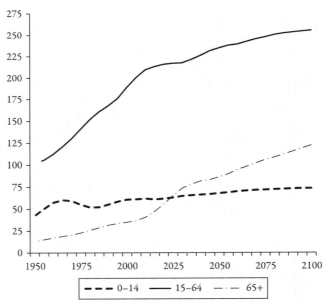

FIGURE 2.12 Population for the United States by major age group, 1950–2100 (in millions).

Note: All figures are using medium variant.

Source: United Nations Population Division, *World Population Prospects: The 2015 Revision*, http://esa.un.org/unpd/wpp/DVD/ (consulted August 12, 2015).

Table 2.7 Immigration Levels and Demographics

	Fertility Rate 2010–2015	Total Number of Immigrants	% of Total Number of Immigrants in the World	Median Age in 2010	Projected Median Age in 2030	Projected Median Age in 2050	Population in 2010	Projected 2050 Population	Projected 2100 Population
United States	1.89	45,785,090	19.8	37	40	42	312,247,000	388,865,000	450,385,000
China	1.55	848,511	0.4	35	43	50	1,359,821,000	1,348,056,000	1,004,392,000
Japan	1.40	2,437,169	1.1	45	52	53	127,353,000	107,411,000	83,175,000
Germany	1.39	9,845,244	4.3	44	49	51	83,017,000	74,513,000	63,244,000
Russia	1.66	11,048,064	4.8	38	42	41	143,618,000	128,599,000	117,445,000
France	2.00	7,439,086	3.2	40	43	44	63,231,000	71,137,000	75,998,000
Britain	1.92	7,824,131	3.4	40	42	43	62,066,000	75,361,000	82,370,000
India	2.48	5,338,486	2.3	26	31	37	1,205,625,000	1,705,333,000	1,659,786,000
Brazil	1.82	599,678	0.3	26	37	45	195,210,000	237,270,000	200,305,000

Notes: All figures are using medium variant. Total number of immigrants and % of total number of immigrants in the world are for 2013.

Sources: United Nations Department of Economic and Social Affairs Population Division, *Trends in International Migrant Stock: The 2013 Revision,* http://esa.un.org/un-migration/TIMSA2013/migrantstocks2013.htm (consulted August 12, 2015); United Nations Population Division, *World Population Prospects: The 2015 Revision,* http://esa.un.org/unpd/wpp/ (consulted August 12, 2015).

an overall decline in educational proficiency in math and science.[34] Everyone
knows that demography is not destiny. But it is an important and predict-
able part of destiny. In explaining why China's growth will be prone to slow
down, demography is notable because its overall trajectory in the next several
decades is so clear and scholars who analyze it all agree that it will have a significant constraining effect on China's growth. Against the backdrop of the
inevitable aging of all the wealthy countries and most of the major powers,
America's "demographic exceptionalism" is widely seen as a comparative advantage in the decades to come.[35]

Moving Beyond GDP

As a way of gauging the role a country plays in the world economy—with all
the implications for a state's power that follow—GDP is becoming increasingly problematic. As Diane Coyle notes in her study of GDP as the central
economic metric, "It is a measure of the economy best suited to an earlier
era."[36] Developed in and for the era of mass production, she argues, it is increasingly misleading because it does not adequately capture the significance
of four important factors of growing salience: (1) innovation, (2) information,
including online activities that do not have a price, (3) "the urgency of questions of sustainability, requiring more attention to be paid to the depletion of
resources and assets, which is undermining potential future GDP growth,"
and (4) economic globalization, in particular the fact that ever more goods
are now "made in complicated global supply chains."[37] Coyle's general argument has been echoed by numerous other economists of late; for example,
Stiglitz, Sen, and Fitoussi conclude that "the time has come to adapt our
system of measurement of economic activity to better reflect the structural
changes that have characterized the evolution of modern economies."[38]

Factoring in Information and Innovation

We discussed above the first major factor not adequately reflected in GDP—
innovation—by presenting a variety of means of measuring the technological
capabilities of nations. The second factor Coyle highlights is information. As
Michael Mandel argues, "Government economic statistics, stuck in the 20th
century, are missing most of the data boom ... [and] dramatically under-
count the growth of data-driven activities."[39] An MIT study illustrated this
phenomenon: "Thousands of new information goods and services are introduced every year. Yet, according to the official GDP statistics, the information

sector (software, publishing, motion picture and sound recording, broadcasting, telecom, and information and data processing services) is about the same share of the economy as it was 25 years ago—about 4%."[40]

The underlying point is that the more knowledge-based an economy is, the more likely it is that GDP underestimates its size. Clearly, innovation and information are central to the US economy. One study estimates that calculating GDP with information as a distinct category alongside goods and services would have added over just over one-half a percent to US real GDP growth in 2012.[41] One economist estimates that a full accounting of the benefits of the technologies associated with the information economy could amount to "trillions of dollars of benefits that are not measured in the Bureau of Economic Analysis's official GDP statistics."[42]

Factoring in Economic Globalization

Economic globalization creates a key statistical problem for GDP because so many goods are no longer made in a single country but instead are constructed using global supply chains. As an OECD/WTO analysis concludes, "With the globalization of production, there is a growing awareness that conventional trade statistics may give a misleading perspective of the importance of trade to economic growth and income and that 'what you see is not what you get.' "[43] This matters greatly for GDP, as Zachary Karabell underscores:

> Well into the twentieth century, there was little ambiguity about who made what where [and] the process of assigning something to a particular country wasn't that challenging. . . . Developments after World War II, especially after the 1990s, shattered that simplicity. As a result, the neat formula of GDP that assumes a basic accounting of exports minus imports and then a plus or minus for the "economy" began to fray. Categories became more fluid, even as there was no change at all in the basic formula we use to calculate GDP and in the way in which we draw conclusions from these numbers.[44]

Estimating China's economic weight on the world stage is now especially difficult because MNCs direct so much of how that country engages with the global economy. As we noted above: (1) the majority of China's exports consists of processing trade, (2) the vast bulk of this processing trade (84%) is directed by MNCs based outside of China, and (3) foreign MNCs based in China are responsible for around a third of China's nonprocessing trade. A recent WTO report underscores that "the notion of 'country of origin' [is] losing much of its significance, since the total commercial value of a product is attributed to the country in which it last underwent processing, regardless of its relative contribution to the value-added chain."[45] A telling, well-documented example is the value of the Apple iPhone and iPad, which are both assigned to China because they undergo final assembly there. In their careful analysis of the iPhone's and iPad's global supply chains, Kenneth Kraemer and his coauthors conclude:

> While these products, including most of their components, are manufactured in China, the primary benefits go to the U.S. economy as Apple continues to keep most of its product design, software development, product management, marketing and other high-wage functions in the U.S. China's role is much smaller than most casual observers would think. . . . Only $10 or less in direct labor wages that go into an iPhone or iPad is paid to China's workers. So while each unit sold in the U.S. adds from $229 to $275 to the U.S.-China trade deficit (the estimated factory costs of an iPhone or iPad), the portion retained in China's economy is a tiny fraction of that amount.[46]

The more general point is that the significance of globalization must be taken into account when analyzing the relative economic heft of the most powerful countries. The premise of Sean Starrs' 2013 study is indeed that a fundamental limitation of recent discussions about the changing distribution of power is "not taking globalization seriously. With the rise of transnational corporations (TNCs), transnational production networks, and the globalization of corporate ownership, we can no longer give the same relevance to national accounts such as balance of trade and GDP in the twenty-first century as we did in the twentieth. Rather, we must summon data on the TNCs themselves to encompass their transnational operations."[47]

Statistics on the stock of outward foreign direct investment (FDI) give some sense of the degree to which firms based in various states have sought to disperse their production activities geographically. As Table 2.8 shows, the outward US FDI level is far beyond that of any other state. For MNCs, the typical guiding motivation for dispersing production is to take advantage of locational differences and thereby reap various efficiencies.[48]

If US MNCs are at the forefront of the geographic dispersal of production activities, then we might expect to find that they are highly competitive in most key sectors. Starrs' study shows that this is indeed the case. Through an analysis of the top two thousand corporations in the world, he finds that

Table 2.8 Stock of Outward Foreign Direct
Investment, 2014

	Foreign Direct Investment (in billions)
United States	5,266
China	793
Hong Kong	1,439
Japan	1,284
Germany	2,048
Russia	534
France	1,510
Britain	1,884
India	130
Brazil	178

Source: Central Intelligence Agency, *CIA World Factbook,* https://www.cia.gov/library/publications/the-world-factbook/rankorder/2199rank.html (consulted August 11, 2015).

"American corporations account for by far the most dominant profit-shares across the most sectors than corporations for any other country, especially in sectors at the technological frontier."[49] Tables 2.9 and 2.10 reproduce Starrs' data but organize it in a different way; Table 2.9 shows that US MNCs have the dominant share of global profits in eighteen of twenty-five sectors, while Table 2.10 shows the seven sectors where US MNCs are not dominant in profit shares. Strikingly, not only are US MNCs ahead in eighteen of the twenty-five sectors, but in many of them they are extremely far ahead: US MNCs account for a majority of the global profit share in eight sectors and at least a third of global profit share in fourteen sectors. A recent OECD report underscores how China is in a fundamentally different competitive position:

> Although China has indigenous technological capabilities to produce competitive products in labour intensive sectors such as apparel, this capability is still limited in high technology sectors where it relies heavily on imported inputs. . . . China's competitiveness within GVCs [global value chains] is still concentrated in processing and assembling activities. However, its role as the world's assembler allows China to generate only limited value added compared to other

Table 2.9 Sectors where the United States is ranked no. 1 in Global Profit Share, 2012

Sector	% of Global Profit Share Held by US Corporations
Aerospace and Defense	67
Business and Personal Services	44
Casinos, Hotels, and Restaurants	64
Chemicals	25
Computer Hardware and Software	74
Conglomerates	43
Electronics	39
Financial Services	53
Food, Beverages, and Tobacco	43
Healthcare Equipment and Services	84
Heavy Machinery	37
Insurance	41
Media	67
Oil and Gas	28
Pharmaceuticals	49
Retail	55
Transportation	31
Utilities	27

Source: Sean Starrs, "American Economic Power Hasn't Declined—It Globalized! Summoning the Data and Taking Globalization Seriously," *International Studies Quarterly*, Vol. 57 (December 2013), p. 822.

countries engaging in more technology and knowledge intensive activities within GVCs.[50]

Starrs notes further that these profit-share data reported in Tables 2.9 and 2.10 actually significantly underestimate the extent of US dominance in the global economy, because they are based on the assumption that US investors own only US firms. Yet as Table 2.11 shows, US investors also own very sizeable amounts of shares of corporations in other countries. The fact that "American firms combined own 46% of all publicly listed shares of the top 500 corporations in the world," Starrs notes, "signifies how globalized American economic power has become. Chinese capital, by contrast, is almost entirely nationally

Table 2.10 Sectors where the United States is not ranked no. 1 in Global Profit Share, 2012

Sector	Leading Country	% of Global Profit Share Held by Leading Country
Auto, Truck, and Motorcycle	Germany	29
Banking	China	24
Construction	China	22
Forestry, Metals, and Mining	Australia	17
Real Estate	Hong Kong	37
Telecommunications	Hong Kong	15
Trading Companies	Japan	87

Source: Sean Starrs, "Economic Power Hasn't Declined—It Globalized! Summoning the Data and Taking Globalization Seriously," *International Studies Quarterly*, Vol. 57 (2013): p. 822.

Table 2.11 Top 10 national owners of the world's 500 top multinational corporations, 2012

	% of Ownership
United States	45.9
Japan	7.9
China	5.9
Britain	5.8
France	3.9
Canada	3.0
South Korea	2.2
Germany	2.2
India	1.7
Australia	1.3

Source: Sean Starrs, "American Economic Power Hasn't Declined—It Globalized! Summoning the Data and Taking Globalization Seriously," *International Studies Quarterly*, Vol. 57 (2013): p. 825.

contained. . . . Chinese ownership of non-Chinese-domiciled firms in the top 500 is negligible."[51] In turn, he finds that not only are US shareholders far and away the top owners of US corporations, but Americans are also top owners of the twenty largest European firms.[52] Because American firms own such a large percentage of many of the world's top corporations and because American citizens own the vast majority of the shares of American firms, Starrs finds that 41% of all global household assets are held by Americans—something that he argues demonstrates "how globalized American capital, American ownership, and American economic power has become. We cannot rely on national accounts to meaningfully assess power in the global political economy."[53]

Factoring In Sustainability

GDP statistics systematically fail to account adequately for sustainability in general and environmental damage in particular. Crucially, GDP statistics do not reliably reflect whether current economic growth occurs in ways that harm the environment and thereby comes at the expense of future growth. While GDP does count the depreciation of man-made objects such as machines and roads, it does not count the depreciation of the physical environment. Karabell illustrates this problem: "If a steel mill produces pollution that then requires a cleanup, both the initial output (the steel) and the cost of addressing its by-product (the cleanup) add to GDP. So, too, would the cost of health care for any workers or residents injured or sickened by the pollution. Conversely, if a company replaces its conventional light bulbs with long-lasting LED bulbs and, as a result, spends less on lighting and electricity, the efficiency gains would detract from GDP. Yet few would argue that the pollution example represents a positive development or that the lighting example constitutes a negative one."[54] A country's long-term economic capacity will obviously be reduced if it has to use relatively more energy and has a larger number of workers who are sick and require expensive treatment, but GDP statistics simply do not take such environmental sustainability dynamics into account.

Although all countries have a lot to do to address global environmental problems such as climate change, developed countries such as Japan and the United States generally shifted decades ago to more strongly prioritize protection of their local environment. Because they were prosperous, they began to address issues such as clean air, clean water, and the prevention of toxic waste dumping when the need became pressing. China is in a different situation: it "is more like a teenage smoker with emphysema. The costs of pollution have mounted well before it is ready to curtail economic development."[55] That China does far less to protect its local environment than more developed countries is well acknowledged. China ranks 118th (out of 178 countries) on the comprehensive Environmental Performance Index and 176th on air quality.[56] What is less well acknowledged is that China's long-term weight on the world stage will not be as high as its current GDP growth statistics would seem to indicate, because they do not properly account for the economic costs of its present practice of environmentally harmful growth and the extent to which current growth comes at the expense of the country's long-term economic growth potential.

A prominent effort to better account for China's environmental damage was advanced by the Chinese government itself in the mid-2000s, when it created a "Green GDP" measure that recalculated GDP to reflect the cost of pollution:

> [The] first report . . . estimated that pollution in 2004 cost just over 3 percent of the gross domestic product, meaning that the pollution-adjusted growth rate that year would drop to about 7 percent from 10 percent. Officials said at the time that their formula used low estimates of environmental damage to health and did not assess the impact on China's ecology. . . . But the early results were so sobering— in some provinces the pollution-adjusted growth rates were reduced to almost zero—that the project was banished to China's ivory tower . . . and stripped of official influence.[57]

Other estimates are much less conservative. In 2006, Zhu Guangyao, then deputy chief of the State Environmental Protection Agency (SEPA), estimated that environmental damage in China is "roughly 10 percent of the country's gross domestic product."[58] A 2001 World Bank study found that "pollution is costing China an annual 8–12% of its . . . GDP in direct damage, such as the impact on crops of acid rain, medical bills, lost work from illness, money spent on disaster relief following floods and the implied costs of resource depletion."[59] And a 2007 study jointly produced by the World Bank and SEPA found that the total cost of just two forms of pollution—air and water pollution—by themselves amount to 5.8% of GDP.[60]

Inclusive Wealth

China's share of global GDP has clearly undergone a dramatic ascent in recent years, and analysts are correct to note that this represents a significant change in the distribution of capabilities. But although GDP reveals a lot about states' economic capacity, it also hides a lot. And it does so in a manner guaranteed to underestimate the economic gap between the United States and China. This is partly because the costs of environmental damage are not properly factored into GDP. In turn, the more knowledge-based and global-ized a country's production is, the more likely it is that GDP underestimates its size: the more an economy resembles the mid-20th century manufacturing model for which the GDP measure was originally developed, the fewer such distortions GDP entails. China is clearly a poster child for the latter sort of economy, while the US economy is among the world's most knowledge-based and globalized.

Given the significance of these distortions associated with GDP, there would ideally be an alternative measure that could be used for making more appropriate comparisons between states that are as divergent as the United States and China. A promising potential candidate that at least partially avoids some of these distortions is the UN's newly inaugurated "inclusive wealth" measure. Although not without its flaws, this measure represents economists' most systematic effort to date to create a rigorous and transpar-ent measure of a state's stock of wealth. Inclusive wealth measures a coun-try's stock of assets in three areas: "(1) manufactured capital (roads, buildings, machines, and equipment), (2) human capital (skills, education, health), and (3) natural capital (sub-soil resources, ecosystems, the atmosphere)."[61] Unlike GDP, which is a measure of a flow of goods and services for a specified time period (typically a short one), inclusive wealth aims to provide information on the state of a country's capital stock for generating wealth over the long term. As the *Economist* put it, "[g]auging an economy by its GDP is like judging a company by its quarterly profits, without ever peeking at its balance-sheet."[62] By contrast, inclusive wealth measures "the stocks of produced capital, natu-ral capital and human capital [and] shows how much wealth a country can potentially create, not just how much is being made right now. . . . The index's transition from measuring flows to accounting stocks provides an intergener-ational understanding of well-being and wealth."[63]

Based on this inclusive wealth measure, America's wealth amounted to almost $144 trillion in 2010—a level 4.5 times that of China's level of inclusive wealth in 2010 ($32 trillion).[64] Although economists did not create this inclu-sive wealth measure to capture what international relations scholars call "latent power"—that is, the key resources that exist within a state that a government can draw upon to advance its geopolitical objectives—it clearly captures this construct much better than GDP does.[65]

Conclusion

The analysis in this chapter reveals that the gap in overall capabilities be-tween the United States and China remains very large. Nothing in the foregoing analysis, however, gainsays China's rapid economic rise in recent years—which has caused it to break away from other leading powers such as Russia, Germany, and Japan in one crucial sense: it alone has at least the potential to someday become a superpower peer with America. Only a highly improbable combination of large scale and rapid growth can put a state in a position like China's: moving in the direction of having the latent material capacity to match the superpower. There is no other candidate today. Indeed, after China the most plausible candidate would be the EU, but it is far from being a state, and its integration trajectory has stalled; moreover, its economic trajectory (like Japan's and Russia's) is moving in the wrong direction. That China's gigantic potential has reached this stage is a significant development, but, as the next chapter shows, this does not mean that China is poised to become a superpower peer of the United States anytime soon.

3

Assessing Change
in a One-Superpower World

CHAPTER 2'S CONCLUSION GENERATES new questions. How long will the United States remain the world's sole superpower? What stages must China or any other rising state pass through on the journey from great power to superpower? How should analysts think about change versus continuity in a one-superpower world with a fast-rising state like China? This chapter addresses these questions. We first assess the speed with which China might bridge the great power/superpower gap. Whereas one might presume that approaching the economic size of the United States would position China to seek superpower status, we conclude that the gap between economic parity and a credible bid for superpower status should be measured in many decades. If the scales are to level out such that there are two or more roughly comparable states at the top—as was the norm for centuries—we thus expect it will be a very long time coming. This puts a premium on addressing the next two tasks: delineating the stages that lie between great power and superpower in the 21st century and providing a way to assess change in today's international system without exaggerating it or downplaying its significance.

Why It Will Long Be a One-Superpower World

Determining the precise economic and technological level a state must attain in order to have sufficient material capacity to bid for superpower status is not straightforward. If a rising state's economy and its technological level match the leading state's, then it is easy enough to conclude that it is in position to bid for superpower status. But what if the rising state is not equal to the leading state in one or both dimensions? If the rising state is comparable to the leading state technologically but is around half of its economic size, then history would suggest that it might have the potential to bid for superpower status, as the Soviet Union did during the first half of the Cold War (though Moscow needed a totalitarian state to distill the needed resources and also challenged the United States in a very different military technological environment). But as the previous chapter established, a different question is relevant today: What if the rising state's economy is approaching the size of the leading state's, but it is at a fundamentally lower level technologically?

There is no modern historical precedent for this situation: the recent rising states of note—namely, the United States in the 19th and early 20th centuries, Germany in the early 20th century, and the Soviet Union in the middle of the 20th century—were not at dramatically different technological levels than the leading state. As a result, when assessing the relative power of Germany or the United States vis-à-vis the United Kingdom and the Soviet Union vis-à-vis the United States, technology essentially faded into the background; the crucial question became the economic size of these rising states and how much they tried to distill their wealth into military power. But when the leading and rising states diverge technologically to a dramatic degree, as is the case today, a critical question is whether the latter has the technological capacity to produce and field a defense force that can effectively match up with the former's. This question would arise in any era, but it is especially salient now given the extraordinarily complicated nature of much modern weaponry. In this respect, Tai Ming Cheung underscores that China now faces "an enormous task of remaking a defense establishment that is still more suited to fighting a Vietnam-era conflict than a 21st century engagement."[1]

To understand the scale of this challenge, it is useful to return to Posen's analysis of the "command of the commons."[2] His examination of the unique set of assets that the United States has developed to sustain this commanding position in the global system reveals four central attributes: (1) a large scientific and industrial base; (2) the particular mix of weapons accumulated over the past few decades of procurement; (3) the ability developed over decades to coordinate the production of needed weapons systems; and (4) the particular skills and associated technological infrastructure the United States has painstakingly developed to be able to effectively employ these weapons in a coordinated manner. In the analysis that follows, we establish the likely time scale each of these four attributes entails, revealing exactly why we expect that China cannot quickly progress from great power to superpower status.

Scientific and Industrial Base

Posen stresses that the "specific weapons needed to secure and exploit command of the commons . . . depend on a huge scientific and industrial base." Having a much larger scientific and industrial base than any other state, he maintains, has enabled the United States to "undertake larger projects than any other military in the world."[3]

There is no reason to think that China will soon be able to develop anything like a comparable scientific and industrial base. The previous chapter established the main reason: China is at a fundamentally different technological level than the United States. Although China is rapidly enhancing its technological inputs—notably, its R&D spending and its graduation rates for science and engineering students—there are natural limits to how fast it, or any state, can do so in a productive way.

For one thing, to educate many more science and engineering students to augment global competitiveness would require significantly increasing the number of institutions (each staffed with the needed, highly trained people) capable of providing appropriate and useful training far beyond the level that China has now. Very few Chinese institutions are regarded as globally competitive, as Table 3.1 shows. As Gary Gereffi and his colleagues report, "The recent surge in engineering graduation rates can be traced to a series of top-down government policy changes that began in 1999 . . . to promote China's transition from 'elite education' to 'mass education' by increasing university enrollment."[4] Enrollment in science and engineering surged after the early 2000s, but the number of technical institutions and teachers and staff was actually lowered, which meant that "graduation rate increases have been achieved by dramatically increasing class sizes."[5] The World Bank concludes that the net result of this "massive expansion of enrollment, which has strained instructional capacity" in combination with other factors—such as "the short duration of Ph.D. training (3 years)"—is that "the quality of the training is weak, and many graduates are having difficulty finding employment."[6] A recent McKinsey report adds that only 10% of Chinese engineers "would be suitable to . . . successfully work at a multinational company."[7] Interviews by Gereffi and his coauthors similarly found that "multinational and local technology companies revealed that they felt comfortable hiring graduates from only 10 to 15 universities across the country. . . . All of the people we talked to agreed that the quality of engineering education dropped off drastically beyond those on the list."[8]

Table 3.1 University Rankings

	QS World University Rankings 2013		Times Higher Education World University Rankings 2013–2014		Academic Ranking of World Universities 2013	
	% Share of Top 20	% Share of Top 50	% Share of Top 20	% Share of Top 50	% Share of Top 20	% Share of Top 50
United States	55	38	75	60	85	70
China	0	4	0	4	0	0
Japan	0	4	0	2	0	4
Germany	0	2	0	0	0	2
Russia	0	0	0	0	0	0
France	0	4	0	0	0	4
Britain	30	16	15	14	10	10
India	0	0	0	0	0	0
Brazil	0	0	0	0	0	0

Sources: QS Top World University Ranking 2013, http://www.topuniversities.com/university-rankings/world-university-rankings/2013#sorting=rank+region=+country=+faculty=+stars=false+search= (consulted March 23, 2014); The Times Higher Education World University Rankings 2013–2014, http://www.timeshighereducation.co.uk/world-university-rankings/2013-14/world-ranking (consulted March 23, 2014); Academic Ranking of World Universities 2013, http://www.shanghairanking.com/ARWU2013.html (consulted March 23, 2014).

In turn, rapidly augmenting spending on R&D is unlikely to produce dramatically improved technological capacity if it is not embedded within an appropriate structure for fostering innovation—something that China is very far away from having. As a recent World Bank report emphasizes, "Increasing R&D spending . . . is likely to have only a small impact on productivity growth, unless the quality of this research and its commercial relevance and uptake are substantially increased." A key limitation, the report stresses, is that

> government and state enterprises conduct the bulk of research and development—and part of this effort still seems divorced from the real needs of the economy. True, China has seen a sharp rise in scientific patents and published papers, but few have commercial relevance and even fewer have translated into new products or exports. . . . A better innovation policy in China will begin with a redefinition of government's role in the national innovation system, shifting away from targeted attempts at developing specific new technologies and moving toward institutional development and an enabling environment that supports economy-wide innovation efforts.[9]

In this regard, China is notably handicapped by insufficient institutions for the allocation of capital and the protection of intellectual property.[10]

Ultimately, it is a formidable task to create a leading-edge scientific and industrial base. China is trying hard to do so and is certainly making significant progress. But given its current technological level and major impediments such as comparatively weak educational institutions and poorly developed institutional structure for fostering innovation, there is every reason to think that it will be a very long time before it will be able to create a scientific and industrial base that is anything like the one that has given the United States a platform for sustaining the command of the commons.

Mix of Weapons Accumulated through Decades of Procurement

The second attribute Posen highlights that sustains America's command of the commons (namely, particular mix of weapons the United States has accumulated over the past few decades) has taken a very, very long time to develop and procure. The main reason is that the ever-growing complexity of many top-end systems has greatly increased their development time. Whereas an advanced system like a combat aircraft had tens of thousands of components in the 1950s, nowadays "a modern weapon system like a jet aircraft . . . consists of hundreds of thousands of different systems, subsystems, components and spare parts, whose individual performance and compatibility with the system depend on extremely small variations."[11] Not surprisingly, as the number of parts and lines of code associated with the production of aerospace vehicles grew, the development time of these weapons concomitantly increased from roughly five years in the 1960s to around ten years in the 1990s. Today, "combat aircraft projects take between 15 and 20 years from research to production," while "the current development cycle for military and intelligence satellites from the initiation of basic research to field deployment is approximately twenty years."[12]

The net result is that in many areas where the weapons systems of other states lag behind those of the United States, the time needed to close that gap is inevitably very long. Even if another state has the necessary scientific and industrial base and the skills and it seeks to produce these weapons *and* all goes well, there will necessarily be a lengthy lag before it actually possesses them. For example, it is projected to take around fifteen years for the United Kingdom to develop a nuclear submarine to succeed its current Trident system. And yet the United Kingdom has significant advantages over China: most notably, it has had more experience producing advanced systems, including submarines, and it receives extensive, direct assistance from the United States in weapons production.

In the end, notwithstanding that much of US military spending does not go toward the accumulation of a larger stock of weapons, the fact that the United States has invested so much more than China in defense spending for so long matters a great deal, in large part because many of the kinds of systems in which China lags take so long to produce. In this regard, consider that during the 2000–2014 period, the United States cumulatively spent nearly $9 trillion on defense, while China spent $1.5 trillion (in constant 2011 US dollars).[13] And although we lack systematic data that can be used to precisely track China's military R&D spending over time compared to that of the United States, there is general agreement that the long-term cumulative gap between the United States and China on this dimension is even more dramatic than it is regarding overall defense spending (recent estimates indicate that China has now become the number 2 global spender on military R&D but that it still is at less than 10% of US spending level, which totaled $79 billion in 2014).[14] Especially given the overall complexity of current military technology, decades of massive US investments in key military capabilities now present formidable barriers to entry.

Nuclear attack submarines (SSNs) are a particularly telling example of how hard it will be for China to catch up in the design and production of weapons systems that are intrinsically complex, take a long time to develop, and in which the United States has made sustained investments over many decades. China is now capable of making SSNs that are roughly comparable in quietness to the kinds that the United States made in the 1950s, but since then the United States has invested hundreds of billions of dollars and six decades of effort to advance its SSN program, and its current generation of Virginia-class submarines has achieved absolute levels of silencing.[15] In those areas such as SSNs where China is far behind the United States in military technology and where the systems in question take a very long time to develop, it will thus require a great many years of cumulative effort by China before it would even be in a position to potentially close the gap that exists due to the United States' own cumulative effort over many decades.

"Systems Integration" in the Design and Production of Weapons Systems

The third attribute Posen highlights is "significant skills in systems integration and the management of large-scale industrial projects."[16] Without these crucial skills, it is impossible to supervise the production of the kinds of weapons systems that give the United States command of the commons. Many top-end weapon systems today require an extraordinarily high level of precision in the design and production process—something that has been elusive in many areas for China. As Richard Bitzinger and colleagues conclude, "Aside from a few pockets of excellence, such as ballistic missiles, the Chinese military-industrial complex has appeared to demonstrate few capacities for designing and producing relatively advanced conventional weapons systems. Especially when it comes to combat aircraft, surface combatants, and ground equipment, the Chinese generally have confronted considerable difficulties in moving prototypes into production, which has resulted in long development phases, heavy program delays, and low production runs."[17]

Aircraft engines are a case in point. Farley recounts that "the problem with Chinese engines is that they've been remarkably unreliable. Engines require extremely tight tolerances in construction; even small errors can lead to the engine burning out."[18] Because of China's "inability to domestically mass-produce modern high-performance jet engines," it continues to be dependent on Russian-made engines in its tactical aircraft; and yet Russian jet engine producers are "a distant second in quality" to the "top jet engine producers," which "are all located in the U.S. and Western Europe."[19] As Sloman and Dickey emphasize, the Russian engines that China relies upon "are no longer cutting edge. The designs of these fighter engines date back more than 30 years and they were intended to be used in aircraft that are much lighter than the new models being tested today."[20]

Many discussions of China's ability to translate its rapidly growing economic capacity into military capacity do not recognize how extraordinarily difficult it is to gain the kind of system integration skill needed to manage the design and production of the panoply of advanced weapons systems that is now needed to project significant military power globally.[i] The actors involved in US defense production decisions have painstakingly accumulated this kind of systems integration skill over decades.[21] In general, China has most consistently made rapid progress in those kinds of weapons systems—such as missiles—in which the "learning curve" is relatively short. In a number of other areas that are more complicated and required much greater skill in production and design—such as aircraft engines—even an extremely high level of Chinese effort and resources has so far not allowed it to be able to learn how to mass-produce effective systems that are comparable even to the kinds that the United States and Soviet Union began fielding in the final phase of the Cold War.[22] And in many other areas, perhaps most notably SSNs and antisubmarine warfare, it would appear that China recognizes that

---

i. As Gilli and Gilli note:

> As the capabilities of military platforms increase, it requires a higher number of more advanced systems, subsystems and components. Integrating them together and ensuring reciprocal compatibility and systemic reliability, while maximizing the platform overall performance is extremely daunting. On the one hand, cutting-edge technologies inevitably give rise to compatibility problems that are difficult to anticipate, understand and to address because of a lack of sufficient knowledge and experience. On the other hand, as the number of systems, subsystems and components grows, the integration process becomes more complex: the F-35/Lighting II Joint Strike Fighter, for instance, features 17 miles of copper wiring while its software contains 8 million lines of code. Minor variations from the expected ideal specification for even marginal components . . . can result in severe malfunctions and possibly even in systemic failure. Anticipating, understanding and addressing the problems emerging from operating in demanding environmental conditions (solar activity, temperature excursion, wind, etc.), as well as designing, developing and integrating systems and subsystems aimed at neutralizing enemy countermeasures add a further layer of complexity that, inevitably, renders production more challenging.

Andrea Gilli and Mauro Gilli, "The Diffusion of Drone Warfare? Industrial, Organizational and Infrastructural Constraints: Military Innovations and the Ecosystem Challenge," *Security Studies*, Vol. 25, No. 1 (Winter 2016), p. 57.

it is so far from being able to manage the production of top-end systems that it has essentially decided not to try. In short, a "selection bias" exists when we observe the speed at which China has moved forward in military technology in the past two decades: it has concentrated much of its efforts on those areas where such rapid progress was feasible.[23]

Note that just being "very good" in the production and/or design of many top-end systems will likely not be sufficient—at least, not in a conflict with a technologically superior competitor. These differences can be pivotal. In the Gulf War, for example, technological superiority gave the American M1 tank a decisive battlefield advantage over the most advanced Iraqi tanks. Due to its advanced computer-guided firing mechanism, the M1 was able to destroy Iraqi tanks from as far as four kilometers away and to regularly score first-round hits of Iraqi tanks from three kilometers away; this is something the Iraqi's T-72 simply did not have the capacity to do. Beyond this, the M1's advanced sights helped give it a marked advantage in detection over the Iraqi T-72 tanks: the M1 had the ability to detect T-72s "four times as far as the Iraqis."[24] As a result of these two technological advantages, US M1 tanks were in a position to "detect and destroy Iraqi vehicles from *outside* the Iraqis' maximum range."[25]

Fighter jets provide another telling example. Given that no air force has risen to challenge the United States' command of the skies since Vietnam, the classic example of what happens when combat aircraft of different generations meet remains Israel's 100% success rate against Syria's Soviet-supplied fighters over Lebanon in 1982.[26] While the analogy is only suggestive, China's combat aircraft clearly have significant limitations when compared with US models. The "problem with Chinese- and Russian-construction stealth fighters is that if there's a bolt out of place, it shows up on a radar signature. Russian and Chinese construction is typically much looser" than American stealth fighter construction.[27] Notably, excellence in production and design must be achieved not just regarding some elements of a fighter; China's advanced aircraft program has achieved many successes, but the significance of these accomplishments is greatly undermined by its lack of ability to produce a capable engine. Regarding its fifth-generation fighter program, Sloman and Dickey underscore that "engines are a critically important component of any fighter aircraft. . . . Without a reliable, high-performance turbofan engine to power them," China's fifth generation fighter program "will be crippled."[28] Because its engine lacks the requisite power, China's fourth-generation fighter, the J-15 (which is a reverse-engineered version of the Russian Su-33), needs to have only a partial fuel load or a light missile load to be able to take off from an aircraft carrier.[29]

For China it is much easier to continue to make improvements in areas where it was already positioned to quickly become very capable, such as missiles, than it would be to gain the ability to effectively produce and design systems across the range of areas where it is not currently close to being capable of matching up with American ones. Catching up in those areas will be very hard, and even if China succeeds, it will almost certainly take an extremely long time to do so.[30] A fundamental reason why is that attaining the necessary knowledge and experience to produce these kinds of top-end systems is "largely a product of a costly and time-consuming process of trial and error."[31] As Mauro Gilli notes, "Significant technological problems emerge when designing, developing, and manufacturing complex . . . weapon systems. These problems stem from the interaction of the high number of sophisticated components integrated together. Anticipating, identifying and addressing these problems can prove extremely difficult, and require extensive experience in the product-area under development and with the technologies involved."[ii]

Some argue that China might leapfrog the painstaking development processes we have described by stealing via cyberespionage.[32] Given the nature of the evidence in question, only intelligence officials are in a position to evaluate this claim. We recently interviewed a former top senior official in the US government with very detailed knowledge of China's cyber capabilities who emphasized that stealing weapons secrets is by far the least useful benefit that China is able to secure via cyberespionage on US firms. Specifically, in descending order from most to least valuable, the official delineated three kinds of information that China is able to secure in this manner: (1) information that helps Chinese firms in negotiations with non-Chinese firms, (2) corporate intellectual property, and (3) information on military technology. As for why information secured via cyberespionage is least useful for military technology, the official emphasized that the situation today with China is different in three key respects from the Soviet experience of securing weapons plans from spies during the early decades of the Cold War: (1) having a spy hand over a single plan is far more valuable than stealing huge numbers of documents and having to sift through them to determine what information

---

ii. He further emphasizes that "the increase in complexity of weapon systems has made the know-how in designing, developing, and manufacturing weapon systems more tacit . . . i.e., it cannot be written down in terms of general rules and principles. It refers mostly to the knowledge derived from experience, and for this reason is retained by people and organizations. As a result, it can be transferred 'only from master to apprentice' through demonstration and instruction." Gilli, "The Struggle for Military-Technological Superiority: Complexity Systems Integration and the Technological Challenges of Imitation," PhD dissertation, Northwestern University, 2015, ch. 3.

is valuable, (2) given the complexity of many modern systems, just getting information on one part without the remainder is unlikely to be especially helpful, and (3) most weapons systems today are not especially valuable on their own, but only as part of an integrated system.

In general, stealing weapons plans is much more likely to be an effective catch-up strategy when the technology gap is small and the range and complexity of the relevant technologies are low, and these conditions do not hold for China today. For essentially these same reasons, reverse engineering (that is, taking something apart to see how it works in order to copy it) is also unlikely to allow China to quickly make gains in those areas where it now greatly lags behind the United States. As Gilli concludes in his systematic analysis of technological imitation, "The increase in complexity of military technology that has taken place over the past century has led to a change in the system of production, which in turn has made the imitation and the replication of the performance of military technology more difficult. . . . The advantages derived from imitating foreign military technology . . . have progressively disappeared because of the increase in complexity. Nowadays, innovating countries can leverage their know-how and experience, which in turn grant them significant performance advantages over potential imitators."[33]

As one of us has stressed previously, a related consideration is that having the requisite domestic production and design skills for modern weaponry must also be complemented in today's world by an ability to tap into global production networks in key dual technologies: states that are unable or choose not to pursue globalization in weapons-related production simply will be unable to be on the leading edge in military technology due to the complexity of modern weaponry, whose production now demands access to a global supply base.[34] The progress of Chinese defense firms has been greatly hampered by the fact that they have thus far made only tentative steps toward pursuing globalization in weapons production, in part due to restrictions on access to key defense-related technologies from Western countries.[35] But even if Chinese defense firms had full access to needed inputs from Western firms and sought them out, it is highly doubtful that many of them would be able to fully exploit such linkages anytime soon; it is extremely difficult, and thus requires a very long time, for firms to gain the requisite experience and managerial capacity to manage the complex global supply chains associated with today's leading-edge weapons, given that they typically involve a mind-bogglingly large number of subcontractors and technological partners.[36]

Skills and Infrastructure for Effectively Using Advanced Weaponry

Finally, Posen highlights the very particular set of personnel skills and technological infrastructure needed to use the weapons systems that give America command of the commons in an effective, coordinated manner. As he stresses, the "development of new weapons and tactics depends on decades of expensively accumulated technological and tactical experience embodied in the institutional memory of public and private military research and development organizations."[37]

More specifically, Posen notes that Washington's ability to use these kinds of systems depends vitally on the "military exploitation of information technology," and "the military personnel needed to run these systems are among the most highly skilled and highly trained in the world."[38] Regarding information technology:

> The effectiveness of many current weapons systems is vitally dependent upon having state of the art battlefield management—that is, having real-time, detailed information about your forces and those of the enemy, being able to quickly and effectively process this information, having seamless command and control, and so on. And effective battlefield management is, in turn, now dependent upon having information that is collected, processed, and distributed through what is sometimes called an "information architecture" that consists of computers coupled with advanced intelligence, surveillance, reconnaissance, and communications technologies.[39]

Chinese military analyst Ren Xiao confirms that "because of the comparatively weak foundation and low starting point for modernization and the incomplete condition of mechanization, the process of informatization in the PLA [People's Liberation Army] remains at an initial stage, and the modernization level still lags substantially behind that of the world's military powers."[40]

Learning how to effectively use many modern weapons is so difficult in part because they are often so complex as individual systems, but more importantly because they typically need to be used as part of a cohesive package. For example, for unmanned combat aerial vehicles "to deliver a marked and enduring combat advantage . . . requires modern battle-networks, C4 architectures, organizational codes, appropriate bureaucratic structures, military doctrines, skilled personnel, and the support of other manned combat air-crafts, among others."[41] Using weapons systems in a coordinated way places a very high premium on delegation. Whether China can develop the ability to use the full range of advanced systems in a coordinated manner in a way that allows it to match up with US forces is unclear, but any effort to do so would be a very long-term process that will be hampered by the highly central-ized, hierarchical structures of China's military—which do not emphasize either delegation or flexibility and thus impair lower-level decision-making.[42] China's lack of actual warfighting experience in combination with deficien-cies in the nature of the training of Chinese military personnel, moreover, also greatly impedes its progress toward developing an ability to coordinate military operations.[43]

A New World for Rising Powers

The upshot is that past historical precedent does not provide a useful guide for understanding the speed of China's upward trajectory. As compared to the recent rising states of note, China is very different because it is so far below the technological level of the leading state. And as important as that gap is, it is only part of the story. The discussion so far reveals two key ways in which the world has changed so as to make it much harder to rise now than in the past.

The first is that developing and using top-end military equipment is much more difficult and complex, and such an effort is therefore much harder and takes far longer. This does not mean that China is incapable of producing any technologically competitive weapons systems. On the contrary, Beijing has been "able to catch up and begin to match the technological standards of other world leaders . . . in a limited, though gradually expanding, number of niche areas, such as precision-strike missiles, space and counter-space systems, and cybersecurity."[44] And due to its rising military capabilities, China has greatly increased the costs and risks of operating US aircraft and surface ships (but not submarines)[45] in its near seas, foreclosing some military options the United States retained in the past.[46] This is a significant change—one that points to the need for some US military adjustments, as we will discuss in chapter 5 of this book. But in many other areas—including many of the kinds of systems that are needed to develop global power projection capacity—such rapid progress is not feasible; building up in these areas requires capacities that must be painstakingly nurtured and developed and even then their ac-quisition cannot be taken for granted. And if China does someday reach a position that allows it to attempt such a buildup and seeks to do so, the very long lead times for many systems would mean that the results would not come to fruition for a very long time even if all goes well. And then once these systems are developed, it would still be necessary to learn how to effectively use them in a coordinated manner, again a time-consuming process.

Compare today's situation with the weapons development process in the early and mid-20th century. At the beginning of the century, Great Britain introduced a revolutionary new battleship—the Dreadnought—which overnight "made all existing battleships obsolete . . . Yet, in less than three years Germany could imitate the British Dreadnought, eliminating any advantage Great Britain enjoyed from its new innovation."[47] Even more impressive in scope was the German rearmament of the 1930s, when it was able in a few short years to shift from being a largely disarmed power to a state that was militarily capable of single-handedly conquering Europe and nearly subduing the Soviet Union. Germany was able to quickly generate a full portfolio of weapons systems that matched or surpassed those of the leading powers of the day. Today, in contrast, China can do this only in a few areas, and even if China someday does have a sufficient technological base to produce the full range of systems needed for power projection, it would require a great many years of cumulative effort in which all goes well before it would be in a position to start closing the gap. Chinese defense planners themselves clearly recognize this: "While China's leaders urge the PLA and defense economy to catch up with the world's advanced military powers as quickly as possible, military planners are more cautious and do not envisage developing the mix of capabilities required to be an advanced military information power until at least the middle of the 21st century at the earliest."[48]

The second key way the world has changed so as to make rising more difficult is that the size of the US military advantage is much bigger than the gap between the number 1 power and the number 2 power in previous eras. The United States is the only state that has for decades made the necessary investment to produce and successfully use the full range of systems and associated infrastructure needed for significant global power projection. Especially in today's technological environment, the choices the United States has made over long spans of time regarding the development of its military capacity have created a reality that will not be easy to overcome. Significantly, closing the military gap would be extremely difficult for China even if it were not chasing a moving target; but this is unlikely: "The technological goalposts of weapons development are constantly moving; as certain nations, particularly the United States, advance the state of the art in defense technology, they create new metrics for defining what is meant by 'advanced' military systems."[49] The fact that China likely faces moving goalposts represents a very significant constraint on its quest for military competitiveness. Regarding naval capabilities, for example, Bitzinger and colleagues conclude that "based on the current trajectory, it seems unlikely that China can catch up with the established naval [science and technology—S&T] leaders unless the latter's defense S&T capabilities erode over time under financial constraints."[50]

The upshot is that it remains a one-superpower world, and nothing will change on this front for a very long time. As Yan Xuetong underscores, while China's "economy has found global impacts . . . the components of Chinese national strength are imbalanced. . . . It is far more difficult for Chinese comprehensive national strength to catch up with that of the U.S. than for its economy to do so. . . . Its military capabilities, the weakest link in terms of national power, have hardly gone beyond perimeter defense."[51]

The Stages between Great Power and Superpower

For a long time China is set to be in some position in between great and superpower, and the analysis here reveals distinct stages along that path. The first is when a rising great power has enough economic resources to try to displace the United States as the sole superpower. With roughly 60% of US GDP, China appears to have met or to be in range of meeting this benchmark, although our analysis of the biases inherent in that measure as well as the huge gap in inclusive wealth between China and the United States are cautionary notes. And in any case, reaching this stage is not as significant as it was for past rising states. Without sufficient technological capacity, a large pool of economic resources alone will not enable China to bring the one-superpower world to an end.

Thus, the second stage is when the rising great power has enough economic resources and technological capacity to be in a position to attempt to match or negate US global power. China has very far to go to reach this stage, and an ongoing task will be to carefully monitor its technological progress. Such an effort will involve both quantitative measures of the kind surveyed in the previous section as well as qualitative assessments. An especially important indicator will be whether China can build effective, replicable prototypes of the core military systems that it would need to be able to project power globally.

The third stage is when the rising great power does not merely have the latent economic and technological capacity to develop the full range of systems needed for global power projection, but has procured these systems and has also learned how to use them effectively in a coordinated manner. This capability would require not just the needed weapons systems but also the "information architecture" that is now a requisite for effective battlefield management. The long lead times associated with developing many modern weapons systems and learning to use them effectively, in combination with the fact that the United States has made massive investments in the key military capabilities over many decades, make this hurdle more formidable than simple indicators imply.

Essentially, the gap between China and the United States can be disaggregated conceptually into different levels, as in Figure 3.1.

LEVEL 4 – SUPERPOWER

LEVEL 3 – POTENTIAL SUPERPOWER

LEVEL 2 – EMERGING POTENTIAL SUPERPOWER

LEVEL 1 – GREAT POWER

FIGURE 3.1 Traversing the Great Power to Superpower Gap

The analysis thus far indicates that China has now risen to the "emerging potential superpower" level—at which it either has or is on track to have enough economic capacity to be able to bid for superpower status but does not yet have the technological capacity to do so. If China can ascend technologically to the point that it has both the requisite economic and technological capacity to be capable of mounting a broad challenge to the United States in the military realm, it would then reach the third "potential superpower" level. At this level, China would have sufficient latent material capacity to match the superpower. For the reasons discussed above, any effort by China to rise yet further and reach a comparable level to the United States—the superpower level—will be fraught with difficulty and will require a lengthy amount of time even if all goes well.

How to Think about the United States' Changing Global Position

In light of this analysis, the global debate on the United States' position seems overwrought. China's rise is real and change is afoot, but the predominant rhetoric about the coming end of the one-superpower world is clearly exaggerated. What accounts for the hyperbole? Part of the problem is that analysts do not systematically assess the distribution of capabilities using measures appropriate for the 21st century, as we did in chapter 2. Also important is the influence of historical analogies to rising powers of the past, which we've shown to be deeply misleading. But another part of the problem is the lack of the right conceptual toolkit and associated terminology for discussing change versus continuity in the current international system. The key is to understand China's ascent without either downplaying it or exaggerating its significance. In the subsections that follow we first show that the most popular concept for organizing discussion of the international system—polarity—is incapable of doing this and then delineate a framework that can.

The Problem with (Uni)polarity

The terminology of polarity dominates the conversation on the United States' global role. Despite decades of intense scholarly criticism, polarity has arguably never been more popular among academics.[52] And despite the oft-lamented disdain that policymakers are said to have for political science concepts, claims about polarity pervade official discourse. The US National Intelligence Council, for example, attracted worldwide notice with its assessment that the "'unipolar moment' is over."[53] And unlike their Cold War predecessors, the highest-level policymakers in some of the world's most important countries do so as well. Chinese president Xi Jinping and Russian president Vladimir Putin are just two leaders who periodically put forward assessments about the polarity of the system: in May 2014, Putin asserted flatly: "The model of a unipolar world has failed. . . . The world is multipolar."[54] And in November 2014 Xi noted a "growing trend toward a multipolar world."[55] Barry Buzan's observation that the concept of "polarity has been hugely influential in public debates about international relations" thus applies much more strongly to the era of unipolarity than to bipolarity's heyday.[56]

The most important idea underlying the concept of polarity is that the key to analyzing any international system is determining the number of powerful states, or "poles," at the top.[57] Does one state stand alone at the top (unipolarity)? Do two roughly comparable states stand significantly above all of the others (bipolarity)? Or do three or more roughly comparable states occupy the highest rung in the system (multipolarity)? Many scholars find the concept useful for explaining how different international systems operate. But as we have shown elsewhere, it is especially misleading when used to understand change in the international system, something scholars learned to their disquiet when they failed to anticipate the end of bipolarity in the 1980s.[58] A key problem is that polarity causes analysts to pay too much attention to the major thresholds that define different system structures and so fosters dichotomous thinking. In 1989 Kenneth Waltz insisted that "the Cold War is rooted in the postwar structure of international politics and will last as long as that structure endures."[59] The system was either bipolar or multipolar. In *Theory of International Politics*, Waltz grappled with the issue of Soviet decline, but the concepts he developed were too blunt to perform the task whose critical importance we just established: determining the stages states must traverse to become—or cease being—poles. The problem is even more salient now. As a result of the increase in China's power, much has changed since the mid-1990s. So is the current system bipolar? Almost no one thinks so. Is it multipolar? Most scholars, at least, are not ready to affirm that. So is everything the same as in 1995 or 2000? The answer is also clearly no.

The bluntness of the polarity framework thus feeds an artificial debate about whether everything is changing or nothing is changing. The minority, contrarian side, mainly comprised of academics, hews closely to the classic structural premises of polarity and generally underestimates how the system is now changing by insisting on a very high bar for shifts in polarity. By Nuno Monteiro's conceptualization, for example, the system will remain unipolar so long as the United States remains the only state with very substantial capacity for global power projection. China could grow to have an economy twice the size of the United States'—or even five or ten times as large—and possess a comparable scientific-technological capacity, but as long as Beijing chooses not to use those resources to develop a superpower's military capability, the world will remain unipolar.[60]

The majority side of the debate, dominated by policymakers, pundits, and government analysts, has the opposite tendency, overestimating the degree to which the system is changing by writing the United States off as the system leader. Briefly examining the three most prominent conceptions of unipolarity that lead to this kind of assessment helps to reveal the need for a different conceptual approach for assessing change in today's system.

In the early 2000s, Joseph Nye prominently argued that the distribution of power among states should not be conceptualized in terms of aggregate capabilities but should be broken into different components (different "chessboards"). Nye concluded: "On the top chessboard, military power is largely unipolar. . . . But on the middle chessboard, economic power is multipolar. . . . On this economic board, the United States is not a hegemon and often must bargain as an equal with Europe."[61] Numerous figures in the current public debate about America's changing role, most notably Fareed Zakaria, also divide up the power of nations into subcomponents and similarly argue that the United States remains the sole superpower in military and political terms, but not in economic ones.[62] Many analysts now assert that China's economic ascent is sufficient to mark the end of America's unique unipole status, even if China remains significantly behind in the military and techno-logical realms.[63] It was precisely this approach to assessing the United States' global position that underlay widely discussed predictions that the EU would either displace the United States as the globe's superpower or join it as a co-equal.[64] But as we stressed above, the interaction between the economic and the political and strategic realms is complex and crucial, and singling out one element is misleading; significantly, this is a point that Nye himself later emphasized, insisting in 2014 that "even if China suffers no major domestic political setback, projections based on GDP growth alone are one-dimen-sional and ignore US military and soft-power advantages."[65] When analysts fail to recognize this interaction, they invariably overestimate the extent of US decline.

According to a second prominent approach, a shift away from America's unique unipolar status is in the offing because of profound changes in the very nature of the international system. In a widely noted application of this approach, the National Intelligence Council (NIC) concluded in 2008 that the "'unipolar moment' is over."[66] Although the NIC traced this polarity shift in part to the relative decline of the United States vis-à-vis other states, it accorded greater significance to a new element in world politics: a dra-matic rise in the significance of nonstate actors.[67] But a rise in the power of nonstate actors does not apply to just some states but to all of them; it thus has limited or no implications for any debate about America's standing among states. The NIC analysis supplied no argument or evidence that any shift in the balance of power between states and nonstates should dispropor-tionally affect the United States. If one wants to analyze whether being the leading state is more or less useful than it used to be, then factoring in the significance of nonstate actors makes a lot of sense. But if the aim is to de-termine how the US position vis-à-vis other states differs from the 1990s or what it might be like in ten or twenty years, then this way of conceptualizing the system is not useful and overestimates the extent of America's decline.

Arguably the most popular conception of unipolarity equates it with the United States' ability to control international outcomes.[68] By this definition the system was unipolar as long as observed outcomes in international poli-tics were widely seen as generally going Washington's way, as they did roughly from 1991 to around 2004. When politicians, pundits, and diplomats use the term, it is very often in this sense; Richard Haass and Timothy Garton Ash are two notable examples along these lines.[69] A careful reading of political leaders' discourse—from Jacques Chirac and Hu Jintou to Xi Jinping and Vladimir Putin—suggests that they most often use polarity language in this sense. Among scholars, arguably the most prominent conception of unipolarity of this kind is Robert Pape's: "As a unipolar leader, the United States is . . . able to determine the outcome of most international disputes, and has significant opportunities to control the internal and external behavior of virtually any small state in the system."[70]

After the victory in Kosovo in 1999 and the seemingly easy victories in Afghanistan in 2001 and Iraq in 2003, many observers seemed to believe that the United States could measure up to this extraordinarily high standard for unipolarity—all the more so given that these three wars came on the heels of the 1990s, a period in which the United States was often seen as having successfully pushed much of the world to embrace the pursuit of economic globalization on the terms that it preferred (most notably by fostering significant openness to flows of international capital).[71] But quickly emerging setbacks in Iraq and Afghanistan along with a range of other foreign policy disappointments—including continued frustration in fostering an Arab-Israeli peace deal and defiance from Iran and North Korea on nuclear proliferation—marked an end to unipolarity in the eyes of most who favor this definition.

The question of how much power as influence the United States really has is important—and one to which we return throughout this book—but it provides a dubious foundation for assessing the relative position of states and the changing dynamics of international systems.[72] The chief danger is inconsistency.[iii] The more capabilities a state has, the more expansive its aims on the world stage are likely to be. Moreover, the stronger an actor is in terms of power capabilities, the larger the set of issues there are for which observers will expect it to be successful in meeting its objectives. Thus, states poor in power resources generally have modest aims and are not expected to exercise immense influence. Weaker states are more likely to meet these lower

---

iii. Key here is that power is an actor's ability to achieve desired outcomes (or prevent undesired ones), and defining unipolarity in these terms requires the analyst to set some threshold (i.e., to define which are the "important" global issues on which the unipole must be successful in obtaining its objectives to deserve that designation). And both desires (preferences) and thresholds are influenced by how many power resources a state has.

expectations and so would seem more "powerful" by this metric. Because preferences vary so dramatically and are influenced so strongly by the specific context, and because expectations about how much influence a state "should" have are so variable, the behavioral approach makes it impossible to maintain a consistent benchmark for assessing states' positions in the international system over time.

This problem of inconsistent benchmarks appears to have affected assessments of the US position. Between 1991 and 2004 US aims on the world stage expanded, but even that was outpaced by what observers expected it to be able to achieve. No one in the early 1990s would have thought that the ability to conquer far-off countries like Iraq and Afghanistan, decisively defeat counterinsurgencies, and build stable democratic states in societies with deep ethnic divisions—all at low cost in lives and treasure—was a reasonable benchmark for unipole status. Yet by the mid-2000s just such a benchmark was routinely applied. It is only because analysts established such an extraordinarily high expectation for American power after the end of the Cold War that it seemed noteworthy that the United States failed to achieve most of the ambitious ends it set for itself. In the end, this behavioral conception of unipolarity leads those who employ it to conclude that America had already decisively fallen in power in the global system over a decade ago.[73]

The Solution: 1 + Y + X

At first blush, assessing the United States' power position in the international system ought to be uncomplicated. There is a clear starting point from which to measure change: the sudden and dramatic collapse of the Soviet Union in 1991, which left the United States in a position of preeminence unparalleled in modern history. And there is a widely accepted concept for understanding this historically novel position—unipolarity—that is used by scholars, policymakers, pundits, and government analysts alike. With such a salient starting point and popular conceptual tool, assessing change in the United States' global position ought to be a straightforward task of determining whether shifts such as China's rise, the 2008 global economic crisis, and Russia's newfound military assertiveness have moved the United States away from the unipolar position it occupied in the 1990s. We have shown that although there is widespread agreement that the United States assumed a unique unipolar status after the Cold War ended, analysts conceptualize this benchmark in radically different ways. As a result, conclusions regarding whether the United States has fallen or will soon fall from this perch are all over the place.

More worryingly, the debate tends to assume an all-or-nothing quality. In response to the financial crisis of 2008 and the continued economic ascent of China, pundits, policymakers, government analysts, and scholars frequently and prominently argued that the United States has tumbled from its previous global position and that a fundamental, system-altering power shift away from unipolarity is occurring. Unipolarity is ending, has ended, or will soon end, goes the gist of much commentary, and the system is reverting to multipolarity or bipolarity or apolarity or whatever neologism the analyst wishes to propound.[74] A minority of contrarians, clinging to classical definitions of polarity, respond that unipolarity persists, often with the implication that no change of significance has occurred.

What now? Should we aim to come up with a better, more refined definition of a unipolar system? The discussion above undermines that option by making clear that this whole conceptual approach to understanding how America's place is shifting is inadequate. The need to avoid concepts that force either-or choices is especially important because they exacerbate an already strong bias in the popular discourse toward proclaiming fundamental change. It is much more exciting to claim that the system has changed than to note that the current system is basically in place, but changes are underway that may eventually change it. Would Fareed Zakaria's *The Post-American World* have been a bestseller if the title had more accurately reflected the contents, which really add up to *Why a Post-American World Is Far Away but Movement in This Direction Has Begun*? Would the National Intelligence Council's *Global Trends 2030* report have gotten as much attention had it said, "The rise of nonstate actors is making the US role as leader more complicated and difficult than before" rather than proclaiming that the unipolar moment is over due to rise of nonstate actors?

A seemingly reasonable response might be to avoid conceptual frameworks altogether. Why not just take a broad approach to assessing power and leave the concepts aside? Indeed, several recent studies of the US-China power relationship that adopt this approach reach overall conclusions generally consistent with ours.[75] But just including many wellsprings of state power is not enough. If too many hard-to-measure, subjective, or behavioral elements are included, the analysis runs into the problem of inconsistency we discussed above. More importantly, without some larger framework to guide the examination, it is hard to connect the results of any broad-based study to the underlying question of how close the international system might be to fundamental change. So some conceptual apparatus is needed to organize the inquiry, set consistent benchmarks for assessing change, and ensure that careful findings are not shoehorned into the all-or-nothing debate the unipolarity concept helps sustain. Ultimately, we agree with David Baldwin that "without clear concepts . . . scholars are apt to talk past each other and policy-makers will find it difficult to distinguish between alternative policies."[76]

How then can we capture the structural nature of debates about the current international system while avoiding the pitfalls of the polarity framework for assessing change? Barry Buzan's "1 + X" terminology for describing system structure helps here.[77] Buzan uses this classification to argue (as of 2004) that the system is a "1 + X" world—that is, a system with one superpower (in this case, the United States) and X number of great powers (four in his understanding: Russia, China, Japan, and the EU).[78] Key for Buzan, as for us, is the distinction between superpowers and great powers, which reduces to the former's "broad-spectrum capabilities exercised across the whole of the international system."[79] Great powers, by contrast, lack such capabilities, although they may aspire to achieve them. Buzan also defines a third group of states—regional powers—as ones that "loom large in their regions, but do not register much in a broad spectrum way at the global level" (he identifies Israel, India, and Iran as being states of this type).[80]

Of key importance is that the very notion of an "X" term for the great powers means that the specific number does not alter the system's basic properties. The rise of, say, India to great power status could increase the value of X, and the decline of an existing great power could decrease it, without altering the fundamental nature of the system. To do that, the number of superpowers has to change.

Buzan's "1 + X" framework meets the test of intuitive plausibility by differentiating the United States from all other states without putting it on too high a pedestal—standing alone at the top of the hierarchy but not all powerful—while also providing a useful means of distinguishing states such as China and Japan from smaller, yet still consequential, regional powers such as Iran and Israel. More generally, this framework provides a means of classifying states into different power categories that is cleanly and clearly distinguished from the theoretical architecture of polarity and its attendant problems. His framework thus has the benefit of classifying states into different categories while avoiding the dichotomous thinking associated with polarity.

Although Buzan's 1 + X framework is very useful, it needs modification. Most notably, because the gap in capabilities between great power and superpower is so large in today's system, it is necessary to carefully differen-tiate between great powers that are not in a position to bid for superpower status and those that are. We need to be open to the possibility of a $1 + Y + X$ system, in which one or more Y powers—as is the case with China—have the potential to rise to superpower status or are moving in this direction and thus need to be differentiated from the other great powers. Again, this is cru-cial because the main question is not the size of the X term but whether the superpower term is 1, >1, or <1.

Conclusion

With their alarmist rhetoric about "the end of unipolarity," observers are saying that China has risen from the position it held in the 1990s. The prob-lem is that we have lacked a firm basis for understanding how much it has risen and how fast it can continue to ascend. As we showed, the past histori-cal experience of rising powers is simply a poor guide in this respect, because China is very different from them, and the world in which it is rising is also very different. The analysis advanced here makes it possible to understand why there will be an extremely long lag between when China achieves some-thing like economic parity with the United States and when it can bid to become a superpower peer.

A key reason for the fascination—indeed obsession—with changes in the system's structure is that it has significant consequences for policy. In the aftermath of the collapse of the Soviet Union, a prominent policy ar-gument that emerged was that America's new global position accorded it great freedom of action in the international realm. In particular, the United States could choose to sustain the deeply engaged grand strategy it inherited as a legacy of Cold War containment or it could disengage strategically. If America no longer possessed such a dramatic power advantage over other states, it would lose this freedom of choice (a key takeaway that we under-scored almost a decade ago in a previous analysis of America's position within the global hierarchy of power[81]).

Perhaps not surprisingly, some prominent advocates of pulling back have argued that the United States has fallen so far in its global position that it will be forced to retrench and shift away from the pursuit of deep engagement.[82] That argument is wrong. It is driven by a problematic understanding of the United States' global role. A comprehensive assessment of the distribution of capabilities tailored to the nature of power in the 21st century shows that the

United States is and will long remain the globe's sole superpower, uniquely capable of pursuing a world-shaping grand strategy. China has risen from the position that it held in the 1990s, a change that eludes the unipolarity concept. In the terminology we borrowed from Barry Buzan, the system has shifted from 1 superpower plus X great powers to 1 + 1 + X, with China occupying a middle category as an emerging potential superpower.

4

America's Grand Strategic Choice

FOR SEVEN DECADES the United States has pursued a singular grand strategy—"deep engagement"—that features an extensive array of security guarantees to allies and partners across Eurasia. This basic strategic choice has been sustained so long and is so deeply enmeshed in the global status quo that it is easy to forget the extraordinary nature of its purpose: to shape the environment in the world's most important regions in fundamental ways that support US national interests in security, economic prosperity, and cooperation on important global issues.

The previous two chapters showed that the United States is and will long remain the world's only state in a position to sustain a grand strategy with this kind of global scope. America thus faces a unique choice: Should it? In the remainder of this book, we answer this question by conducting a comprehensive analysis of deep engagement's costs and benefits. In this chapter we set the stage for this analysis by accomplishing three crucial tasks. First, we unpack the logic of the United States' grand strategy, distinguishing its defining elements from optional choices it enables but does not necessitate. These key pillars of deep engagement have underlain US foreign policy since the dawn of the Cold War. Second, we explain the seemingly puzzling decision to retain the strategy even after 1991, when the Cold War conditions that initially gave rise to it ended. Third, we clarify the grand strategy debate, stressing the crucial distinction between deep engagement itself and additional objectives such as democracy promotion, fostering human rights, humanitarian interventions, and the spread of other liberal values. Much of the debate in Washington, both at present and in the past, concerns the advisability and practicality of these "deep engagement plus" add-ons. In contrast, the scholarly debate directly centers on the sustainability and value of the strategy itself.[i]

There are thus three broad grand strategic options for America: (1) focusing on deep engagement, (2) a "deep engagement plus" stance that embraces the core grand strategy as a foundation but also expands beyond it by adding new missions and obligations, or (3) pulling back from deep engagement by disengaging from some or all of its key strategic commitments. The chapters that follow demonstrate how the grand strategy resonates with theory and research findings emerging from all major schools of international relations scholarship. We assess the strategy's benefits and costs, and show that the knowledge about the workings of international politics that emerges from this scholarship validates its essential conceptual blueprint. The clear implication is that disengaging from the strategy's core commitments is not only unnecessary but also inadvisable. Less obviously but equally importantly, in demonstrating the grand strategy's substantial net benefits, we also undermine the case for more expansive visions of the US role in the world. Most notably, those who advocate ambitious projects to assertively spread democracy and liberal principles and foster dramatic improvements in human rights, by the sword if necessary, make the same mistake as proponents of pulling back: they fail to appreciate the major benefits America derives by sustaining its long-standing grand strategy. In a world of budgetary pressure, public weariness, and decreasing (if still substantial) margins of US material preeminence, our findings support focusing on and sustaining deep engagement, not curtailing it or moving beyond it.

---

i. As we noted previously, scholars on all sides of this discussion now generally are "in favor of 'restraint' in the use of American power . . . [and] see military interventions in places such as Haiti and Kosovo as optional choices that are outside [the] grand strategy's logic. The debate is clearly . . . about whether the United States should remain deeply engaged in the security affairs of East Asia, the Middle East, and Europe or should instead retrench." Stephen Brooks, John Ikenberry, and William Wohlforth, "Correspondence: Debating American Engagement: The Future of U.S. Grand Strategy," *International Security*, Vol. 38, No. 2 (Fall 2013), pp. 181–199. See also the discussion in Evan Braden Montgomery, "Contested Primacy in the Western Pacific: China's Rise and the Future of U.S. Power Projection," *International Security*, Vol. 38, No. 4 (Spring 2014), p. 118, and Zack Beauchamp, "How to Think about the Future of American Foreign Policy," *Thinkprogress*, October 30, 2013, available at http://thinkprogress.org/security/2013/10/30/2860641/think-future-american-military-power/.

Defining US Grand Strategy

Grand strategy is a set of ideas for deploying a nation's resources to achieve its interests over the long run.[1] The descriptor "grand" captures the large-scale nature of the strategic enterprise in terms of time (long-term, measured in decades), stakes (the interests concerned are the large, important, and most enduring ones), and comprehensiveness (the strategy provides a blueprint or guiding logic for a nation's policies across many areas).[2] Grand strategy is thus far less variable than foreign policy, which changes from one administration to the next or even within a single presidency (as when Ronald Reagan shifted from a hard line toward a more accommodating approach to the Soviet Union in his second term). While foreign policy analysis is often preoccupied with such shifts, the study of grand strategy invites a longer-term view that looks broadly at all of the issues encompassed by the US approach to the world. That perspective reveals a set of core pillars that have underlain US foreign policy for seven decades.

Ever since the dawn of the Cold War, the United States has sought to advance its fundamental national interests in security, prosperity, and domestic liberty by pursuing three overlapping objectives: (1) managing the external environment in key regions to reduce near- and long-term threats to US national security; (2) promoting a liberal economic order to expand the global economy and maximize domestic prosperity; and (3) creating, sustaining, and revising the global institutional order to secure necessary interstate cooperation on terms favorable to US interests. The connection between essential American interests and these three larger objectives did not spring forth from the pen of George F. Kennan or any other single strategist. It emerged from the rough-and-tumble process of solving more immediate problems, as US leaders progressively discovered the interdependence of security and economic goals and the utility of international institutions for attaining both.[3]

The pursuit of these three core objectives underlies what is arguably the United States' most consequential strategic choice: to maintain security commitments to partners and allies in Europe, East Asia, and the Middle East. US administrations have consistently maintained that the security commitments in these three key regions are necessary to shape the global environment and thus advance the grand strategy's three core objectives.[4] During the Cold War, the commitments served primarily to prevent the encroachment of Soviet power into regions containing the world's wealthiest, potentially most powerful, and resource-rich states. But it is only in hindsight that Cold War containment seems so simple. As John Lewis Gaddis demonstrated, containing Soviet military might demanded economic recovery, which in turn appeared to require military assurances to instill the confidence needed to save, invest, and trade.[5] So even though the Soviet military threat was not imminent (it was initially widely assumed that Moscow would be in no position to attack for a decade at least) the United States found itself organizing political, military, and economic activity around the world to assemble a "preponderance of power" over its Soviet adversary.[6]

Discrete choices about how to respond to immediate challenges ultimately added up to a choice for a grand strategy of deep engagement. Each choice entailed rejection of an alternative—and these alternatives, taken together, would have added up to a different grand strategy. The United States worked long and hard to foster an open global economy rather than adopting a noncommittal stance or, as it did in the 1930s, actually taking very significant actions that moved the world toward economic closure. In turn, the United States made a decided effort to advance necessary cooperation through international institutions rather than relying only on a mix of ad hoc cooperative efforts and a unilateral approach. And in the security realm, the United States opted for formal alliances and a significant forward presence in Asia and Europe rather than relying entirely on local actors to prevent either of these key regions from falling under the domination of a hostile power.

In the security realm, the problem with pursuing the alternative, less engaged "offshore balancing" approach in Asia and Europe was that local states were too weak to counter Soviet power without US help, and it was ultimately hard to see how to make them strong enough to balance the Soviet Union on their own without scaring neighbors and thus ruining alliance cohesion. In Europe, making frontline Germany strong enough to check the Soviet Union without a major US presence would have demanded German rearmament and acquisition of nuclear weapons, which risked alienating France and other neighbors and wrecking the alliance.[7] To paraphrase Lord Ismay's famous dictum regarding NATO's purpose, US officials concluded that keeping the Americans in was the ideal method for keeping the Soviets out while simultaneously keeping the Germans down.

The same story replayed in the looser Asian alliance setting, as US officials understood that a move by Japan toward remilitarization and nuclearization would radically destabilize the alliances that were thought just barely able to contain Soviet and Chinese power. US leaders concluded that the only way to achieve "alignment despite antagonism" among prospective US partners was through active regional security management.[8]

In the Middle East, limiting Soviet leverage over major oil producers and securing a steady supply of oil became a key interest, and, as was not the case in the other regions, it was generally seen as one achievable from offshore, without a permanent military presence on the ground. But the logic of US security engagement bore key similarities to that governing American security provision in other regions: achieving its aims in the region required active efforts to ameliorate conflicts among regional actors.

Early in the Cold War, the United States had successfully put in place the fundamental building blocks for pursuing its three core objectives. Most prominently, this involved the creation of NATO and the associated large presence of American troops on a network of bases throughout Western Europe and the establishment of global economic institutions such as the International Monetary Fund and the General Agreement on Tariffs and Trade (GATT). Once these building blocks had been put in place to advance the three core objectives, a central guiding element of US foreign policy was to keep this basic structure in place, and no American president since has refrained from doing so.[9] As we will discuss later in this book, this did not involve a rigid acquiescence to the existing structure; sometimes presidents sought to build upon it (as with the shift from the GATT to the World Trade Organization) or revise it on more favorable terms (as when the United States altered the rules of the Bretton Woods regime during the 1971–1973 period by suspending the convertibility of the dollar into gold as part of an effort to gain cooperation on a new set of principles for a system with reduced capital controls). Key here, as we stress in chapter 9, is that order maintenance and creation go together: maintaining an order still demands the creation of new and/or revised structures so that it does not stagnate or become too unwieldy.

The "Puzzle" of Post–Cold War Continuity

Viewed over the very long term using the widest lens, the big story of US grand strategy in the Cold War was constancy: a decision for deep engagement involving an American presence on the ground in Europe and East Asia, institutionalized alliances, and active efforts to shape the regional security setting, foster an open global economy, and sustain multilateral institutions to manage interstate cooperation. When the Cold War ended and the Soviet Union collapsed, there was, as far as we know, no single moment when the US government made a clear, discrete decision to retain that basic approach. Rather, the choice to adapt rather than replace the deep engagement grand strategy emerged from a series of more immediate choices: to address the issues of German unification and ultimately the security of newly Western-oriented states in Eastern and Central Europe via NATO expansion;[10] to respond to China's rise, Japan's uncertainty over its foreign policy direction, and North Korean security challenges via renewing and upgrading the mutual security ties with Japan, South Korea, and other Asian partners in the 1990s and 2000s; and to respond to concerns over US competitiveness and Asia's economic rise via new economic institutions like NAFTA or using leverage to upgrade old ones, most notably the GATT-WTO transformation. Each of these decisions elicited debates, and each debate provided evidence of the reasons US officials advanced for revising and updating rather than revoking the alliances, institutions, and other commitments that had taken shape in the Cold War. Taken together, the actions and supporting ideas are consistent with John Lewis Gaddis's realistic definition of grand strategy as "the process by which a state relates long-term strategic ends to means under the rubric of an overarching and enduring vision to advance the national interest."[11]

The "striking continuity" of US grand strategy in the face of structural change puzzles many scholars.[12] "It's possible that US leaders in the late 1940s hit on the ideal grand strategy for any and all structural conditions," observes Stephen Walt, "but it is surely odd that an event as significant as the Soviet collapse can have so few implications for how America deals with the other 190-plus countries around the globe."[13] For many scholars, the puzzle can only be explained by reference to peculiarities of US domestic politics or ideology.[14] But determining how "odd" America's grand strategic choice really is demands a careful study of its premises in light of what scholars know generally about international politics.

In the security realm, the key point is that by the time the Soviet Union collapsed, the United States had been preoccupied with managing relationships within the three core regions for four decades, making the decision to continue doing so seem less puzzling than many scholars assume. Over the four decades of Cold War rivalry, the United States built up complex relationships of influence that allowed it to shape the strategic environment to facilitate highly effective balancing against Soviet power. When Soviet power receded, the United States chose to sustain those complex relationships of influence. The primary aim of its security commitments remained to make the core regions more secure, and so make the world safer and thus more hospitable for the pursuit of America's national interests. At the same time, defense commitments in these regions also allow the United States to shape the security environment facing potential rivals to induce them to accommodate its main interests and, should that fail, constitute a hedge against the need to contain a future peer rival. The web of alliance relationships, moreover, serves as a resource that can be drawn upon to address new security challenges, such as terrorist threats against the US homeland.

Similarly, the interconnection between security commitments and other US interests was well established in the Cold War. Given the widely appreciated reality of what scholars often call "complex interdependence" (in which states have a multitude of complex linkages), there are many issues whose management requires institutionalized cooperation, not least of which is the stability of the global economy. As we will discuss in chapter 10, the United States, as by far the largest economic player in the system, has immense stakes in the continued stability and expansion of economic globalization. Little wonder that US decision-makers opted to maintain the economic and institutional pillars of their grand strategy and that they continued to recognize the value of a close connection between those pillars and security provision.

Woven through official US foreign policy statements and documents is a set of arguments that explain post–Cold War grand strategic continuity. The security commitments are a necessary condition of US leadership, the argument goes, and that leadership is necessary to pursue the strategy's three interdependent objectives: managing the security environment to ward off threats to the US homeland and its interests abroad, fostering economic globalization, and sustaining institutionalized cooperation on key common problems. Without the security commitments, US leverage for leadership on both security and nonsecurity issues declines. As we will review in detail in chapters 10 and 11, not only does US leadership facilitate cooperation on security challenges and the global economy, but the commitments and associated leverage are also necessary pillars of a larger institutional and normative order whose maintenance makes the United States more secure and prosperous over the long term. Embedding US leadership in these institutions has major benefits for Washington and its partners—functional benefits that make cooperation more likely and more efficient[15] as well as political and legitimacy benefits (mitigating politically awkward aspects of US leadership). Embedding US leadership in less formal institutions—for example, international law and other informal rules—also pays in more diffuse ways. It is easier to pursue a national interest when it can be expressed as a rule or principle to which others have formally subscribed. And because the United States is not strongly constrained by these institutional commitments, the benefits far outweigh the costs.[16]

Although US officials prefer the term "leadership," social scientists would be inclined to call it "power." If power is conceived as the ability to make things happen or prevent things from happening, then the United States' long-standing security relationships are key power assets. To be sure, they are not free. They require constant management and attention, the allocation of significant resources, and the acceptance of real risks (which we analyze in depth below). But what they promise in return is an unparalleled ability to shape the global environment, both to prevent undesired outcomes and to foster desired ones over the long term. In this sense, the decision to maintain the deep engagement grand strategy after 1991 is consistent with the axioms of practical "realist" statecraft. Realism 101 would stress that in an uncertain world prudential leaders should maintain power, not throw it away. No one knows exactly what new threats or challenges might emerge. Under these circumstances, one would expect the heirs of Machiavelli and Bismarck to say: Do not choose to be less powerful unless there are compelling reasons to do so.

Debating US Grand Strategy

Grand strategy is not foreign policy. It is the foundation, the anchor, the center of gravity—"the intellectual architecture that gives form and struc- ture to foreign policy," as Hal Brands aptly puts it.[17] A definitive core has anchored US foreign policy for seven decades: the three interlinked objec- tives (managing the security environment, fostering economic globalization, and sustaining institutionalized cooperation on key problems) and the set of arguments for the central role of US security commitments in pursuing them. If grand strategy is strategy conceived on the largest scale of time and comprehensiveness, then this core *is* US grand strategy. From the very be- ginning of the Cold War, this core and the set of supporting arguments un- derlying it lay at the center of America's basic strategic choice. They supply the overarching logic behind the United States' most consequential commit- ments in multiple regions and issue areas. They differentiate Washington's deep engagement grand strategy from the less deeply engaged, embedded, and institutionalized grand strategies favored by past leading states—and by the United States itself until the middle of the 20th century. They remained constants throughout the four decades of the Cold War. And it was the deci- sion that emerged under Presidents George H. W. Bush and Bill Clinton to retain these foundational elements after the Soviet Union's dissolution that first attracted scholars' critical attention.[18]

The rest of this book is a comprehensive assessment of the grand strat- egy's costs and benefits. It is clearly directly relevant to the unambiguously grand strategic debate now ongoing between those who favor continued deep engagement and those who advocate fully "coming home," or at least substantially drawing down US overseas commitments. For many years, the idea of pulling back from deep engagement was hardly considered outside a few political science departments. Now, however, the debate has reached a "crossover point between academic critiques of U.S. grand strategy and the policy mainstream."[19] As the Iraq War ended and the vast bulk of troops were withdrawn from Afghanistan, the United States seemed to face quantitatively and qualitatively new pressures on its grand strategy: rising and/or newly assertive powers, a continuing terrorist threat, demographically and politically driven constraints on the defense budget, weakening allies, domestic weariness from lengthy and inconclusive wars, and a public opinion shift away from internationalism.[20] Against the backdrop of a widespread sense of a lack of foreign policy successes, these long-term trends place the grand strategy under new and intense scrutiny among the public, pundits, and policymakers.

Focused as it is on the overarching grand strategy debate, our analysis cannot resolve every question about US foreign policy—or even every important question. In any given period, the United States does many things other than those related to the basic grand strategy, and many foreign policy debates are about those issues rather than directly about the core. Focused as it is on interstate relationships, the grand strategy's implications for nonstate and transnational policy challenges like terrorism tend to be indirect—though crucial. But the grand strategy anchors those debates, just as it anchors foreign policy itself over the long run, and so our analysis has important implications beyond the debate over retrenchment.

Adjustment Debates

Much of the foreign policy discourse between the political parties and among experts is about how best to sustain deep engagement, reduce its costs or risks, or get the right balance among the regions. The Obama administration's "rebalancing" toward Asia is merely a recent example in a long line of such adjustments. Practically every president since Truman has introduced (or tried to introduce) a course correction of one sort or another, from Eisenhower's "new look," to Kennedy's "flexible response," Nixon's "Guam Doctrine," and Carter's "Carter Doctrine." Even though analysts sometimes characterize these shifts as changes in grand strategy, the debates surrounding them are not about the optimality of sustaining the core of the grand strategy but rather about how best to do so.

Deep Engagement versus
"Deep Engagement Plus" Debates

Another set of debates concerns whether deep engagement is enough or whether America should seek to do more on the world stage. As the grand strategy increasingly became taken for granted with the passage of time, much of the foreign policy discourse seemed to be about other issues. But these debates are never about abandoning the grand strategy and replacing it with a new set of aims and commitments. Rather, these debates treat deep engagement as a foundation from which further tasks, humanitarian or otherwise, can be attempted.

The less salient the classical great power issues are—most notably in the post–Cold War era—the more the debate is prone to veer toward "deep engagement plus." Calls to go beyond the grand strategy stem from different traditions in American foreign policy such as liberal internationalism and neoconservatism. Often these arguments reflect normative aims, such as spreading democracy or defending human rights, as in the case of Carter's human rights agenda. But normative aims are often intertwined with arguments that US material interests in security and prosperity demand more than the basic grand strategy can deliver. Such arguments often amount to a claim that new aims and missions need to be added. In the Cold War, the major debate of this type was whether the United States needed to "bear any burden" to combat communism outside the core regions. After the Cold War, Clinton's "enlargement and engagement" and George W. Bush's "democracy agenda" were portrayed as being about both US values and more prosaic objectives in Europe and the Middle East. Notwithstanding their differing intellectual roots, "deep engagement plus" prescriptions generally converge on dissatisfaction with the status quo and the claim that the United States can be even safer and more prosperous if it assertively seeks to foster desired changes, such as a world with more democracies.[21]

The American impulse to go beyond deep engagement is strong enough to cause many analysts to see it as definitive of US grand strategy. Frequently used terms such as "liberal hegemony" and "primacy" are meant to capture this strain in US rhetoric and behavior.[22] Thus, Colin Dueck asserts that the strategy's goal is "not only US dominance, but an Americanized international order, characterized by an expanding zone of market-oriented democracies—what Robert Kagan and William Kristol call a 'benevolent global hegemony.' "[23] Barry Posen adds that the strategy is based on the premise that "the United States can only be truly safe in a world of states just like us."[24] If one assumes that a "deep engagement plus" stance is the historical norm, then focusing on the grand strategy itself might actually look like retrenchment.[25] But that is wrong, mistaking a course correction for a truly grand strategic change.

There is no question that the United States has often sought to do more on the world stage than sustain deep engagement. Democracy promotion, in particular, is so dear to the hearts of the American people and elites that presidents generally express fealty to the idea. But that does not mean that these additional elements define the grand strategy or are somehow necessitated by it. While "deep engagement plus" debates are commonplace, the specific policies involved are neither constant nor defining elements of US grand strategy. Rather, the United States' commitment to them has varied from administration to administration, and even within a single presidency. And while American presidents' expressed commitment to the idea of spreading democracy has been constant, their willingness to expend blood and treasure in pursuit of this objective has been anything but. Even as it pursued deep engagement during the Cold War, for example, the United States routinely and systematically allied with and supported various antidemocratic military dictatorships from Greece, Spain, and Portugal to Turkey, Pakistan, South Vietnam, the Philippines, and too many others to name. Of course, most US officials would have preferred to support democracy and human rights, and the impulse to do so has always remained present in the American body politic. But that preference could never consistently prevail.

Similarly, battling communism everywhere was the sine qua non—at least until it wasn't, and Nixon normalized relations with the People's Republic of China. Jimmy Carter began his administration with a strong emphasis on human rights, but shifted course in midterm. After the Cold War, George W. Bush began by emphatically eschewing democracy promotion, then shifted to make it a central feature, only to back away again toward the end of his second term. The commitment to humanitarian intervention is even more variable, with Presidents George H. W. Bush, Bill Clinton, George W. Bush, and Barack Obama veering between seeming to deny any US obligation, soaring rhetoric affirming the responsibility to protect, and case-by-case conditional arguments. Amid all this variation, the deep engagement grand strategy remained the anchor—unseen, often unremarked upon, but constant.

Debates about Deep Engagement's Edge

The logic of that grand strategic anchor helps address a final type of perennial foreign policy debate: whether some existing or prospective commitment is worth the expected costs and risks. For us, the first crucial step is to determine whether the commitment is necessary for the grand strategy. That is not the end of the debate, for, as we have noted, the American public or its elected leadership may want to undertake a commitment even if it is not necessary for the strategy. But it is important to know where deep engagement ends and when the country is contemplating a move beyond it. US presidents are understandably wary of drawing lines between core and noncore commitments, but analysts can and should do so.

One way to think about the grand strategy's edge is to ask what best explains the constants amid the variation, what has differentiated long-standing from more passing commitments over all the decades of deep engagement. When the chips are down and the costs of adding too many missions become punishing, or when the risks and dangers of pulling back from deep engagement seem too great, the United States tends to tack back to those commitments most central to the grand strategy's logic. Looking over the decades, four desiderata that emanate from the logic of deep engagement help differentiate its core commitments from "deep engagement plus" add-ons:

1. Power—the centrality of the state, region, or territory to the global distribution of capabilities. If things were to go badly and a given state or territory were to become part of a hostile alliance, would it meaningfully alter the global distribution of capabilities?
2. Threat—the degree to which a commitment will prevent or forestall a significant threat to the US homeland. This generally covaries with power, but not always, as in the case of potential nuclear proliferation to relatively weak states or a small state that becomes not only a base but a direct sponsor of major terrorist activities directed at the US homeland.
3. Economic importance. Is the commitment or potential commitment central to the functioning of the global economy? If things were to go badly in this territory, country, or region, would economic globalization likely be imperiled to a significant degree, or would it likely be sustained with essentially little or no interruption?
4. Importance to core international institutions. Is the commitment or potential commitment central to the functioning and stability of the network of core international institutions the United States built after World War II to fulfill its grand strategy—most notably, NATO and the network of formal alliances that were constructed in Asia as well as the remaining Bretton Woods institutions (the International Monetary Fund and the World Bank) and their immediate successors (the World Trade

Organization)? If things were to go badly in this territory or country, would any of the core international institutions likely be meaningfully endangered in any way?

This list makes it clear that the grand strategy does not require making the world look just like America; as desirable as it may be for democracy to spread, it is not a necessary element of the grand strategy. Nor does it require "general stability." Rather, what it requires is a certain kind of stability. It is vital that some key elements of the global order are not threatened, but some turbulence, perhaps a great deal, need not be addressed if it will have little effect on America's main objectives. As George Kennan argued at the outset of the formation of America's deep engagement strategy, there are only a few core regions that are of vital importance to the United States. It is only in these regions where it must prize stability and be willing to expend effort to maintain it. And even in these regions, what is required is not general stability, but merely "enough" stability to sustain America's central objectives.

The significance of this point is especially apparent and important with respect to the Middle East, which for many reasons has been very unstable over the decades and will likely continue to be for a very long time to come. As Steven Simon and Jonathan Stevenson underscore, the United States sought merely to maintain those aspects of the status quo in the region that were vital to its interests throughout the Cold War and afterward until 9/11. As a result, it undertook "military interventions in the region only in exceptional circumstances. Direct US military involvement was nonexistent, minimal, or indirect in the 1948 Arab-Israeli war, the 1956 Suez crisis, the Six-Day War in 1967, the Yom Kippur War in 1973, and the Iran-Iraq War in the 1980s."[26] Simon and Stevenson's analysis provides a helpful reminder that the restrained approach that Barack Obama took toward the region in his second administration is merely a return to this long-standing US approach; it only looks like "retrenchment" when compared to the highly activist 2001–2013 period.

The Value of Anchoring Debates about Grand Strategy

By providing the most comprehensive evaluation of the cost/benefit ratio of sustaining deep engagement yet attempted, our analysis has major implications for debates about how to execute the grand strategy and whether it is sufficient for the major US interests. To determine how best to implement deep engagement or what kinds of military posture it requires, we need to be clear about precisely what it is and what it does for the United States. Too often debates about "how much is enough" fail to distinguish between the grand strategy itself and additional missions it may enable but does not necessitate. As we will show below, classical and modern scholarship on strategy and international politics reveals a critical difference between the requirements of a strategy aimed at revising the settled status quo as opposed to one aimed at defending it. "Deep engagement plus" missions that entail challenging a settled status quo thus have major implications for the resources the United States will need and the risks it may have to run.

The question of whether deep engagement is sufficient can only be answered by comprehensively assessing what it achieves for US interests. To be sure, we cannot settle every debate about how much "plus" to add—how much the United States should actively foster liberal values as well as prepare for and be willing to execute humanitarian or stability enhancing operations outside the core commitments we have discussed. We cannot rule out that the American public and political elite may come to see some missions of this type as ethical imperatives. What our analysis does allow us to recommend is that such operations should not be pursued at the expense of sustaining the grand strategy.

Conclusion

We have established what the deep engagement grand strategy is and why understanding its costs and benefits matters—not just for the grand strategy debate about retrenchment but also for debates about how to sustain the strategy and whether it is sufficient. Only a few years ago, our focus on deep engagement might have seemed academic. After all, if the grand strategy has been the lodestar of US foreign policy for so long that leaders, analysts, and pundits take it for granted and tend to debate other things, does it really require such a fulsome reckoning? But times have changed. In this respect, Richard Betts argues, "For a quarter century, Washington had the luxury of concentrating on second- and third-order challenges: rogue states, medium-sized wars, terrorists, peacekeeping operations, and humanitarian relief. But the time has come to focus again on first-order dangers. Russia is back, and China is coming."[27] While terrorism and other transnational issues are not going away, the challenge they pose depends critically on the interstate setting and the United States' position within the international system. The long-standing scholarly debate over whether to abandon the deep engagement grand strategy is more relevant than ever. In a world of rising powers and constrained resources, the widespread calls to "come home" need to be addressed with research-based analysis.

Once again, as so often in the past, the foreign policy debate is itself returning to the core issues. Our focused assessment engages the overarching questions at the center of the debate. From the moment America's strategic choice to retain deep engagement after the Cold War became clear, a large and growing number of security-studies scholars have subjected it to withering criticism. Three questions lie at the center of this debate. First, should the United States continue to maintain a wide roster of global security commitments? Second, should it sustain a significant overseas military presence? And third, should it seek to lead the institutional order? On many other pressing foreign policy questions—notably armed humanitarian intervention and democracy promotion—supporters and critics of deep engagement do not have uniform opinions. On these three questions, however, supporters of deep engagement uniformly answer yes, whereas critics invariably answer no.[28] The question is: Who's right?

In positing that certain kinds of actions will cause outcomes favorable to a state's long-term interests and prevent unfavorable ones, grand strategy in essence constitutes a country's bet on how the world works. Evaluating grand strategic choice therefore inevitably engages scholarly knowledge about international politics. The critical analyses of US grand strategy that proliferated over the last decade have the virtue of connecting the grand strategy debate to international relations scholarship. As we will see, however, those advocating retrenchment engage only pieces of that knowledge, often ignoring all theoretical approaches other than realism, all issues other than security, and uncritically adopting models developed in earlier eras that do not apply today. The chapters that follow remedy these shortcomings, and in so doing render a radically different verdict than the conventional view among security-studies scholars on one of the major questions of our time.

5

The Security Logic of Deep Engagement

AS FAR AS we know, the George H. W. Bush and Bill Clinton administrations did not undertake a comprehensive assessment of scholarly knowledge about international politics before deciding to retain NATO and the major East Asian alliances and security partnerships in the new post–Cold War setting. But what if they had? What verdict would international relations scholarship have rendered on the value of continued pursuit of deep engagement? To answer this question, they would have to imagine what the world would be like if they decided to abandon the old commitments. The thinking of many American officials on this score is well captured by the recollections of President Bush and his national security advisor, General Brent Scowcroft, concerning the decision to retain the NATO alliance:

> Our first requirement was to prevent yet another repetition of the turmoil which had beset Europe in the twentieth century. American isolation had played its part in those tragedies. The lesson we drew from this bloody history was that the United States had to continue to play a significant role in European security, whatever developed with respect to the Soviet Union. The vehicle for that role must be NATO. The alliance was the only way the US could keep forces in Europe as a visible commitment to its security and stability. In addition, a united Germany as a full member of the alliance was key to our presence.[1]

In short, *après nous, le deluge*: if the United States comes home, the world courts disaster. That was the gut feeling of these two seasoned statesmen, reasoned by analogy to the 1930s, when US failure to engage was associated with very bad outcomes. But this was the 1990s, not the 1930s. There was no Hitler, Stalin, or Mussolini; there were nuclear weapons, deep economic globalization, and many other major changes. What would revoking US security guarantees do to *this* world? Though practitioners may be loath to admit it, the only way to answer that question is with theory. Bush and Scowcroft's expectation that, absent US security guarantees, the world would become more insecure in ways that would put the long-term core objectives of US foreign policy at risk was based on their informal theory about what a counterfactual post-American world would be like.

Scholars have labored for decades to produce an intellectual apparatus that could help check their informal theory against more explicit, developed, and rigorous arguments. Here we conduct just such an assessment by performing two tasks. First, we unpack the logic of how deep engagement produces security. Second, we assess its most important mechanisms for influencing the strategic environment in light of relevant international relations theories. To be sure, this scholarship does not yield the expectation that American withdrawal would plunge the world into 1930s levels of insecurity. But it does say that Bush and Scowcroft were right to be concerned that regions unmoored from US security engagement would likely be less secure in ways that could compromise important US interests.

Our overarching argument in this chapter is that security provided from the outside is likely to make these regions more secure than they would be if security were provided locally. Although this key conclusion is implied by existing scholarship, the analysis in this chapter is the first systematic account of all the varied theoretical arguments that explain why this is the case.

How Deep Engagement Produces a Favorable Security Environment for the United States

The essential claim advanced for a grand strategy of deep engagement is that it allows the United States to shape the strategic environment in favorable ways. The premise is that key security outcomes favorable to the United States—including balances of power to contain potential aggressors, freedom of action for the United States, relative stability in core regions of importance, reduced prospects for the proliferation of nuclear weapons, enhanced cooperation on terrorism and other major security problems on terms favorable to US interests—are more likely to eventuate when the United States pursues a globally engaged grand strategy. The strategy reflects skepticism that a world as congenial to US interests as the one we now observe would emerge if the

international system were left to its own devices. By sustaining security commitments to allies and partners, the strategy seeks to put Washington in a
stronger position not simply to exercise positive power and make desirable
things happen but, even more importantly, to exercise "blocking power"—
that is, to prevent undesirable changes to the status quo.

As we discuss below, deep engagement fosters a more favorable strategic
environment for the United States via four key mechanisms: deterring potential adversaries, assuring allies' security, providing positive leverage over both
allies and potential adversaries, and creating more and better opportunities
for institutionalized security cooperation than would be possible with a less
deeply engaged strategy.

Deterrence

A central, if understated, aspect of deep engagement is deterrence—that is,
maintaining a military posture that discourages others from undertaking
undesirable actions. More specifically, deep engagement seeks to dissuade potential adversaries from using force in ways that would undermine American
interests in regions far from US territory, with the cardinal example being the
US effort to deter the Soviet Union from attacking, coercing, or intimidating
Western Europe during the Cold War.[i] Today, an often discussed example is
US support for Taiwan, which is aimed at deterring China from pursuing
its claim to sovereignty over the island militarily. The aim in this situation
and all others in which Washington has issued deterrent threats is not only
to make it prohibitively expensive for other actors to use forceful policies to
change the status quo but to do so in a way that does not transform potential partners into enemies or provoke other dangerous reactions. Thus, in the
Taiwan case, the United States also seeks to reassure Beijing that it supports
the ultimate aim of one China as long as it is achieved peacefully. US security
alliances, moreover, are also closely coupled with efforts to give potential adversaries options other than challenging the status quo militarily. The higher

---

i. Within the context of deterrence theory, the most accurate technical term for its current
role in US grand strategy is extended general deterrence (preventing an attack on another
state), as opposed to immediate deterrence (concerning an imminent decision to attack)
or central deterrence (concerning an attack on the homeland). For these distinctions, see
Patrick Morgan, *Deterrence: A Conceptual Analysis* (Beverly Hills, Calif.: SAGE, 1977); Paul
Huth, *Extended Deterrence and the Prevention of War* (New Haven, Conn.: Yale University
Press, 1988); and Vesna Danilovic, *When the Stakes Are High: Deterrence and Conflict among
Major Powers* (Ann Arbor: University of Michigan Press, 2002).

the expected costs of using military force to challenge the status quo, the greater the incentives to accommodate it or at least seek nonviolent means of altering it. Lawrence Freedman nicely sums up the purpose of the deterrent piece of this overall strategy:

> Once certain courses of action have been precluded through fear of the consequences should they be attempted, this conclusion may become embedded. It requires little further deliberation. In this way, at one level deterrence never goes away. Certain options—whole categories of actions—are precluded because of the possible reactions of others. Land may be coveted but not grabbed; the unacceptable practices of foreign governments are denounced but they are left untouched; ideological ambitions are shelved; inconveniences, disruptions, outrages are tolerated; punches are pulled.[2]

In addition to this "deterrence that never goes away," which applies even to periods and regions with no observable major power challenger, US security alliances also serve as a hedge against the emergence of a more immediate threat. The capabilities and alliance relationships needed to signal a would-be challenger that altering the status quo in ways inimical to US interests would be prohibitively costly are essentially the same as those needed to constitute a hedge against the emergence of an overt challenge some time in the future.

Assurance

Deep engagement seeks not only to deter potential adversaries but also to assure allies. It is premised on the proposition that US alliances make the key regions more secure. As noted in the last chapter, this strategic move had its origins at the very outset of the Cold War when policymakers discovered that containing Soviet power required solving incipient local security dilemmas among potential US allies. Thus, US alliances always served not only as capability-aggregating mechanisms against potential adversaries but also as tools for controlling risks and exerting influence among its allies. The Cold War's end and the Soviet Union's dissolution simply caused the balance to swing toward the latter two functions. If in the Cold War the fear was that without direct US security provision interallied friction would frustrate efforts to contain Soviet power, after the Cold War the concern was that former allies, if cast loose from US protection, would adopt solutions to security problems that would exacerbate regional insecurity and run counter to important US interests.

Sustaining security commitments thus not only removes incentives for allies to adopt policies the United States prefers that they not adopt but also nudges allies toward security policies in concert with US global interests. A salient example of this interaction is nuclear proliferation. By providing security guarantees to partners and allies, the United States seeks to reduce their incentives to proliferate. At the same time, the guarantees underwrite positive leverage for inducing allies to actively support US approaches to preventing proliferation by other states, such as the economic sanctions used against Iran. And these commitments may also limit the downstream consequences of any such proliferation that does occur by reassuring neighboring states.

Leverage

US and allied officials insist—usually sincerely and often accurately—that the alliances reflect common interests. There are also many circumstances in which common interests are nurtured and potential disagreements that might have otherwise occurred never become actualized. But when disagreements do occur, deep engagement presumes that in general the balance of bargaining leverage favors the United States as the more powerful, less dependent partner that acts as a security patron. There are exceptions, as circumstances inevitably occur in which an ally may provide assets that cannot be substituted or has some other source of leverage. But the unwritten clause in all the alliance relationships is that Washington is the senior partner and provider of security assurance whose preferences tend to prevail when allies differ.

This leverage matters not only for influencing allies but also for potential adversaries and other nonallied powers. Most of their interests concern their own neighbors. Much of what potential US rivals want to achieve requires negotiations with those neighbors. If Washington has leverage on those neighbors then it has leverage on potential adversaries as well.

Institutionalized Cooperation

The final key mechanism through which deep engagement fosters a more favorable strategic environment is cooperation. US security alliances are institutions and as such have the potential identified in institutionalist international relations theory to facilitate cooperation that would not otherwise occur, an effect strengthened further by the presence of the US as an unambiguous hegemon to help solve "collective action problems" (in which cooperation would make a group of states better off but with a cost each state individually is reluctant to pay).[3] We discuss the underlying logic behind this phenomenon as well as its implication for nonsecurity cooperation in chapter 9. Here the main point is that deep engagement yields both leverage and extensive networks that Washington can draw upon to help solicit cooperation on whatever security issue commands the day. In the Cold War, the key cooperative outcome in the security realm was an effective effort to balance Soviet military power. That outcome was quite unusual in the history of international politics. Usually, collective action problems bedevil balancing alliances, as each state seeks to avoid paying the cost of containing a potentially threatening rising rival. This is arguably the main reason that balancing is inefficient and that it often takes years of war for credible counterbalancing coalitions to form.[4] US leadership, however, helped overcome those challenges to foster the most potent long-standing balancing alliance the world has ever known. This potential remains nascent in Europe and especially Asia today. As long as US-led alliances remain intact, any power contemplating major, forceful alteration of the status quo would have to expect more efficient US-led balancing than would otherwise occur.

More readily observable are the ways in which institutionalized alliances also facilitate cooperation on a large array of security issues, ranging from counterterrorism, intelligence sharing, and piracy to large global security operations. In this sense, institutionalized alliances are attractive as hedging devices, because institutions created for one purpose can facilitate cooperation on new, previously unforeseen issues.[5] Security cooperation also involves military forces and other security institutions from allied countries working together to share information and practices as well as ensure interoperability. US troops deployed permanently in allied countries make this kind of cooperation far cheaper and more effective than "rotational" deployments, where military units periodically visit a country for training purposes and then rotate back to the United States.[6] The result of this security cooperation is a net increase in military effectiveness: working and training together makes both US and allied forces more capable than they would otherwise be.[ii] And because deep engagement places Washington at the center of the world's most important security and intelligence networks, it puts US officials in

---

ii. This does not mean the multilateral operations are always or even generally more effective than US-only ones. Rather, the point is that each military is improved through working with the other, and thus that cooperation enhances the total military capacity of the alliance.

a uniquely strong position to foster cooperation even with non-allies as the situation demands. Thus, on a range of issues from counterpiracy to counterterrorism, the US can sometimes sustain surprisingly deep cooperation even with potential adversaries.

An Interaction Effect

Each of these mechanisms is important, but they are also interdependent: leverage enhances cooperation and deterrence, cooperation enhances deterrence and assurance, assurance feeds leverage, and so on. And all of these security mechanisms interact, in turn, with nonsecurity aspects of the grand strategy to generate the capacity to affect the United States' strategic environment. That is, the security mechanisms discussed here are integrated with the institutional and economic ones we analyze in chapters 9 and 10 to support US goals internationally.

Evaluating Deep Engagement's Causal Mechanisms

Are there good reasons to think that these mechanisms—assurance, deterrence, leverage, and cooperation—will work as advertised? Given the complexity of each mechanism and the complicated ways in which they interact with each other, answering this question is hard. The standard approach in the grand strategy debate is to plunge immediately into evidence concerning US policy in various regions where it is easy to find salient cases of apparent success and failure for each of the basic mechanisms. Here we first take a step back and ask whether the ways in which these mechanisms are postulated to produce a favorable security environment are consistent with what scholars know generally about international politics.

Deep engagement is a massive policy intervention intended to make the world more favorable for the United States. Assessing it requires rendering a verdict on a complex counterfactual about what the world would be like if the United States retrenched.[7] To tame the analysis, we focus on the two mechanisms most directly related to the strategy's purported aim of increasing regional security in ways favorable to US interests: deterrence and assurance. Theory is thus crucial to the enterprise, as it inevitably informs any counterfactual about the world. In the analysis that follows we shall engage most major international relations theories, but two bodies of theory matter most: realism and deterrence theory. Realist theories loom large not only because they address international security issues so extensively, but also because many of the most salient criticisms of deep engagement come from scholars steeped in this intellectual tradition. For a large portion of the expert community engaged with this issue, realism's verdict on the strategy thus carries special weight. And the large and closely related scholarly literature on deterrence is tailor-made for assessing that important aspect of deep engagement.

Deterrence

The alliances at the heart of deep engagement are meant to enhance US security by deterring potential adversaries from using force in ways that would undermine American interests. The scholarly literature on deterrence is one of the oldest and biggest in international relations, benefitting from over a half-century of rigorous theorizing, quantitative testing, and in-depth case analysis.[8] What does it say about the security commitments of the type the US sustains? Does it predict that they will work as advertised?

To start with theoretical logic, deterrence hinges on assessments of capability and intent. When contemplating the use of force to challenge the status quo, states assess expected benefits minus costs, which include the capabilities of all potential opponents as well as their willingness to use those capabilities to make good on their deterrent threat. Theorists identify multiple logics that may be in play: the defender's reputation for resolve in general or regarding a specific commitment; the manipulation of commitments and risks to increase any challenger's estimate of the probability that the defender will follow through on its threat to use force; the intrinsic interests of the parties to fulfill alliance obligations; and the actual capability to thwart or retaliate against the challenger's use of force.

While theorists debate the relative significance of these various logics, two broad implications are apparent. First, US alliances tend to have features that trigger all or most of the basic deterrence logics. If the framers of US grand strategy after the Cold War had consulted the huge literature on deterrence theory and then tried to fashion alliances to maximize extended deterrence—without seeking to adjudicate among various schools of thought within this literature, simply weighting all of the various logics roughly equally—they would have wanted the following features:

- A long history and deep institutionalization with allies, reinforcing the inference for potential adversaries that strong mutual interests are engaged

- Deep nonsecurity relationships with allies on economic and cultural levels, again signaling to potential adversaries that strong intrinsic interests exist
- A markedly favorable balance of military forces, especially in the regions where the status quo is being defended, which would both signal real interest and make deterrence intrinsically more credible[9]
- Actual US forces deployed abroad in order to:
  - show that both the United States and its allies are willing to bear costs to make the alliance credible, justifying the inference on the part of potential adversaries that the alliance reflects important interests and therefore that the alliance treaty is more than just a piece of paper[10]
  - act as tripwires, generating what Thomas Schelling called "pre-commitment," strongly raising expectations of US involvement in case of armed conflict and raising the credibility of commitment[11]
  - increase the speed and firepower of early responses to any use of force, decreasing the chances for quick victory by adversaries, thus reducing a crucial precondition for deterrence failure[12]
- That as many allies as possible—but especially the US—be democracies, because democratic governments may be better able to pre-commit to honor commitments via the well-known "audience cost" mechanism: because leaders of democratic states may suffer political penalties if they back down from a salient public commitment, scholars argue, they are better able than their authoritarian counterparts to make deterrence credible[13]

Needless to say, alliances with precisely these features are just what the Clinton administration inherited as legacies of the Cold War. If the US alliances do not fit the conceptual parameters for sustaining deterrence, it is hard to think of any that would. And the evolution of deterrence theory puts a premium on exactly these properties of the US deterrent posture. The deterrence theorists of the postwar "golden era," such as Bernard Brodie, Herman Kahn, and especially Thomas Schelling, highlighted the hyperrational manipulation of risk, the supremely modulated signaling of commitment, and, above all, the overarching importance of sustaining a reputation for resolve. These works conjured the image of a nuclear-era Bismarck in total control of his rhetoric, moving military forces like chess pieces to create unassailable positions of strength in the tense standoffs of the Cold War. It was reasonable to wonder whether real presidents operating in the competitive pluralism of American domestic politics could possibly measure up. The trend in the theoretical literature over the last generation, by contrast, has been increased emphasis on the interdependent interests and capabilities logic that emerges from nurturing and sustaining alliance relationships over the long haul.[14] Rather than perfectly controlled signaling and obsessive concern with appearing tough and resolute, it is more the natural evolution of alliance ties and the development of close mutual interests that make deterrence work. The US set of alliances generally scores especially well in precisely those areas. Little wonder that most studies of the deterrence effect of alliances find that defense ties like those that bind the United States to its allies are especially effective.[15]

The second widely accepted theoretical implication from this literature is just as relevant: it is easier to deter forceful challenges to the status quo than to compel their reversal after the fact. Schelling originally argued that compellence (which involves getting another actor to take some positive action) was harder than deterrence; the reason is that a compellent threat is much less likely to succeed than a deterrent threat, and so the compeller is much more likely to have to actually use force to attain its objective.[16] Schelling established several arguments for this proposition. The challenger to the status quo must make the first move, he argued, and it is intrinsically harder to make such a first-move threat credible. Deterrence upholds a known status quo, while compellence seeks to change to some unknown future state. When a potential challenger acquiesces and chooses not to challenge a status quo, the move's implications are fairly clear. In contrast, when the recipient of a compellent threat acquiesces to a demand, it is less clear how the interaction ends. Compellence thus lacks the limits and manageability of deterrence. All these arguments, other scholars contend, apply with special force to nuclear weapons, which are widely seen as being much more effective at deterring challenges than reversing challenges that have emerged.[17]

Scholars have since adduced numerous additional reasons, many of which center on the simple fact that acceding to a deterrent threat is unobservable, whereas it is much harder to back down in the face of a compellent threat. After all, it is hard for one actor to tell another "Do this or else suffer the consequences" without others knowing about it.[18] Thus, Barry Posen argues that acquiescing to a compellent threat is more likely to invite further predation than giving in to a deterrent threat, and Robert Art maintains that national honor is invoked in acceding to compellence in ways that do not occur with deterrence.[19] Decades of well-established research findings in psychology also show that people fear losses more than they crave gains, and so are far more likely to run risks to prevent loss than to acquire gain.[20] The leaders of a state that is the target of a compellent threat are likely to be willing to run higher risks to avoid losses. The opposite is true of the leaders of the state issuing such a threat in search of gain. The implication strongly supports the weight of scholarship behind the expectation that revising a settled status quo is much harder than defending it.[21]

Assurance

As chapter 4 made clear, deep engagement's security alliances have always been about more than deterring potential adversaries; they are also about assuring allies to shape their security policies in ways that enhance US interests in interallied cooperation, avoiding regional tensions and inhibiting the spread of nuclear weapons. This mechanism assumed much greater salience after the Cold War's end. Although the US interests served by assurance are many, at root is the claim that it makes regions more secure than they would otherwise be. Why should US assurances from the outside be preferable to security provided purely by local actors in the absence of a Soviet-scale great-power challenge? Ironically, the answer can be found in realist theory. Realists are among the most numerous and prominent critics of deep engagement. Many critics question the security benefits of US assurance by relying on propositions that flow from the theory.[22] Yet realism actually contains strong theoretical arguments for the security benefits of US assurance. Bearing in mind the difficulty of summarizing such a complex literature, it is fair to say that the preponderance of contemporary realist theorizing predicts net security gains from US assurance.

Let us start with "offensive realism," a branch of realism whose baseline prediction is a deeply insecure and violence-prone world, with core regions beset by dangerously shifting power balances, preventive war temptations, widespread nuclear proliferation, runs at regional hegemony, great power security competition, and even major-power war. According to the theory's principal proponent, John Mearsheimer, a key reason why this world has not yet emerged is security provision by the "American Pacifier."[23] "There is no question that the presence of US troops in Europe and northeast Asia has played an important role in moderating security competition and promoting stability over the past decade," he insists.[24] How? External security assurance solves the collective action problem among local actors, making it possible to band together in credible coalitions and thereby deter adversaries. The collective action problem is a major reason for states failing to act together to advance their collective security interests, according to Mearsheimer. Each state's individual incentive is to try to avoid the costs and risks of balancing by passing the buck to other states and free riding on their efforts. A credible outside superpower willing and able to overcome this problem by creating and sustaining alliances reduces the expectations of any revisionist that it can take a "divide and rule" path to regional dominance.

But the key trick the strategy demands is to generate that certainty without sparking as much security competition as would occur in America's absence. For Mearsheimer, geography solves this problem. It makes an overseas superpower like the US more capable than local powers of creating deterrence postures that do not threaten regional hegemony. The difficulty of projecting military power over long distances and especially across oceans means that a state like the United States cannot seriously contemplate attaining hegemony in a different region. Its aim must remain defensive: to prevent any other power from attaining hegemony in the key regions outside North America. The result is a comparatively nonoffensive defense of the regional status quo that is less likely to stoke security competition than purely local attempts at self-help would.

Another branch of realist scholarship, "defensive realism," provides a more nuanced portrayal of the baseline security problem than its offensive cousin. The theory considers variation in key "structural modifiers," notably the "offense-defense balance" and the ease with which states can distinguish offensive from defensive military postures.[25] If defense is relatively easy compared to offense, states may be able to secure themselves without threatening others, lessening the overall security problem that figures so prominently in offensive realism. And if states can easily tell the difference between offensive military postures and defensive ones, they may be able to signal that they lack aggressive intentions, reducing the pervasive uncertainty about intentions that drives offensive realism's grim portrayal of incessant security competition. In particular, nuclear weapons provide defense from threats to states' core security, and postures can be created that are good for defense and deterrence but little else. In addition, geography and conventional military technology may allow states to construct military postures that are relatively unthreatening to neighbors, reducing the incentives for the cutthroat security competition offensive realism forecasts. The theory thus considers the possibility of strategic settings that allow states to signal that they are "pure security seekers" with no aggressive intentions, thus ameliorating the uncertainty about intentions that drives the security dilemma—and offensive realism's dire forecasts.

Applying the theory to the effects of US security commitments is complicated, however. Recent research on nuclear weapons casts doubt on the most sanguine arguments about their security effects and especially their ability to deter conventional security competition. Other structural modifiers such as the offense-defense balance remain contested theoretically on various grounds and are very hard to measure.[26] Moreover, we lack a systematic scholarly analysis that applies the logic of the theory to either Asia or the Middle East, which is exactly where such analysis is most needed, since scholars of all theoretical traditions—realists, liberals, institutionalists, and constructivists—predict that these regions are likely to be less stable than Europe.[27]

The most important point about defensive realism for our purposes here is that its logic predicts net security gains from US assurance even in regions seemingly primed for peace. Critics of deep engagement who rely on the offense-defense balance and other defensive realist precepts argue that US alliances are not worth their high cost (discussed in chapters 7 and 8) because security in these regions is either already robust enough or because the United States can and should wait to intervene until after a truly threatening scenario has emerged. They do not deny that US assurance adds to the robustness of security in these areas. The theory's logic clearly shows that it is easier for an overseas major power to provide security in a way that is comparatively less threatening to the local great powers. US assurance thus makes security dilemmas, dangerous arms races, and rivalries even less likely. If cost were not an issue, defensive realism would therefore imply that security assurance by an overseas superpower is to be preferred to purely locally supplied security.

A more general limitation of the standard conception of defensive realism is that it relies on a very particular—and very restrictive—assumption about state preferences. Specifically, as Randall Schweller stresses, the theory assumes a world of purely security-seeking states.[28] It models a post-American Eurasia populated with states whose only relevant preference is security, with security defined narrowly in terms of protection from violent external attacks on the homeland. Needless to say, burgeoning research across the social and other sciences undermines that core assumption: states have preferences not only for security but also for prestige, status, and other aims, and they engage in tradeoffs between the various objectives.[29] It follows that rationally led states must allow for the possibility that other states may have "greedy" nonsecurity motivations for competitive behavior.

Charles Glaser's important book *Rational Theory of International Politics* theoretically allows for this possibility while retaining all other key elements of defensive realism. Glaser's theory allows for the possibility that regional interstate settings primed for peace in material terms may nonetheless risk creating a spiral of dangerous security competition, because states still can't determine whether others are motivated by security alone or some more dangerous drive for expansion.[30]

In a very careful application, Glaser models hypothetical post-American security settings in Northeast Asia and Europe, and his theory captures the greater pessimism about Asia that is common among many analysts. "U.S. security guarantees reduce incentives for competition in both regions," he finds, but "a continuing American military commitment makes a larger contribution to regional security in Northeast Asia than in Europe."[31] In a hypothetical post-American Northeast Asia, the theory predicts, "the most likely outcome would be a competitive peace supported by defensive advantages and strained by unresolved territorial disputes possibly resembling the dangerous major-power relations of the Cold War."[32] Because US security guarantees prevent that more competitive security situation from emerging without themselves generating additional insecurity, the net effect is positive.

Limiting nuclear proliferation is an especially salient part of the larger security benefit that assurance is meant to generate. By standard realist logic, demand for nuclear weapons is a function of insecurity. Making allies more secure should make them less willing to absorb the considerable costs associated with acquiring nuclear weapons. Of course, if making allies more secure makes non-allies even less secure, then assuring allies is a poor choice for counterproliferation. But if security assurances generate a net increase in security, the consequence is a net decrease in demand for nuclear weapons. Needless to say, many realists are highly critical of US counterproliferation policies, as indeed they are of deep engagement more generally. But the narrow question here is whether the theory predicts that the core US commitments to allied security, setting aside other US policies, will serve to limit proliferation or not. And the bottom line is that in either the extremely dangerous post-American world envisaged by offensive realism or the less apocalyptic but still more competitive world predicted by defensive realism, the demand for nuclear weapons would be greater than it is today if the US pursued retrenchment.[iii]

---

iii. By the same realist precepts, however, any increase in proliferation caused by US retrenchment might enhance security, such that the net effect of retrenchment could be neutral. We address this issue in the next chapter.

Conclusion

The statesmen who decided to retain the deep engagement grand strategy as the Cold War ended and the Soviet Union entered its death throes believed that US security commitments would help prevent the reemergence of a more unstable and threatening world. Many scholars are highly critical of that decision and skeptical of the intuition behind it. Perhaps the decision to retain NATO and the Asian alliances reflected sheer inertia, a lack of strategic vision, or just the hubris of a great power convinced of its own indispensability and addicted to an overweening global role. In this chapter, we scrutinized the basic propositions underlying the strategy and found that the decisions by Bush, Scowcroft, and their colleagues to stay the course regarding US alliances were right. Even in the nuclear age, even in a world without a geopolitical challenge on the scale of the Soviet Union, there are strong reasons to believe that US provision of security to overseas allies generates a net increase in security compared to what would occur if local actors were left entirely to their own devices.

We reached this conclusion by examining the logic of security provision in the deep engagement grand strategy, highlighting two mechanisms that all agree have been absolutely central for seven decades: deterrence and assurance. We found that the oldest and arguably most relevant international relations theories—ones often favored by advocates of retrenchment themselves—predict that US disengagement would decrease security. According to the well-established logic of deterrence theory, moreover, the key alliances at the core of US grand strategy have most of the properties for a strong deterrent effect, notably the presence of deployed military forces, the capability to bolster them quickly, a robust nuclear deterrent posture, and extensive observable evidence of strong interest in upholding the status quo. In addition, there are compelling theoretically grounded reasons to expect that deterring challenges to the status quo is far easier than compelling or coercing states to relinquish gains acquired by force. All of this suggests that sustaining alliance commitments is a sensible move for a major power interested in fostering a security setting hospitable to its interests and deterring or hedging against potential challenges to a favorable status quo.

6

Assessing the Security Benefits of Deep Engagement

CONSISTENCY WITH INFLUENTIAL relevant theories lends credence to the expectation that US security commitments actually can shape the strategic environment as deep engagement presupposes. But it is far from conclusive. Not all analysts endorse the theories we discussed in chapter 5. These theories make strong assumptions that states generally act rationally and focus primarily on security. Allowing misperceptions, emotions, domestic politics, desire for status, or concern for honor into the picture might alter the verdict on the strategy's net expected effects. And to model the strategy's expected effects we had to simplify things by selecting two mechanisms—assurance and deterrence—and examining their effects independently, thus missing potentially powerful positive interactions between them.

This chapter moves beyond theory to examine patterns of evidence. If the theoretical arguments about the security effects of deep engagement are right, what sort of evidence should we see? Two major bodies of evidence are most important: general empirical findings concerning the strategy's key mechanisms and regionally focused research.

General Patterns of Evidence

Three key questions about US security provision have received the most extensive analysis. First, do alliances such as those sustained by the United States actually deter war and increase security? Second, does such security provision actually hinder nuclear proliferation? And third, does limiting proliferation actually increase security?

Deterrence Effectiveness

The determinants of deterrence success and failure have attracted scores of quantitative and case study tests. Much of the case study work yields a cautionary finding: that deterrence is much harder in practice than in theory, because standard models assume away the complexities of human psychology and domestic politics that tend to make some states hard to deter and might cause deterrence policies to backfire.[1] Many quantitative findings, meanwhile, are mutually contradictory or are clearly not relevant to extended deterrence. But some relevant results receive broad support:

- Alliances generally do have a deterrent effect. In a study spanning nearly two centuries, Johnson and Leeds found "support for the hypothesis that defensive alliances deter the initiation of disputes." They conclude that "defensive alliances lower the probability of international conflict and are thus a good policy option for states seeking to maintain peace in the world."[2] Sechser and Fuhrmann similarly find that formal defense pacts with nuclear states have significant deterrence benefits.[3]
- The overall balance of military forces (including nuclear) between states does not appear to influence deterrence; the local balance of military forces in the specific theater in which deterrence is actually practiced, however, is key.[4]
- Forward-deployed troops enhance the deterrent effect of alliances with overseas allies.[5]
- Strong mutual interests and ties enhance deterrence.[6]
- Case studies strongly ratify the theoretical expectation that it is easier to defend a given status quo than to challenge it forcefully: compellence (sometimes termed "coercion" or "coercive diplomacy") is extremely hard.[7]

The most important finding to emerge from this voluminous research is that alliances—especially with nuclear-armed allies like the United States—actually work in deterring conflict. This is all the more striking in view of the fact that what scholars call "selection bias" probably works against it. The United States is more inclined to offer—and protégés to seek—alliance relationships in settings where the probability of military conflicts is higher than average. The fact that alliances work to deter conflict in precisely the situations where deterrence is likely to be especially hard is noteworthy.

More specifically, these findings buttress the key theoretical implication that if the United States is interested in deterring military challenges to the status quo in key regions, relying only on latent military capabilities in the US homeland is likely to be far less effective than having an overseas military posture. Similarly, they lend support to the general proposition that a forward deterrence posture is strongly appealing to a status quo power, because defending a given status quo is far cheaper than overturning it, and, once a favorable status quo is successfully overturned, restoring the status quo ante can be expected to be fearsomely costly. Recognizing the significance of these findings clearly casts doubt on the "wait on the sidelines and decide whether to intervene later" approach that is so strongly favored by retrenchment proponents.

The Causes of Nuclear Proliferation

Matthew Kroenig highlights a number of reasons why US policymakers seek to limit the spread of nuclear weapons: "Fear that nuclear proliferation might deter [US leaders] from using military intervention to pursue their interests, reduce the effectiveness of their coercive diplomacy, trigger regional instability, undermine their alliance structures, dissipate their strategic attention, and set off further nuclear proliferation within their sphere of influence."[8] These are not the only reasons for concern about nuclear proliferation; also notable are the enhanced prospects of nuclear accidents and the greater risk of leakage of nuclear material to terrorists.[9]

Do deep engagement's security ties serve to contain the spread of nuclear weapons? The literature on the causes of proliferation is massive and faces challenges as great as any in international relations. With few cases to study, severe challenges in gathering evidence about inevitably secretive nuclear programs, and a large number of factors in play on both the demand and the supply sides, findings are decidedly mixed.[10] Alliance relationships are just one piece of this complex puzzle, one that is hard to isolate from all the other factors in play. And empirical studies face the same selection bias problem just discussed: Nuclear powers are more likely to offer security guarantees to states confronting a serious threat and thus facing above-average incentives to acquire nuclear weapons. Indeed, alliance guarantees might be offered to states actively considering the nuclear option precisely in order to try to forestall that decision. Like a strong drug given only to very sick patients, alliances thus may have a powerful effect even if they sometimes fail to work as hoped.

Bearing these challenges in mind, the most relevant findings that emerge from this literature are:

- The most recent statistical analysis of the precise question at issue concludes that "security guarantees significantly reduce proliferation proclivity among their recipients."[11] In addition, states with such guarantees are less likely to export sensitive nuclear material and technology to other nonnuclear states.[12]
- Case study research underscores that the complexity of motivations for acquiring nuclear weapons cannot be reduced to security: domestic politics, economic interests, and prestige all matter.[13]
- Multiple independently conceived and executed recent case studies nonetheless reveal that security alliances help explain numerous allied decisions *not* to proliferate even when security is not always the main driver of leaders' interest in a nuclear program.[14] As Nuno Monteiro and Alexandre Debs stress, "States whose security goals are subsumed by their sponsors' own aims have never acquired the bomb. . . . This finding highlights the role of U.S. security commitments in stymieing nuclear proliferation: U.S. protégés will only seek the bomb if they doubt U.S. protection of their core security goals."[15]
- Multiple independently conceived and executed recent case research projects further unpack the conditions that decrease the likelihood of allied proliferation, centering on the credibility of the alliance commitment.[16] In addition, in some cases of prevention failure, the alliances allow the patron to influence the ally's nuclear program subsequently, decreasing further proliferation risks.[17]
- Security alliances lower the likelihood of proliferation cascades. To be sure, many predicted cascades did not occur.[18] But security provision, mainly by the United States, is a key reason why. The most comprehensive statistical analysis finds that states are more likely to proliferate in response to neighbors when three conditions are met: (1) there is an intense security rivalry between the two countries; (2) the prospective proliferating state does not have a security guarantee from a nuclear-armed patron; and (3) the potential proliferator has the industrial and technical capacity to launch an indigenous nuclear program.[19]

In sum, as Monteiro and Debs note, "Despite grave concerns that more states would seek a nuclear deterrent to counter U.S. power preponderance," in fact "the spread of nuclear weapons *decelerated* with the end of the Cold

War in 1989."[20] Their research, as well as that of scores of scholars using multiple methods and representing many contrasting theoretical perspectives, shows that US security guarantees and the counter-proliferation policy deep engagement allows are a big part of the reason why.

The Costs of Nuclear Proliferation

General empirical findings thus lend support to the proposition that security alliances impede nuclear proliferation. But is this a net contributor to global security? Most practitioners and policy analysts would probably not even bring this up as a question and would automatically answer yes if it were raised. Yet a small but very prominent group of theorists within the academy reach a different answer: some of the same realist precepts that generate the theoretical prediction that retrenchment would increase demand for nuclear weapons also suggest that proliferation might increase security such that the net effect of retrenchment could be neutral. Most notably, "nuclear optimists" like Kenneth Waltz contend that deterrence essentially solves the security problem for all nuclear-armed states, largely eliminating the direct use of force among them.[21] It follows that US retrenchment might generate an initial decrease in security followed by an increase as insecure states acquire nuclear capabilities, ultimately leaving no net effect on international security.

This perspective is countered by "nuclear pessimists" such as Scott Sagan. Reaching outside realism to organization theory and other bodies of social science research, they see major security downsides from new nuclear states. Copious research produced by Sagan and others casts doubt on the expectation that governments can be relied upon to create secure and controlled nuclear forces.[22] The more nuclear states there are, the higher the probability that the organizational, psychological, and civil-military pathologies Sagan identifies will turn an episode like one of the numerous "near misses" he uncovers into actual nuclear use. As Campbell Craig warns, "One day a warning system will fail, or an official will panic, or a terrorist attack will be misconstrued, and the missiles will fly."[23]

Looking beyond these kinds of factors, it is notable that powerful reasons to question the assessment of proliferation optimists also emerge even if one assumes, as they do, that states are rational and seek only to maximize their security. First, nuclear deterrence can only work by raising the risk of nuclear war. For deterrence to be credible, there has to be a nonzero chance of nuclear use.[24] If nuclear use is impossible, deterrence cannot be credible. It follows that every nuclear deterrence relationship depends on some probability of nuclear use. The more such relationships there are, the greater the risk of nuclear war.[i] Proliferation therefore increases the chances of nuclear war even in a perfectly rationalist world. Proliferation optimists cannot logically deny that nuclear spread increases the risk of nuclear war. Their argument must be that the security gains of nuclear spread outweigh this enhanced risk.

Estimating that risk is not simply a matter of pondering the conditions under which leaders will choose to unleash nuclear war. Rather, as Schelling established, the question is whether states will run the risk of using nuclear weapons. Nuclear crisis bargaining is about a "competition in risk taking."[25] Kroenig counts some twenty cases in which states—including prominently the United States—ran real risks of nuclear war in order to prevail in crises.[26] As Kroenig notes, "By asking whether states can be deterred or not . . . proliferation optimists are asking the wrong question. The right question to ask is: what risk of nuclear war is a specific state willing to run against a particular opponent in a given crisis?"[27] The more nuclear-armed states there are, the more the opportunities for such risk-taking and the greater the probability of nuclear use.

It is also the case that for nuclear weapons to deter a given level of conflict, there must be a real probability of their use at that level of conflict. For nuclear weapons to deter conventional attack, they must be configured in such a way as to make their use credible in response to a conventional attack. Highly controlled and reliable assured-retaliation postures might well be credible in response to a conventional attack that threatens a state's existence. But as newer research shows, the farther the issue in question is from a state's existential security, the harder it is to make nuclear threats credible with the type of ideally stable nuclear posture whose existence proliferation optimism presupposes.[28] If a state wishes, for example, to deter a conventionally stronger neighbor from seizing a disputed piece of territory, it may face great challenges fashioning a nuclear force that is credible. Following Schelling's logic about the "threat that leaves something to chance," it may face incentives to create a quasi-doomsday nuclear posture that virtually locks in escalation in response to its rival's attempt to seize the territory conventionally.

Key here is that nuclear spread cannot be treated as binary: "You have 'em or you don't." States can choose the kind of nuclear postures they build.

---

i. If proliferation strictly substitutes for US nuclear guarantees (that is, the only states that proliferate are those with US nuclear guarantees), then the net number of nuclear deterrence relationships stays constant. But as we argue later, proliferation to current US allies is likely to generate further spread to states not currently allied with Washington. And there are strong reasons to expect it to be harder to build robust low-risk postures in the case of many potential proliferators.

Some states may choose to build dangerous and vulnerable nuclear postures. And because they lack the money or the technological capacity or both, many states may not be able to create truly survivable forces (that is, forces that can survive a nuclear first strike by a rival power) even if they wanted to.

The links between nuclear possession and conflict are hard to assess empirically. Still, there are relevant findings that are probative for this debate:

- Nuclear weapons are most credible at deterring the kind of conflict— threats to a state's core territorial security—that is least relevant to the actual security concerns of most states most of the time. Both quantitative and case study research validates the claim that territorial conquest is rarely an issue in armed conflicts in the present era. Yet states that are bullish on their prospects for territorial survival as sovereign units still have plenty of security concerns and also often find plenty of reasons to use force and plenty of ways to use force other than by conquering other states.[29]
- Robust, secure nuclear postures do not stop states from engaging in intense security competition. Though the United States and Soviet Union did not fight each other during the Cold War, their nuclear arsenals did not prevent them from engaging in one of history's most costly rivalries, complete with intense arms racing and dangerous crises that raised the specter of nuclear war.
- Though they built massive arsenals, at various junctures the two superpowers adopted dangerously escalatory postures to attempt to deter various levels of conflict.[30]
- The mere possession of nuclear weapons does not deter conventional attack, as both India and Israel discovered.
- In both statistical and case study tests, Vipin Narang finds that the only nuclear posture that has any effect on conventional conflict initiation and escalation is a destabilizing "asymmetrical escalatory" force, a doomsday posture designed to create intense incentives for early use, such as that constructed by Pakistan in the 1990s.[31]

In short, nuclear spread is a Hobson's choice: it will inevitably increase the chances of nuclear use, and it will either not deter conventional war or will do so only by raising the risks of nuclear war even more. Add to this the risk that states in the real world may not behave in ways consistent with the assumptions underlying proliferation optimism. That is, some subset of new nuclear-armed states may not be led by rational leaders, may not prove able to overcome organizational problems and resist the temptation to preempt before feared neighbors nuclearize, may not pursue security as the only major state preference, and may not be risk-averse. The scale of these risks rises as the world moves from nine to twenty, thirty, or forty nuclear states. In addition, many of the other dangers noted by analysts who are concerned about the destabilizing effects of nuclear proliferation—including the risk of accidents and the prospects that some new nuclear powers will not have truly surviv-able forces (making them susceptible to a first-strike attack and thus creating incentives for early first use)—are prone to go up as the number of nuclear powers grows. Moreover, the risk of unforeseen crisis dynamics that could spin out of control is also higher as the number of nuclear powers increases. Finally, add to these concerns the enhanced danger of nuclear leakage to dan-gerous, undeterrable nonstate actors, and a world with overall higher levels of security competition becomes yet more worrisome. And all of these con-cerns emerge independently of other reasons the United States is generally better off in a world with fewer nuclear states, notably increased US freedom of action.

Regionally Focused Research

Based on what scholars know generally about international relations, deep engagement should work to produce a security setting favorable to US inter-ests in key regions. Regionally focused research reveals strong though hardly universal support for this proposition. Prominent general studies of regional security orders and the sources of war and peace yield conclusions consistent with the foregoing analysis.[32] In explaining how US assurances from the out-side enhance regional security over local self-help, these studies highlight sev-eral mechanisms in addition to those discussed so far (deterrence, assurance, cooperation, and leverage), in particular the United States' ability to serve as a mediator and partial guarantor of commitments among local parties to a dispute.

East Asia

Most experts on East Asia's security ratify what general international rela-tions scholarship has to say about deep engagement's security-enhancing and security-deterrent effects. Numerous studies of Asian security support the prediction that were the United States to pull back from the region, security competition would rise.[33] Indeed, this is the dominant view among experts on Asian regional security.[34] The assessment is very close to Charles Glaser's theoretically derived forecast that abrogation of US security alliances risks bringing major-power security competition to Cold War levels, including arms racing, nuclear proliferation, militarized crises, and competitive support for rivalrous smaller-power allies and the like.[35]

The best way to sum up the dominant scholarly perspective is that most analysts expect the probability of more militarily competitive policies to rise if the US security guarantees are withdrawn. For any country, there is always a range of choice, and experts debate the probabilities for each option in a world with a reduced US regional role. Concerning Japan, for example, Barry Posen's own survey of the expert literature identifies four options for Tokyo: finding a new nuclear protector, bandwagoning with China, continuing the current nuclear hedge (maintaining a relatively rapid breakout capacity), and nuclear breakout of some type.[36] While these responses are all possible, ultimately Posen concludes that nuclear breakout is most probable—in accord with careful studies by many Japanese security experts.[37] Replicate this kind of analysis for the other key regional players, and what emerges from this literature is a strong expectation that more competitive policy responses become more likely in the absence of the US security presence.[38]

Regional studies also generally leave little doubt that deep engagement increases the efficiency of balancing or deterring China.[39] This is the case even though they vigorously debate China's interest in and capability for revising the regional status quo coercively. On one end of the spectrum are those who follow Mearsheimer in arguing that absent the United States, and provided it continued to grow rapidly, China would seek regional hegemony.[40] On the other end are those who hold that China is very far from attaining the capabilities needed to overwhelm local resistance to its dominance in the region and, in any case, is unlikely ever to conceive such an aim.[41] But even as they debate whether the US presence is necessary to contain or deter China, experts largely confirm the expectations from theory and more general studies that US security alliances do make it much harder for China to exploit its local military advantages to revise the status quo in its favor.

Needless to say, the US-China relationship is far from being as antagonistic as the term deterrence may imply. Christensen's argument that US alliance commitments "shape China's choices" resonates most closely with how many observers see the state of play.[42] For Christensen, the alliances help sustain the more important elements of a regional status quo favorable to the United States in part by raising the costs to China of exploiting its geographic advantage (as well as mutual antagonisms among neighbors) to settle out-standing disputes coercively.

In a region with relatively few local stabilizers, some security crises are bound to emerge, and when they do, the assurance and deterrence sides of deep engagement facilitate another role stressed in accounts of regional security: that of mediator. Needless to say, parties to disputes can resolve them without high-leverage mediators like the United States. But taking the United States out of the equation increases the probability that issues will be settled in ways that upset the regional status quo in China's favor or that they will be settled violently, or both. In a counterfactual world of American retrenchment, security crises such as the Senkaku/Diaoyu Islands dispute would have to be settled by the immediate participants (in this case Japan and China) themselves, without the involvement of an actor with a strong interest in peaceful resolution and strong levers to influence the disputants. In this case, the United States is in a position to use the leverage flowing from its status as the security provider for Japan to warn Tokyo that provocative Japanese actions would be counterproductive. At the same time, a forwardly engaged United States remains capable of deterring China: Beijing knows that it is not in a position to effectively match US and Japanese forces in an air/naval conflict so far from its borders. As Thomas Christensen notes, these and other similar episodes show that "a combination of U.S. power and resolve on the one hand, and diplomatic assurances on the other, can calm potentially volatile situations involving emotional sovereignty claims and a rising China."[43]

Assessing Escalation Risks

In recent years, a key question that many analysts have raised in response to China's rising military capabilities is whether Washington's assurance and deterrence missions can be achieved in a manner that does not court insecurity and crisis instability. As was noted in chapter 3, China's rapid augmentation of its anti-access and area denial (A2/AD) capabilities has greatly raised the costs and risks of operating US aircraft and surface ships (but not submarines) near China's coast.[44] In response, US defense planners have bruited potential military strategies that many analysts worry could run contrary to our basic argument about the security-enhancing effect of security provision by an offshore superpower.[45] Of all the recent developments discussed in the expert literature on East Asian security, this poses the greatest challenge to our analysis. For if, in seeking to assure allies and dissuade China from resorting to force, the United States ends up adopting a military posture that sparks more severe security problems than would exist without American engagement, our core argument no longer applies.

The severity of this challenge depends on how the United States defines its strategic goals. If the aim is to regain all the military options that the US enjoyed in the 1990s, then the challenge can appear daunting, demanding potentially expensive and/or risky counters. With its emphasis on a "disrupt, destroy and defeat approach," the much debated AirSea Battle[ii] concept reflects this mentality.[46] Yet deep engagement's core objectives are defensive: securing regional allies, raising the costs to China of coercively upsetting the status quo, sustaining the favorable institutional and economic order, and continuing to provide China with incentives to cooperate with rather than combat that order. And the requirements necessary for sustaining such a defensive stance appear by all accounts to be manageable and sustainable.

Reflecting the changed military reality owing to China's rise—in particular its rapidly augmented capacity to strike targets with accurate missiles—a growing number of analysts argue that the United States' core defensive goals of deterrence and security provision can be well served by a denial strategy. Using terms such as "mutual denial," "sea denial," "maritime denial," and the "mutually denied battlespace strategy," analysts argue that the United States can and should develop strategies and postures to avoid the need to undertake potentially escalatory strikes on the Chinese mainland of the type purportedly envisioned in AirSea Battle. They posit that the United States should take advantage of maritime geography in order to "deter Chinese land or maritime aggression and, failing that, deny China the use of the sea inside the first island chain (a conceptual line from Japan to Taiwan and the Philippines) during hostilities."[47]

A central notion undergirding the approach is "A2/AD reversed": curtailing the ability of China's military to operate within the so-called first island chain during a conflict and thereby prevent it from prevailing in scenarios such as an attack on Taiwan or an effort to close or control key strategic waterways by employing the same basic strategy and mix of capabilities—mines, mobile antiship missiles, and so on—that China itself has used to effectively push the US surface ships and aircraft away from its coast.[48] A related key theme these analysts emphasize is to turn the tables and focus on exploiting areas of relative Chinese weakness, most notably by leveraging US undersea

---

ii. Note that the AirSea Battle concept did not initially include a role for the army and that the Pentagon has now incorporated it within the strategy and relabeled it Joint Concept for Access and Maneuver in the Global Commons (JAM-GC).

dominance, which is poorly countered by China's weak antisubmarine warfare capacity.[49]

Ultimately, the premise of the denial strategy is that even if China is able to effectively deny US surface ships and aircraft access to the area close to its coast, China can be prevented from using this geographic space as a launching pad for projecting military power in a conflict. In this view, the geographic area close to China's coast is not poised to flip from being a potential launching pad for the United States to use surface ships and aircraft to project power against China in a conflict to being a potential launching pad for China itself to use these military assets to project power. Instead, the zone close to China's coast is poised to turn into a no man's land (or no man's sea) in which neither state can effectively use surface ships or aircraft for force projection during a conflict.[50] This change is notable but needs to be kept in perspective. The 1990s baseline had China, a putative great power, incapable of preventing the globe's leading military power from having essentially unfettered access to its airspace and ocean surface right up to its territorial border. That it has begun to remedy this unusual vulnerability after spending tens of billions of dollars over decades is hardly surprising.[51] It is a noteworthy change, but not one that undermines the United States' ability to pursue deep engagement in the region.

Given its proximity and importance to China, Taiwan might create the greatest challenge to a denial strategy, especially given that the United States faces limits on what kinds of capabilities it can share with Taipei. Yet, William Murray convincingly shows that there is a range of technologically feasible, affordable steps that Taiwan can take on its own to turn itself into a "porcupine" that would "offer Taiwan a way to resist PRC military coercion for weeks or months without presuming immediate U.S. intervention."[52] For different reasons, Japan would also create a potential challenge: even if it breaks its self-imposed limit of 1% of GDP for defense spending, its highly strained diplomatic relationship with China means that investing in new capabilities could generate a dangerous spiral. Yet as Toshi Yoshihara underscores, Japan can adopt a range of affordable and defensively oriented measures to create "an anti-access strategy of its own. . . . Japan is well-positioned and -equipped to draw lines on the map beyond which Chinese anti-access/area-denial forces can expect to encounter stiff, deadly resistance. Access and area denial works both ways."[53]

Needless to say, there are other potential challenges that might call for tough choices, especially surrounding maritime disputes. As Christensen argued over a decade ago, China can "pose problems without catching up."[54] But the conclusion emerging from the voluminous literature on East Asian security is that the United States' position of global primacy gives it options to address those problems other than by decisively countering each new Chinese military capability. As strategic thinkers from Liddell-Hart to Schelling remind us, using military power to challenge a settled status quo is very hard to do. As long as the United States keeps its focus on deep engagement's core defensive mission, it will long retain options to sustain the strategy in Asia.

Europe

How would a US pullback from Europe affect America's security interests? For twenty-five years after the collapse of the Soviet Union the debate hinged on NATO's purpose given a benign regional security setting. With Russia treated officially as a partner and conventional security threats to the wealthy, powerful, and institutionally robust states of the EU/North Atlantic area considered extremely low, the chief argument was that the alliance had to "go out of area or out of business," as Senator Richard Lugar put it in 1993. Analysts and policymakers tended to measure the value of US security commitments to Europe by the degree to which they nurtured an alliance that was able and willing to act as a global security provider. NATO contributions to operations in Afghanistan, Iraq, and Libya were scrutinized in this light. Yet with its interventions in Georgia (2008), Ukraine (2014), and Syria (2015), its ongoing military reforms, and its increasingly pugnacious foreign policy, Russia has swung the pendulum back toward Europe itself. As of 2015, the alliance's official view was that efforts to integrate Russia into a stable partnership had failed, at least for the time being, and that NATO's Article 5 commitment to collective defense once again could apply to a threat from the east.[55]

European security analysts generally concur that Russia's military challenge is of a different order than China's in East Asia.[56] Russia is a declining economic power that has invested heavily in military capabilities even as NATO has disinvested (with European and US defense cuts as well as withdrawal of most US forces from Europe).[57] To be sure, unlike China, Russia benefits from the defense-industrial infrastructure developed at massive expense over many decades in the Soviet era. Some of the results of Moscow's new investments and military reforms were on display in operations in Ukraine and Syria.[58] But Russia's military modernization confronts demographic, political, social, and especially economic challenges.[59] NATO can deploy some two million troops (compared to Russia's eight hundred thousand), and its dramatically larger and more advanced economy allows it, if provoked, to mobilize and rearm far more effectively and quickly than Russia.[60] In this perspective, Russia's "non-nuclear military power is woefully insufficient for the conquest of the major states of Eurasia."[61]

Given the overall imbalance in favor of the West, the focus of both NATO and Russia is on potential "asymmetric," "hybrid," or "ambiguous" noncontact conflicts where coercion might occur at levels well below what most see as traditional Article 5 red lines.[62] Worries centered on the Russian capability to quickly obtain control over territory near its borders by such means—including within Baltic NATO members—which it could then defend via formidable A2/AD capabilities. The circumstances under which Moscow might risk such a move are hard to define. But most assessments suggest that NATO can "develop the capability to deter this type of Russian operation, not necessarily to comprehensively defeat it . . . at a reasonable cost."[63] The trick, as in East Asia, is to accomplish this without foreclosing a rapprochement with Russia if possible—to shape Moscow's choices without instigating more intense security competition or adopting overly escalatory postures. NATO's answer is to make "persistent but not permanent" military commitments to the eastern front, including redeployed equipment and dedicated forces not necessarily stationed in the Baltics as well as command and control, intelligence reconnaissance, and infrastructure improvements that would make such a move extremely risky and costly for Moscow and yet keep both overall costs and potential escalation risks low.

In light of this assessment of the security setting, the debate over the US role in Europe centers on two issues: whether US security guarantees to NATO are necessary and the net value they add to the United States' overall security.[64] Most analysts—even those who argue for the need to "shock" the alliance into better performance by reducing the US role—agree that the commitment does improve the regional security setting, and thus accept the need to maintain the core Article 5 commitment for the policy-relevant future.[65] Why? The main reason is that NATO's Article 5 guarantee is an important part of the current institutional equilibrium in Europe.[66] Revoking it would destabilize the system, potentially tearing apart the security policies of key European actors. The key for experts on the region's security is less the return of security competition than the decline of security cooperation. For some, the shock of strategic decoupling would "cause a collapse of concerted power in Europe. [It would] incapacitate European foreign policy, [and] invite Russian and other outside meddling."[67]

This brings us to what is arguably the more germane question for students of the region's security: Do the commitments yield a net plus for US security? US commitments are advertised both as responses to incipient local security challenges and as adding to global security via strengthening the overall military capacity of North Atlantic countries. It is widely agreed, however, that though the alliance will remain capable of deterring Russia, declining US and especially allied defense efforts will steadily weaken NATO's capability for out-of-area expeditionary operations.[68] Most assessments nonetheless amount to the conclusion that NATO is a net security plus. Although NATO's capability for large-scale optional expeditionary operations to address conjectural security threats or humanitarian ideals is declining, the alliance retains value for a number of US security interests:

- Bolstering the region's security in light of a resurgent Russia and strengthening overall US and European bargaining leverage with Moscow
- Maintaining an institutional framework for coordinating and fostering transatlantic security cooperation
- Sustaining a reduced but still significant capacity to assist the United States in out-of-area operations (some forty thousand allied troops served alongside US personnel in Afghanistan)
- Preserving US access to permanent bases, logistical assets, overflight rights, etc.
- Maintaining key infrastructure and lines of communications to sustain even "light footprint" US-led military action in western and central Eurasia, the Middle East, or Africa
- Preserving US influence and leverage over allies
- Institutionalizing intelligence cooperation among like-minded allies

What is disputed is less the existence of these benefits than their value to the United States. For the most expansive conceptions of US foreign policy that call for Washington to pursue an expansive "deep engagement plus" kind of leadership, NATO's value added continually falls short. The vision of a militarily potent "global NATO" adding major capability for large-scale operations around the globe is partly what drives a strong narrative of an underperforming alliance. Conversely, if the United States engineers a dramatic shift in its grand strategy to a retrenchment that devalues the capacity to mount light footprint military operations around Eurasia as well as the incipient "coalition in waiting" represented by NATO, then the alliance's net security value added would decrease. But for a grand strategy of deep engagement, these benefits are considerable. Retrenchment would put them at risk by reducing security cooperation, resulting in a region less militarily capable of handling even Balkans-scale problems within the region or on its periphery.

The Middle East

The perennial US aims in the Middle East have been to prevent adversaries from dominating the region, to maintain access to the region's oil and waterways, to reduce proliferation risks, to support Israel and other friendly states in order to increase regional security, and, especially since 9/11, to prevent the region from becoming a platform for mass-casualty terrorist attacks against the US homeland.[iii] In pursuit of these objectives, Washington has cultivated a range of different kinds of partnerships with a long list of states, including one NATO ally (Turkey), six officially designated "major non-NATO allies" (Israel, Jordan, Egypt, Kuwait, Bahrain, and Morocco), and a varying group of security partners ranging from Saudi Arabia (with which the United States has had a security relationship since the 1930s) to more recent collaborators such as the United Arab Emirates and Qatar. Needless to say, the configuration of this set of partnerships has not been stable, nor should it be expected to remain so.

While deep engagement has translated into remarkable continuity concerning the US position in Europe and East Asia, Washington's role in the Middle East has been much more volatile. The region lacks a great power anchor; US interests vary substantially between the broader region and the Persian Gulf subregion; and US commitments are more fluid and far less institutionalized than in other core regions. In the post–Cold War era alone, US regional postures have ranged from the "dual containment" of Iraq and Iran under Clinton, to the Bush administration's putatively transformational "freedom agenda," to the restrained post–Arab Spring approach of the Obama administration. The military posture veered from essentially offshore during the Cold War to an onshore presence in the 1990s (dual containment) and most

---

iii. US support for Israel's security is clearly not reducible to America's regional security interests but reflects, to some degree, at least, nonstrategic American preferences. See Jerome Slater, "Is It Love or the Lobby? Explaining America's Special Relationship with Israel," *Security Studies*, Vol. 18, No. 1 (January/March 2009), pp. 58–78. Deep political and social changes in both countries may weaken these bonds in coming years. See Steven Simon and Dana Allin, "Our Separate Ways: The Struggle to Save the US-Israel Alliance," book manuscript, Dartmouth College.

dramatically in 2003–2011 (Iraq). Much of the most relevant recent literature is understandably focused on debating that shift, even as the United States has already begun to transition back to a much lighter footprint in the region.[69]

While we cannot settle the debate on the optimal regional posture, five propositions about the relative effectiveness of the baseline US security partnerships in the region emerge from the literature.

First, the heavy onshore presence of the 2003–2011 period was not needed for the core deep engagement missions. Indeed, even the less extensive onshore role in the 1991–2002 period may have been overkill for attaining the traditional US aims. Concerning the Gulf, Joshua Rovner and Caitlin Talmadge find that "a relatively light military posture—akin to that of the British in the post-war period and backed by a modest US land force—can achieve US goals in the region today while avoiding many of the costs that the United States incurred through its heavy forward presence in the 1990s and 2000s." They consequently "reject calls for the United States to leave the region, because the historical evidence shows that hegemonic stability is a very real phenomenon in the Gulf. This same evidence, however, also suggests that a hegemon—in this case, the United States—can achieve stability at a relatively low cost."[70]

Second, when regional peace is a priority for the United States, security relationships facilitate that goal. This is not surprising. As we argued concerning East Asia, if parties to a conflict are dependent on the United States and the United States wants peace, Washington can use its allies' mutual dependence to generate incentives for conflict resolution. Egypt embarked on the peace process in part due to expectations of US pressure on Israel as well as in exchange for economic and security benefits. In turn, Israel made territorial concessions only when compensated by US aid and security assurance. This Camp David effect persisted and proved robust even during the period of Muslim Brotherhood governance in Cairo. The post-9/11 experience amply demonstrates that democracy promotion and nation building are beyond America's capabilities. But it is also the case that the era of major interstate wars between Israel and its neighbors would likely not have ended, or would not have ended so soon, without US engagement in the region.[71]

Third, the same logic applies to more recent conflicts involving US security partners—either directly (as in Israel-Turkey tension in 2011) or indirectly (as in Israel-Hamas tension in which the United States had ties with Tel Aviv and Hamas' key interlocutors—Turkey, Qatar, and Egypt). In these cases, the security role does not prevent conflict, but it can make it possible for the United States to act as a mediator with leverage.[72]

Fourth, the region's three interstate wars since the Camp David era are cases in which other US interests trumped regional security and peace. In two of these, the United States used its security ties and military capabilities in pursuit of the traditional deterrence/containment objective. In the Iran-Iraq War, US support for Iraq reflected its classical interest in preventing regional dominance by a hostile state. The same logic underlay the US-led war to expel Iraq from Kuwait in 1990. The outlier was the 2003 Iraq invasion, in which the complex congeries of motives that brought the Bush administration to decide for war featured not the traditional emphasis of deep engagement on forestalling a rival's regional hegemony but a "transformational" solution to the region's perceived security problems.[73]

Fifth, on most accounts the standard assurance mechanism is in play in the region. While the US role can be a threat to local actors (especially in the highly active 2003–2011 period), the net effect of security provision is to decrease demand for nuclear weapons. Most analyses forecast that there would be a significant increase in nuclear proliferation in the region if the United States were to withdraw, with poor prospects for stable nuclear deterrence. That is, the main argument advanced for why Washington need not fear a proliferation cascade if Iran were to obtain a nuclear weapons capability is continuing US security assurance for Tehran's regional rivals.[74]

Key for our analysis is that the much more activist onshore US role, especially after 2003, was a dramatic shift from the long-standing US stance in the region.[75] Steven Simon and Jonathan Stevenson underscore that from the dawn of the Cold War until the 9/11 terror attacks, "the United States was the quintessential status quo power in the Middle East . . . . Washington's post-9/11 interventions in the region—especially the one in Iraq—were anomalous and shaped false perceptions of a 'new normal' of American intervention, both at home and in the region."[76] An array of forces including the shale oil and gas revolution, US public opinion in the aftermath of the Iraq War, and political shifts inside several partner states seems to be pushing for a more limited definition of US security commitments to the region over the long term that is consistent with the core defensive mission of deep engagement that the United States had long pursued in the region before 9/11. (The wild card in the short term is the nature of the terrorist threat and whether policymakers regard significant offensive military actions in the region as being beneficial for reducing it.) While it may seem minimalist compared to the activist approach of the Bush administration, this posture nonetheless delivers real security benefits—namely, more leverage and less nuclear proliferation.

Conclusion

Given the upshot of the previous analysis, that the shifting distribution of capabilities will not soon compel US retrenchment, only three general ways remain to make the case against deep engagement: to object that it actually does not yield power to influence the strategic environment; to show that having such power is not beneficial but is actually a bad thing; or to demonstrate that the power comes at an unacceptably high cost.

This analysis presented here and in chapter 5 has largely addressed the first two objections. Overall, we find that security provided from the outside is superior to security provided locally. The upshot of theory, evidence, and relevant regional research is that the security setting in core regions would worsen substantially without US security guarantees. The US security commitments and associated relationships and nascent capabilities constitute a hedge, providing the potential ability to deal with as yet unforeseen threats. Finally, coming back to address security threats after the United States has come home would be much harder and more expensive—and more likely to actually require large-scale fighting—than deterring them in the first place.

The next four chapters address the remaining arguments in play. Chapters 7 and 8 assess arguments about the strategy's costs, while chapters 9 and 10 consider the strategy's net benefits in the nonsecurity realms of institutionalized cooperation and the global economy.

7

Assessing the Economic Cost
of Deep Engagement

THE CASE FOR the security benefits of deep engagement is strong. The key relevant theories predict that the strategy's security commitments augment the United States' capacity to shape the security environment in desired ways and to hinder those who wish to revise the system in ways disadvantageous to America's interests. Both general and more focused empirical studies provide substantial support for these expectations. Together, these large swaths of scholarly knowledge strongly suggest that severing US security commitments would risk a much more dangerous world that would be harmful to America's security and prosperity.

Why then do so many analysts advocate retrenchment?[1] Part of the answer is a lower estimate of the strategy's security benefits than we reached in chapters 5 and 6. Our overarching argument that security provided from the outside is likely to make the core regions more secure than they would be if security were provided locally is implied by existing scholarship, but the significance of this point has not yet been properly appreciated. An additional reason is retrenchment advocates' general optimism about nuclear proliferation. As we stressed, there are many reasons for doubting that optimism, however, and if it is removed from the equation, then the gap between our assessment of deep engagement's security benefits and theirs narrows considerably.

More than any other factor, however, it is critics' high estimate of deep engagement's cost that drives their recommendation to retrench. They highlight both economic cost, which we address in this chapter, and security risks, which we assess in chapter 8. Their arguments about economic cost fall into two broad categories. First is the budgetary cost of deep engagement.

Retrenchment proponents argue that the United States' high budget deficits make the fiscal burden of its grand strategy ever harder to bear—which is all the more concerning given that wealthy US allies could, in their view, easily defend themselves. The second category concerns the deeper and potentially much more significant economic cost of global leadership. Drawing on venerable studies of hegemony in international politics, critics argue that deep engagement's focus on leadership hastens US economic decline vis-à-vis both rivals and partners.

Budgetary Costs

Almost no call for retrenchment is complete without invoking the budgetary costs of deep engagement, which is arguably the most prominent argument for pulling back in the wider public debate about US foreign policy. In pursuit of its "ambitious agenda," Barry Posen argues, "the United States has consistently spent . . . far more than the sum of the defense budgets of its friends and far more than the sum of those of its potential adversaries . . . levels of spending that the Great Recession and the United States' ballooning debt have rendered unsustainable."[2] "The nation's ballooning budget deficits are going to make it increasingly difficult to sustain [the United States'] level of military commitments," Christopher Layne warns; "its strategic commitments exceed the resources available to support them."[3]

The budgetary cost of deep engagement is the difference between the expenditures the strategy demands and the amount required for its replacement. Consensus estimates for either number do not exist, and a comprehensive exercise in budget forensics lies outside the parameters of this book. Defense has claimed an average 3.8% of GDP in the post-Cold War era (3.5% in 2014). But that figure includes outlays supporting activities that go beyond deep engagement.[4] The contrast that needs to be made is between the expenditures that are needed to sustain the grand strategy (as opposed to expensive add-ons) and realistic alternatives that meet minimum capability requirements set by retrenchment advocates themselves, who invariably support the maintenance of a force projection capacity that is second to none. When such a comparison is made, it is clear that the budgetary premium of deep engagement is far more modest than it is often portrayed to be.

In estimating deep engagement's cost, it is especially vital to distinguish between the strategy's defining commitments as spelled out in chapters 4 and 5 and the optional "war on terror" ramp-up that occurred in the decade after 2001. After the September 11, 2001, attacks, defense spending increased dramatically owing in large part to the wars in Iraq and Afghanistan. Between 2003 and 2013, those wars added an average of $125 billion annually to total defense expenditures.[5] But the post-9/11 decade also saw the "base" nonwar budget skyrocket 40%, from $390 to $540 billion in constant (2010) terms— what former defense secretary Robert Gates termed a "gusher" of spending.[6] That increase had two main causes: an augmented effort to field and use military tools in the wider war on terrorism and, as Defense Secretaries Gates, Panetta, and Hagel stressed repeatedly, a dramatic decrease in Pentagon spending discipline.

All of these drivers of defense spending began to reverse after 2010 as the United States wound down the Iraq and Afghanistan wars and began seriously to trim nonwar spending. In a sense, the United States began to retrench not from but rather back to deep engagement levels of expenditure, as US officials continued to stress their intent to preserve and even buttress the strategy's core commitments in a tight budget climate.[7] The expected budgetary costs for this strategy are dramatically lower than those the country became accustomed to in the 2001–2011 period. As of January 2016, the Pentagon based planning on defense budgets that would decline from 2.8 percent of GDP in 2016 to 2.6 percent by 2020 and 2.3 percent by 2030.[8] This projection reflects the estimate by the Congressional Budget Office (CBO) of the costs of the Pentagon's current plans, and thus is higher than the budget authorized by Congress in the Budget Control Act (the so-called sequester). The key is that if the forecast is based on current Department of Defense (DoD) plans and past budget realities, "the growth in DoD's costs over time would be slower than CBO's projection of the growth of the U.S. economy, so costs would decline as a share of gross domestic product."[9]

To be sure, some analysts question whether even the CBO's estimates are sufficient to sustain the strategy as envisioned by the Pentagon. Yet many of those analysts favor an expansive "deep engagement plus" stance.[10] For many of these critics, the 2012 defense budget proposed by Secretary Gates in 2011—the last year the Pentagon followed a "normal" planning process not influenced by sequestration—is the benchmark for sustaining the strategy.[11] That budget, which would have entailed modest increases in the base budget over the ensuing five years, would still have increased more slowly than the economy and so claimed a shrinking share of GDP (approaching 3% of US GDP in 2016).[12] Importantly, many of these same analysts also identify feasible reforms to the way the Pentagon does business—including procurement practices and compensation policies—that potentially could save significant additional sums.

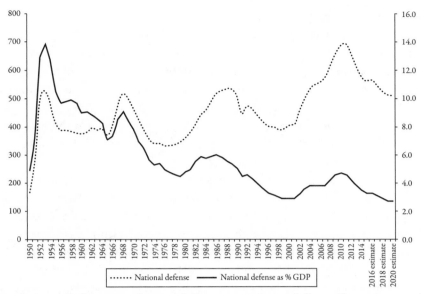

FIGURE 7.1 Defense expenditures in billions constant 2009 dollars and as percentage of Gross Domestic Product (GDP).

Note: "National defense" here includes supplementary spending for overseas contingency operations.

Source: "Composition of Outlays: 1940 to 2017," Historical Tables of the Budget of the United States, Fiscal Year 215 (Washington, D.C.: Office of Management and Budget, 2015), Table 6.1, available at: http://www.whitehouse.gov/omb/budget/Historicals.

The budgetary savings that a switch to retrenchment would yield are unclear. They depend on which security commitments are to be abandoned outright and over what period of time, how US allies would respond, and how many new capabilities would be needed to facilitate a switch to an "over the horizon" stance with US forces stationed offshore or back in North America, ready to redeploy if needed.[i] If the alternative strategy requires keeping a similarly sized force in the United States, then the expected savings are much

---

i. To simplify a complex literature, the alternatives suggested by retrenchment advocates fall into three broad categories: those who would maintain the existing roster of US security commitments but would move US forces offshore (e.g., Robert A. Pape, *Dying to Win: The Strategic Logic of Suicide Terrorism* (New York: Random House, 2005); those who would cut a subset of commitments, while reducing US forces in various regions (e.g., Barry R. Posen, *Restraint: A New Foundation for U.S. Grand Strategy* (Ithaca, N.Y.: Cornell University Press, 2014); and those who call for a more general curtailment of US security commitments, as well as a widespread shift to move US forces offshore (e.g., Eugene Gholz, Daryl G. Press, and Harvey M. Sapolsky, "Come Home, America: The Strategy of Restraint in the Face of Temptation," *International Security*, Vol. 21, No. 4 [Spring 1997], pp. 5–48).

more modest, given that host governments cover many infrastructure costs of US forces and bases. As a comprehensive study concludes, "From the grand strategic perspective, personnel and force structure, not presence or basing, is the biggest cost driver for DoD. The overall size of U.S. non-naval forces, and therefore the vast majority of their cost, is only minimally linked to where DoD has bases."[13] And if it requires the maintenance of major expeditionary capacity, again, the savings, if any, might be modest owing to the need for continued or even enhanced investment in the kinds of weapons platforms that now eat up so much of the defense budget.[ii]

Even if we assume an unambiguous retrenchment that entails abrogation of all alliances, the savings are unclear unless the size and cost of the remaining military posture are carefully estimated. Cato Institute analysts Benjamin Friedman and Justin Logan helpfully provide such an estimate for a strategy that would revoke all US security guarantees and alliances, bring all overseas deployed troops home, reconfigure the navy to "surge to fight rare wars rather than patrol the world in the name of stability," decommission large numbers of personnel in all branches, slash the nuclear deterrent force, and dramatically scale back weapons procurement.[14] This posture would either vitiate or radically curtail each of deep engagement's key mechanisms for influencing the strategic environment—deterrence, reassurance, leverage, and security cooperation. Yet Friedman and Logan rightly stress that those seemingly dramatic cuts would still leave a "U.S. military with global reach far exceeding any rival: roughly 230 ships, including eight full-sized aircraft carriers and 40 attack submarines; roughly 1,400 fighter and bomber aircraft aided by airborne refueling tankers; the bulk of the Army, Marines, Special Operations Forces; and 500-plus nuclear warheads deliverable by submarine or land-based ballistic missiles."[15]

Of course, the United States could conceivably undertake an even more substantial retrenchment than Logan and Friedman recommend, with an even smaller defense force. But their posture arguably reflects the realistic lower bound in the grand strategy debate. Retrenchment advocates are not isolationists; they agree that the United States has global interests that it may need to defend militarily. Even those calling for the most decisive break with

---

ii. If the United States is unable to use its overseas bases in regions where it has abandoned its security partnerships, then it may have to compensate by investing in platforms for projecting force that are particularly expensive. In turn, if the United States truly abandons its overseas bases, then they may have little utility: bases in places such as the Middle East cannot be mothballed and left empty, but instead require a significant, permanent source of noncombat personnel to remain effective. Adm. William Fallon, interview by Stephen Brooks, Hanover, New Hampshire, July 19, 2012.

deep engagement still want to allow for these types of contingencies.[16] The difference is that, rather than actively managing the security environment to try to reduce their likelihood, a retrenchment strategy steps back and adopts a "wait and see" attitude. Retaining that global intervention capacity, however, comes at the cost of reducing the potential net budgetary savings as compared to maintaining deep engagement. Friedman and Logan estimate that the force sketched above associated with their comprehensive conception of retrenchment would save some $900 billion over ten years, but that was based on projected spending as of 2011 and thus misses two subsequent rounds of substantial defense cuts. A rough estimate based on projected DoD spending as of fall 2014 halves those projected savings.[17] Against the backdrop of a $3.5 trillion federal budget, it is hard to see how annual savings in the $40 billion range make the difference between a grand strategy that is fiscally sustainable and one that is not.

Barry Posen provides another benchmark for the potential budgetary savings of retrenchment. His "restraint" grand strategy calls for the United States to abrogate key security treaties (NATO, Korea), "shock" other allies into greater autonomous military effort via major force reductions (Japan), curtail subsidies to key allies/partners (e.g., Israel), and exit or at least radically downsize its presence in the Middle East, yet maintain "command of the commons" via a navy-dominant global posture. He estimates that this would yield roughly a 20% reduction in overall force structure and a corresponding reduction in defense outlays from 2013 levels.[18] He maintains that if this were accomplished over five years, it would bring defense expenditures to 2.5% of GDP. As noted, current projections are for outlays to fall below 3% of GDP in 2018 and below 2.7% by 2024. Bearing in mind the radical uncertainty attending these estimates, the implication is that ten years hence Posen's version of retrenchment thus might allow the United States to shave 0.4% of GDP in five years, falling to below 0.2% in ten years.[iii]

The gap between the budgetary cost of deep engagement and retrenchment that retains global power projection capacity is thus much more modest than the language of many critics would imply. To be sure, the politics of the defense budget may well become contentious in a tough fiscal climate.

---

iii. Neither we nor Posen pretend precision here. The idea is to get a general sense of savings. For his part, Posen focuses on assessing force reductions, not budget savings. His estimate is based on the assumption that reducing the force structure by 20% will reduce costs over the long term by 20%. His approach is appealing, given the uncertainties attending budget forecasts noted above. The precise base structure he recommends is not spelled out, however, nor are any of the one-off (but large) closure/relocation costs considered.

However, that prospect hardly means that deep engagement cannot be sustained. Few contend that defense expenditures below 3% of GDP are unsustainable—after all, the global average for all countries is 2.5%.[19] Rather, it underlines the need for a proper reckoning of the strategy's net benefits and the need to avoid a shift to a "deep engagement plus" stance.

The fact that the expected savings associated with switching away from deep engagement are less than they are often portrayed to be probably explains why budgetary costs do not figure more prominently in the scholarly case for retrenchment. Arguably the most influential scholarly article on retrenchment yet written—Eugene Gholz, Daryl Press, and Harvey Sapolsky's "Come Home, America"—was published in 1997 just as US defense spending was approaching a fifty-year low as a percentage of GDP at 3% and the US Treasury was registering record budget surpluses.[20] Deep engagement's other costs are clearly the centerpieces of the case for retrenchment.

Hegemonic Decline and Imperial Overstretch

In making the case for the high costs of deep engagement, many realists highlight the works of scholars such as Robert Gilpin, Paul Kennedy, and David Calleo concerning the connection between hegemony and US decline.[21] The substantive implications of this scholarship are potentially important, but the terms used to express them bear close scrutiny.

In invoking this scholarly literature, retrenchment advocates are claiming that the United States is a hegemon and that deep engagement is a hegemonic grand strategy. These claims are true only with minimalist definitions of the main terms. Gilpin defines hegemony as "the leadership of one state (the hegemon) over other states in the system."[iv] That constrained definition applies, with two key provisos regarding "leadership:" that it is relative, not

---

iv. Robert Gilpin, *War and Change in World Politics* (Cambridge, UK: Cambridge University Press, 1981), p. 116. A loaded term, hegemony means different things to different people and in different scholarly literatures. The United States is clearly materially the most capable state in the international system by far, but it falls short of many definitions of a hegemon. In the balance-of-power literature, hegemony often refers to a condition under which one state can physically conquer all other major powers. See R. Harrison Wagner, "What Was Bipolarity?" *International Organization*, Vol. 47, No. 1 (Winter 1993), pp. 77–106. In the world systems literature, hegemony often refers to a relationship of political control only slightly less hierarchical than empire, under which the hegemon exercises dominant political influence, resolving or arbitrating all major disputes and exercises decisive influence even over the domestic affairs of other states. See David Wilkinson, "Unipolarity without Hegemony," *International Studies Review*, Vol. 1, No. 2 (Summer 1999), pp. 141–172.

absolute, and that it concerns the preservation of the status quo, not revisionism. Deep engagement entails the United States taking a more prominent role overall than any other state in organizing collective action to uphold the global order. That does not mean that Washington must be in charge of every collective endeavor. Nor does leadership as implied by the grand strategy of deep engagement mean that the United States must preserve stability everywhere or crusade forcefully to expand its values or approach to governance. Its meaning is spelled out in the two proceeding chapters: the United States maintains a more extensive web of influence than any other state, which it uses to advance its fundamentally status quo interests, frequently through organized and institutionalized collective action.[22]

Retrenchment proponents' essential substantive claim is that deep engagement actually hastens US relative decline. For one thing, monetary and human resources devoted to deep engagement are unavailable for other, possibly more productive purposes—infrastructure, education, civilian research and development, innovation, and so on—that would enhance US competitiveness. Further, they contend that a globally engaged grand strategy creates incentives for allies to free ride. With lower military expenditures, the argument goes, they are able to grow faster than they otherwise would, and do so at the United States' expense. In this view, deep engagement will ultimately fall prey to the same fate as many leading states' grand strategies of the past: it will tend to be self-defeating over time, ultimately causing other states to increase capabilities faster—and the United States to decline faster relative to those other states—than would be the case if the United States retrenched.

In this vein, Layne concludes that "the United States now is facing the dilemmas that Gilpin and the other declinists warned about."[23] Layne's observation may be true, but it does not mean that the United States' deep engagement grand strategy is the problem or that major retrenchment is the solution. Newer scholarship has transformed 1980s-vintage conventional wisdom about hegemonic decline and imperial overstretch. Key is that the canonical works (and many of today's retrenchment advocates) fail to distinguish between causes of decline that have nothing to do with a state's international position or its grand strategy and those that are causally connected to being the system's most powerful state or pursuing leadership. Mechanisms of decline that directly stem from being the hegemon or pursuing leadership have rarely been identified, and those that have are weakly grounded in logic and poorly supported by evidence. A new wave of scholarship has emerged over the last two decades showing that, if anything, leading states can use their position to slow decline and mitigate its effects.

Most of the causes of decline featured in the 1980s texts have nothing to do with the United States' current situation. Kennedy's *Rise and Fall of the Great Powers,* for example, did indeed document repeated overextension of great powers—but in every case the key mechanism causing overstretch was counterbalancing by other major powers. Yet as we review in the next chapter, the counterbalancing constraint does not operate against the United States in a system with one superpower in the same potent way it did against leading states in the multipolar and bipolar systems Kennedy analyzed, so the historical cases he assesses are not probative for the current debate.

Gilpin's *War and Change in World Politics* presented a theory of decline that has implications for hegemony, but did not establish a causal connection between the pursuit of hegemony and decline. Gilpin identifies a tendency "for the economic costs of maintaining the status quo to rise faster than the economic capacity to support the status quo."[24] He explains this by reference to a set of processes, most of which are entirely unrelated to the international system: declining rates of economic growth (essentially the neoclassical growth model, which stipulates that as a country gets richer, it becomes harder and harder for it to sustain rapid economic growth); the rising costs of military power; the tendency of private and public consumption to grow; the tendency for economic activity to shift to services; and the "corrupting influence of affluence."[25] These can be expected to bedevil any rich state regardless of its position in the international system. They all affect a state's ability to sustain hegemony, but none is caused by being a hegemon or pursuing policies of leadership. Indeed, they would presumably all conspire to hinder any state on the same growth path as the hegemonic leader from mounting a challenge. For example, were the European Union to become a state and seek hegemonic leadership, it would be just as susceptible to these processes as the United States—as would China if it were to become rich.

The main link between hegemonic grand strategy and decline that figures for Gilpin, as well as in the works of Calleo and Kennedy, is diversion of resources away from productive investment toward system maintenance and protection.[26] The argument is that simply paying the costs of protecting clients and maintaining the system—military expenditures, subsidies to allies, and so on—exacerbates the larger growth-sapping trend toward consumption and away from investment. This amounts to a claim that the opportunity cost of its grand strategy will cause a hegemon's rate of growth to slow more markedly than a nonhegemonic state as it proceeds along the path from poor and rapidly growing to rich and slowly growing. Conversely, other states whose security and prosperity are underwritten by the hegemon will be spared this opportunity cost and will perform relatively better. Always present in realist arguments for strategic retrenchment, this proposition began to figure even more prominently as US defense expenditures began to rapidly climb after 2001.[27]

The problem with the claim that pursuing leadership imposes significant growth-sapping opportunity costs for the United States is that subsequent research does not provide a basis for supporting it. For a long time, the consensus in the economics literature was that military spending spurred growth.[28] The consensus shifted in recent years; as one review essay summed it up, the "literature in economics has not found military expenditure to be a significant determinant of growth."[29] Taken together, hundreds of studies conducted over decades of sustained research focused on this core question, using multiple theoretical models and empirical strategies, yield no reason to believe that military spending saps growth or that reducing military spending speeds growth.[30]

Unlike the broader research in economics, political scientists Karen Rasler and William Thompson conducted a study tailored to the specific claims about the costs of hegemonic grand strategies. Their findings do not support claims that the diversion of resources away from investment and toward defense and foreign policy plays any role in understanding why leading states decline.[31] Obviously, there are some limits to this overall claim: if the United States were a dramatic outlier among the advanced economies, spending Soviet Union-type levels on defense (20–25%) over decades, this would surely complicate its growth trajectory and relative competitiveness. But as noted above, defense spending in 2014 was 3.5% of GDP, with planning based on a decline to below 3% in 2018.

The flip side of this finding is that the economic performance of US allies is largely unrelated to any security subsidy they receive from Washington. The contention that lower military expenditures facilitated the economic rise of Japan, West Germany, and other US allies seemed plausible when Gilpin, Calleo, and Kennedy were publishing their signature books in the 1980s. Their relative position vis-à-vis the United States essentially stopped improving subsequently, however, as their per capita wealth approached US levels—just as standard growth models would expect. Over the past twenty years, the United States' total and per capita GDP relative to key European allies and Japan has improved despite a growing gap in respective military efforts.[32]

In sum, there is scant theoretical or empirical reason to link rates of growth to either the distribution of power or the specific policies the United

States pursues to sustain deep engagement.[v] As Thompson notes, it is unclear "why uneven growth should be viewed as a function of unbalanced power."[33] The revival of Gilpin/Calleo/Kennedy arguments coincided with America's still heavy commitments to Iraq and Afghanistan and the 2007–2009 financial collapse and subsequent "great recession." That correlation gave "imperial overstretch" arguments a superficial appeal. But no scholarly theory or empirical findings clearly link the 2007–2009 financial collapse, great recession, and consequent ballooning of the US budget deficit to the international system at all (at least as scholars of international security construe it). Nor does any established research finding show a connection between any US security commitment and the causes of the economic downturn. Nor is there reason to expect that resources freed up from global commitments would necessarily be diverted to uses more advantageous for long-term US growth.

Thus, even if US allies are free riding, it will likely not affect US long-term economic performance and so will not conspire to make the pursuit of deep engagement self-defeating. On the contrary, to the degree that other states' reliance on US security guarantees means that they fail to invest in significant military modernization, it simply serves to entrench US military

---

v. Our focus is on the putative connection between deep engagement and US growth and competitiveness because that is the key claim of the original scholarship on hegemonic decline and it remains a mainstay of the case for the grand strategy's high economic cost. As noted above, many versions of retrenchment would likely allow somewhat lower military expenditures, and some proponents of retrenchment highlight a different economic benefit that would result from reduced Pentagon spending: improved welfare; see, for example, Barry R. Posen, *Restraint: A New Foundation for U.S. Grand Strategy* (Ithaca, N.Y.: Cornell University Press, 2014). Would Americans not be better off if fewer of their tax dollars were used for military purposes? Retrenchment advocates sometimes write as if the answer is self-evident, assuming that every dollar freed from the Pentagon's clutches would presumably go to welfare-enhancing purposes. But there is no reason to make that assumption, and, even if one does, the answer is anything but self-evident. In a recent analysis, Robert Pollin and Heidi Garrett-Peltier estimate the welfare effects of shifting away from defense spending and find that "both the total number of jobs created as well as the average pay are both higher" through spending on education as compared to spending on the military, but the welfare effects of shifting away from defense spending are more ambiguous for the other categories of spending they investigate: tax cuts which produce increased levels of personal consumption, health care, mass transit, and construction targeted at home weatherization and infrastructure repair; see Pollin and Garrett-Peltier, "The U.S. Employment Effects of Military and Domestic Spending Priorities" (Department of Economics and Political Economy Research Institute working paper, 2007), available at http://www.peri.umass.edu/fileadmin/pdf/other_publication_types/PERI_IPS_WAND_study.pdf. Overall, the anticipated "peace dividend" is unlikely to be large enough (0.4% of GDP in five years, falling to below 0.2% in ten years in the case of Posen's recommended defense budget) to transform American civilian life. It should also be noted that in any assessment of the welfare effect of retrenchment, the costs and risks it would impose on US security (chapters 5 and 6) and other nonsecurity aims (chapters 9 and 10) must be included.

dominance. Moreover, as we underscore in chapters 9 and 10, the United States derives some positive economic benefits from its global security role.

Retrenchment advocates' focus on allied free riding faces an even bigger challenge, however. It is far from clear that lower allied military expenditures actually constitute free riding.[34] For allied security behavior to be considered free riding, US security provision must be a collective good. Collective goods have two key properties: nonexcludability (once it is provided, the good may be enjoyed by all parties) and nonrivalry (the consumption of the good by one does not reduce its consumption by others). As recent scholarship stresses, US security guarantees violate these two assumptions.[35] The consumption of US security guarantees by some states (e.g., NATO) arguably can reduce the security of others (e.g., Russia). In addition, Washington can exclude any state it wants, which means that its bargaining leverage is greater than the theory implies. Indeed, Michael Beckley argues that foreign aid and peacekeeping more closely resemble true public goods, and there it is the United States that is actually the free rider, contributing far less than its allies.[36] In other words, collective goods theory is misleading. What really appears to be going on is a kind of bargain under which allies undersupply conventional military capabilities but oversupply foreign aid and postconflict peacekeeping. The question—which we address in more detail in subsequent chapters—is whether the bargain is favorable to US national interests.

Conclusion

The verdict on the economic cost of deep engagement is remarkably favorable. To be sure, the military posture required to sustain deep engagement is almost certainly more expensive than retrenchment. But when we compare realistic replacement grand strategies with deep engagement, the budget cost differential shrinks dramatically. The economic argument with the most potential to undermine the case for deep engagement has always been that it will confront the punishing, long-term economic costs featured in classical works on the rise and fall of hegemons in world politics. Our analysis, building on decades of newer research, finds no support for those classic arguments as applied to the United States today. Past leading states have indeed become overstretched and declined economically, but there is no good theory or evidence to suggest that deep engagement is having or will have any such effect on the United States today. If deep engagement's cost is going to compel a negative verdict, it will thus have to be measured in the realm of security; we address this issue in the next chapter.

8

Assessing the Security Costs
of Deep Engagement

IN LIGHT OF chapter 7's finding concerning the economic costs of deep engagement, it is clear the critics' case for the cost of deep engagement hinges on
the security realm. Retrenchment advocates have identified a large number of
potential costs of deep engagement that would be measured in terms of increased security challenges or threats to the United States. They fit into three
overall categories. First is "global pushback": in their view, America's intrusive
grand strategy generates counteraction and resentment among both governments and foreign publics, producing various forms of balancing against US
power. And if those state-centric forms of pushback were not enough, many
retrenchment advocates also argue that stationing US troops abroad dramatically increases the threat of terrorist attacks. Second is a set of arguments
that stress the potential cost of maintaining alliances: obligations to fight on
allies' behalf that might entangle the United States in wars that are not in its
national interest. Finally, retrenchment proponents stress the cost of simply
being so powerful: with unsurpassed globe-girdling military capabilities and
forces positioned and ready to use worldwide, Washington periodically faces
the temptation to use this awesome capability, whether out of humanitarian
impulse or an inflated sense of threat, and may end up embroiled in costly,
challenging conflicts as a result.

Global Pushback

Critics contend that deep engagement causes both state and nonstate actors
in the international system to push back against the exercise of US power.
The more the United States seeks to lead, the more others conspire to thwart

its aims. As Barry Posen puts it, US grand strategy is "self-abrading": "The very act of seeking more control injects negative energy into global politics as quickly as it finds enemies to vanquish."[1] In the view of these critics, the problem is not the United States' underlying material capabilities. If it were, then resentment and pushback would happen whether the United States retrenched or not. Rather, the argument is that seeking to translate those capabilities into an effort to shape the global environment generates responses from other actors that lead to pushback and speed the diffusion of capabilities away from the United States. As Richard Betts puts it, "Attempts at running the world generate resistance."[2] Retrenchment proponents highlight two forms of resistance to deep engagement: balancing and terrorism.

Balancing

Some advocates of retrenchment suggest that deep engagement in the security affairs of the world's key regions "prompts other states to balance against US power however they can."[3] Such balancing could take the form of alliance formation (institutionalized interstate security cooperation against the United States that would not occur if America retrenched), "internal balancing" (the conversion of economic and technological capacity into military power that would not occur if the United States retrenched), or "soft balancing" (the use of institutions and other nonmilitary means to hamstring US policy that would not occur if the United States retrenched).

Derived from long-established theories of the balance of power, this line of argument posits a direct connection between the United States' position as the most capable state in the system, its strategic choice to pursue a grand strategy stressing engagement in the security affairs of other regions, and pushback from other major powers.[4] The United States' large share of global capabilities primes other potential great powers to ramp up their power in order to restore balance, the argument goes, and a forward leaning grand strategy is just the trigger needed to get the process going. Being number one is thus a dubious honor, and the temptation to pursue deep engagement in order to influence the strategic environment should be resisted, for the result is likely to be a more rapid decline as other major powers' capabilities rise faster than they would if the United States cut a lower profile on the world's stage.

Such arguments have not fared well in scholarship over the last two decades. The initial claim that unipolarity was especially unstable because it would invoke particularly strong balancing reactions was ultimately largely supplanted by the opposite view: that by making counterbalancing prohibitively costly, the post-1991 concentration of capabilities in the United States rendered balance-of-power theory essentially inoperative.[5] This proposition rests on two key features of the system: the large aggregate power gap between the United States and the other powers and the geographical fact that the former is in North America while the latter are all clustered in and around Eurasia. As we discussed earlier, the bigger the power gap, the harder it is to restore balance in the system. And geography matters because power is a function of distance: efforts by other states to generate capabilities to match the United States or negate its ability to act as a superpower will tend to elicit counterbalancing from regional neighbors.

But do these conclusions from the literature on balancing still hold in light of China's and Russia's enhanced military capabilities and the apparent uptick in the salience of major-power competition? The answer requires attention to three key distinctions that are often elided in discussion of the balance of power by retrenchment proponents.

First is the distinction between what Evan Braden Montgomery calls "local balancing" and "global balancing."[6] Global balancing is about the international system: it concerns shifts in the distribution of power that move the international system back toward a more even distribution by negating or matching US global capabilities. Such balancing is what classical balance-of-power theory is all about. Local balancing, in contrast, is about self-defense within a regional context. Deep engagement makes the United States a key factor in at least two regions, Europe and East Asia, and so may affect the nature of local balancing by the major regional players. By failing to maintain this distinction, however, retrenchment advocates miss the possibility that local balancing may not contribute to global balancing, and, indeed, it may undermine it.

Second is the distinction between balancing and other phenomena that work against the longevity of the United States' position as the globe's sole superpower. To say that balance-of-power theory is inoperative does not mean that there are no other forces in the world pushing it back toward balance, nor that local balancing is somehow precluded.[7] The growth of China's economy has nothing to do with balance-of-power theory, but it is pushing in the direction of balance. And as China has grown, so has its ability to defend itself—not only territorially but also against some kinds of potential intimidation by the United States. The claim that the United States is unconstrained by global balancing in practice means that the barriers to balancing are so high for China and the X powers that Washington would have to go to improbable lengths to cause those states to seek to overcome them. It follows that a deep asymmetry remains. The United States does not in practice face a balancing constraint on its grand strategy, which is conducted across the entire system. In contrast, the other great powers, with only regionally focused grand strategies, do face a balancing constraint.

Third and most important is the distinction between the United States' underlying material capabilities and its grand strategy. The difference of interest here is between the degree of balancing the United States confronts when it pursues deep engagement and what it would confront if it retrenched. If the United States did retrench and ended up with fewer alliances, fewer forward-deployed forces, a smaller army, and a reduction in defense spending, these would be consequential changes, to be sure, but from the perspective of balance-of-power theory they are subtle, especially given that the United States' capacity to generate military power would remain. Retrenchment advocates have not explained why we should expect a difference of that scale to result in substantially decreased incentives for the X powers to balance.

In light of these key distinctions, how does the shift from a 1 + X to a 1 + 1 + X world, with China in a class by itself as the one state that might someday emerge as a potential superpower, affect the core argument that balance-of-power theory is inoperative? In chapters 2 and 3, we showed that, unlike past rising powers, China is at a very different technological level than the leading state and thus its ability to distill raw economic resources into top-end military capabilities is much more constrained. And the technological playing field itself has changed to make it even harder for new entrants to get into the top league.[8] Ultimately, the military and technological hurdles to internal balancing by China will remain formidably high for decades. Our analysis thus confirms that true global balancing—creating an equipoise in the system by either matching or negating America's superpower capabilities—will long remain effectively out of reach for China, which alone among states has the scale and raw economic heft to make such counterbalancing even a notional option. And the absence of global balancing matters: it enables freedom of action for the United States and dramatically constrains choices for all others. US security policy remains relatively unconstrained by a significant Chinese ability to "channel a rivalry away from its territory and challenge [the US] in far-flung locations,"[9] while China, as well as Russia and the X powers, must concentrate their resources on navigating a local security environment shaped by US power.[10]

That leaves external balancing—alliances—as the potential route back to global equilibrium. But our analysis in chapters 2 and 3 makes clear how improbable that option remains. If capabilities are presented as simple aggregates like GDP or military spending that can be added up as states combine in alliances, it might seem easy for states to band together to match the US. If we look instead at the number of superpowers and the underlying capabilities needed to produce them, however, a very different picture emerges. The kinds of capabilities and investments needed to be a 21st-century superpower require the politically and organizationally integrated setting only a state can foster. It remains exceedingly unlikely that any alliance of great powers could replicate that kind of setting.

It would take a threat of massive proportions to cause states to overcome these formidable barriers to balancing. Deep engagement, as irksome as it may appear to China and Russia, simply does not rise to that level. Stephen Walt, the author of balance-of-threat theory and the leading realist scholar of alliance formation, concludes that because of the numerous factors that mitigate other powers' perceptions of US threats to their security, the United States would have to "have the same expansionist ambitions [as] Napoleonic France, Wilhelmine and Nazi Germany, or the Soviet Union" to spark a hard balancing coalition.[11] Expanding the theoretical lens to encompass domestic and international institutions only strengthens the case: deep engagement allows the United States to embed its dominant role within heavily institutionalized alliances and exploit the rules-based order it fostered to dampen some of the more politically toxic elements of its grand strategy. The result is to make the US alliance system—especially among its core liberal members—far more robust and harder to challenge than if the United States were to disengage.[12]

Deep engagement may affect Chinese and Russian incentives for local balancing, but recent scholarship strongly supports the proposition that overall the strategy slows rather than increases the rate at which capabilities might diffuse to a more balanced distribution. As chapters 5 and 6 established, securing partners and allies in key regions reduces their incentives to generate military capabilities (most notably, nuclear weapons). Moreover, deep engagement gives America leverage to prevent US allies—which comprise most of the most modern and effective militaries in the world—from transferring military technologies and production techniques to potential rivals. The United States' predominant position in the high-end defense industry also allows Washington to trade access to its defense market for compliance on key security issues, notably technology transfers to potential geopolitical opponents.[13] The continued European embargo on military sales to China—in place since 1989—is a case in point.

In contrast to the unipolarity concept, however, this book's focus on the stages that bridge the great-power/superpower gap suggests that the balancing constraint is not a dichotomous either/or proposition. As an X power traverses this gap, its costs of balancing decline and the constraint on the reigning superpower comes gradually into play. To be sure, a Level 2 power—an emerging potential superpower—lacks a realistic global balancing option vis-à-vis the system's sole superpower. As it acquires both the technological and economic requisites and ascends to Level 3—a potential superpower—it incrementally begins to be in a position to choose whether to build counterbalancing capacity. And even in Level 2, at some stage balance-of-power theory may come into play—notionally, at least—as efforts at advancing its military capacity in its own region may help nurture the preconditions that hasten the day when true global balancing becomes feasible. Whether such local balancing speeds or slows a power's journey from Level 2 to Level 3 remains an open question; resources devoted to countering a superpower locally cannot be used immediately for countering its global power, yet they may sow seeds for future global capacity.

But the main implication is the massive lag between any incentive to balance the United States globally and the realistic ability of other powers to do so regardless of whether it sustains deep engagement or retrenches. In contrast to the current setting, the classical European systems in which balance-of-power theory developed featured much smaller aggregate capabilities gaps between leading states and challengers, technology that allowed for comparatively swift transformation of economic resources into top-end military capability, contending states at roughly the same technological level, and geography that placed contenders in close proximity and thus vitiated the distinction between local and global balancing. In such systems a leading state was often on tenterhooks, sensing that its position was inherently unstable and easily negated by others. That was the kind of world in which balance of power dynamics could quickly kick in against a leading state as an immediate, dangerous, and powerful constraint. The contrast to today's world is stark.

Soft Balancing

Because it is a slippery concept that is difficult to distinguish from standard diplomatic bargaining and competition, so-called soft balancing is harder to evaluate.[14] Case studies of headline episodes widely seen as soft balancing fail to find much evidence that balancing dynamics were really in play.[15] Michael Beckley's efforts to evaluate quantitative indicators (voting patterns at the United Nations, arms sales to US adversaries, and foreign public opinion) also show no consistent trend other than evidence of political resistance to the US invasion of Iraq in 2003.[16] Comprehensive studies of global public opinion also do not find patterns consistent with soft balancing propositions.[17]

For the purposes of assessing US grand strategy, however, the most important point about soft balancing is that it is defined in a way guaranteed to miss the real question: Does the current grand strategy give the United States or its potential adversaries more soft balancing–style leverage? Almost all definitions of soft balancing are about actions below the significance of hard balancing that other states can take to constrain the United States. They focus on the use of international institutions and coordinated action to restrain the United States, in part by denying it legitimacy.[18] Yet precisely the same tools are available to the United States: it too can use international institutions and undertake coordinated actions to constrain other powers. In this sense, the United States is "soft balancing" other states all the time.[19]

Studies that focus only on actions directed against the United States thus cannot address the question of whether deep engagement, on net, leads to more such constraints or fewer. The only way to gain leverage on that question is to study efforts on all sides—the United States, its allies, potential rivals, and nonaligned countries. Empirical studies examining that question generally provide strong evidence of deep engagement's utility to the United States in institutionally and normatively constraining others.[20] For example, in 2011 Washington coordinated action with a number of Southeast Asian states to oppose Beijing's claims in the South China Sea by highlighting established international law and norms to deny China's claim legitimacy. This fits all definitions of soft balancing—except that it is directed against China. It takes only a moment's thought to see that this sort of action goes on constantly—sometimes explicitly, often implicitly. The United States is clearly the world's number one "soft balancer." Moreover, the institutions, norms, rules, and standards of legitimacy that it uses to constrain others are largely of its own creation.[21] A core proposition of the deep engagement strategy is that sustaining a global presence enables systematic use of soft balancing–style tools to restrain and shape others' behavior. To be sure, other powers sometimes use the same tools, but to define soft balancing as action that can be taken only against the United States misses the forest for a few trees.

Terrorism

US officials periodically hail counterterrorism cooperation with allies, a benefit of deep engagement we discuss in more detail later. But what if the strategy's forward-leaning military posture actually significantly increases the terrorism threat in the first place? Proponents of retrenchment frequently invoke this objection. The argument that the United States should pursue retrenchment in order to reduce the supply of terrorists that target America is largely due to Robert Pape's prominent research.[22] Pape focuses specifically on suicide terrorism, and his overall conclusion is that "over 95% of suicide attacks are in response to foreign occupation" and thus "the more occupation, the more suicide terrorism."[23] The validity of Pape's overall conclusion that foreign occupation by democracies causes suicide terrorism has been critiqued on various grounds,[24] but here we wish to focus on whether it is reasonable to extrapolate from Pape's analysis to his underlying foreign policy recommendation. To avoid suicide terrorism, he counsels, the US must take one clear step: avoid having *any* "boots on the ground" and instead rely on "over-the-horizon air and naval forces and rapidly deployable ground forces, combined with training and equipping national armies and local militias to oppose the terrorist groups."[25]

It is important to note that even if we accept Pape's argument uncritically, it only bears on one of the three main regions featured in deep engagement. In some of his later writings, Pape implies the sweeping policy recommendation that the United States should generally pull back its forward-deployed troops in all regions where it has a military presence.[26] Yet his research at most points to a geographically specific recommendation—to remove US troops from the Persian Gulf—and has no bearing on the wisdom of maintaining US forward military presence in all other regions (a limiting condition that Pape does clearly emphasize in some of his writings[i]). The reason for this geographic limitation is that it is only in the Persian Gulf that any possible link between a US military presence and suicide terrorism can be made; suicide terrorists are simply not emerging from Western Europe and

---

i. As Pape notes, "Given the close association of foreign occupation and suicide terrorism, this goal can be achieved only if the United States substantially alters its military policy toward the Persian Gulf. . . . We need to recall the virtues of our traditional policy of 'offshore balancing' in the Persian Gulf and return to that strategy. Offshore balancing is the best way to secure our interests in the world's key oil-producing region without provoking more terrorism." Robert A. Pape, *Dying to Win: The Strategic Logic of Suicide Terrorism* (New York: Random House, 2005), pp. 238, 246–247.

East Asia in response to the extensive US military presence in countries like Germany, Japan, Korea, and Italy.

Even regarding the Persian Gulf, it is not clear how much the threat of suicide terrorism would decline if the United States followed Pape's recommendation and removed its onshore military presence from the region, which follows from his conclusion that it is specifically US boots on the ground that leads to suicide terrorism.[27] It would seem plausible that those who engage in anti-US terrorism are collectively influenced by a variety of factors. Indeed, Pape agrees, noting that suicide terrorism can be spurred not simply by the US military presence in a country but also by US backing of local governments[28] or by the ability of the United States to exert leverage over a country where it does not have many or any troops.[29] Yet if this is so, then would switching to an over-the-horizon military capacity solve the problem? After all, Pape acknowledges that "the key issue with American troops is their actual combat power."[30] And Pape hardly counsels for a comprehensive pullback from the region; he recommends that the United States should maintain "permanent readiness to intervene massively and rapidly if necessary, including maintaining the current infrastructure of military bases in the region."[31]

If the United States retains its bases in the region and has essentially just as much actual combat power after it shifts to an over-the-horizon capacity, then how much difference would it make simply to eliminate US boots on the ground? In other words, is it only a particular mechanism of US control in the Persian Gulf—boots on the ground—that is resented and not the overall level of US control that it can potentially exercise in the region?[ii] More generally, is it the overall US objectives in the region that generate resentment, or is it a narrow set of actions that the United States takes to realize these objectives? Even more generally, looking beyond American actions in the Persian Gulf, is it perhaps the United States' overall position as the sole superpower in the system that is the key source of resentment? The answers to these three questions are not yet clear. Depending on the answer to the last one, it could be

---

ii. Pape's analysis centers on the role of perceptions: he notes that a foreign military presence will produce suicide terrorism only when local actors perceive it as a foreign "occupation" rather than as a "stabilizing" mission (Robert A. Pape and James K. Feldman, *Cutting the Fuse: The Explosion of Global Suicide Terrorism and How to Stop It*. Chicago: University of Chicago Press, 2010). Given the role of perceptions, even an over-the-horizon US could still be seen as an "occupier" given the massive military capabilities the US has as the sole superpower. Ultimately, it is not clear why it would make any difference if the US can mount equally ferocious attacks from platforms at sea versus from air bases on land; either way, US firepower would give it a tremendous capacity for influence.

that it is only the end of a one-superpower world that would meaningfully affect the terrorism problem. And even if the kind of resentment that generates terrorism is driven not by America's sole superpower status but specifically or principally by the nature of its foreign policy, depending on the answers to the first two questions above it may be that the only change in US foreign policy that could meaningfully affect the terrorism problem would be a far more sweeping pullback from the region than is favored by even the strongest proponents of retrenchment.[iii]

In the end, the details of Pape's analysis do not support the contention that maintaining deep engagement necessarily imposes high terrorism costs; we lack a basis for concluding that merely removing US boots on the ground from the region would, by itself, eliminate the terrorism problem. It follows that the kind of over-the-horizon military posture Pape and other proponents of retrenchment call for could impose the same terrorism costs as a continuation of deep engagement. Beyond this region, the overwhelming bulk of the deployments associated with deep engagement are in areas that clearly do not generate these costs. And, as noted in chapter 4, large numbers of boots on the ground in the Middle East—the only region actually relevant to Pape's analysis—are not necessary for deep engagement.[32] The massive ground troop deployment in the region that attended the conquest and long-term occupation of Iraq—and which sparked the intense focus on links between suicide terror and foreign occupation—has ended and is unlikely to return.[33]

Distorting US Interests, Part 1: Entrapment and Entanglement

The costs of US foreign policy that matter most are lives that might be lost if the country's strategy goes awry. Supporters of retrenchment express grave worry that the United States' multifarious commitments might lead it to

---

iii. Even Gholz and Press, who present arguably the clearest and least-hedged version of retrenchment, still see three possible scenarios that would call for quick and potent US intervention in the Middle East if the United States were to pull back from the region: a cross-border invasion by an aggressor, an attempt to block the Strait of Hormuz, or domestic instability in Saudi Arabia. Eugene Gholz and Daryl G. Press, "Protecting 'The Prize,'" *Security Studies*, Vol. 19, No. 3 (August 2010), pp. 453–485. For two of these missions—reversing an effort at conquest and keeping the Strait of Hormuz open—Gholz and Press maintain that although air forces would probably be sufficient, ground forces could need to be reintroduced into the region. Ibid., pp. 476, 481.

be tempted to join an unnecessary shooting war, or that its global military presence feeds a dangerous expansion of interests that ends with young Americans dying in battles that only serve other nations' causes. We consider each of these potential costs in the next two sections, beginning first with the potential entrapment risk.

Drawing on studies of alliance politics by Glen Snyder and others, advocates of retrenchment highlight the risk of entrapment.[34] In this view, securing smaller allies invites the danger of drawing the United States into unnecessary wars. In a pure case of entrapment, an ally deliberately instigates a conflict intending to draw its patron into the fray. But alliances might entail a broader array of mechanisms that are arguably best described as "entanglement."[iv] The concern is that securing allies could pull the superpower sponsor into costly wars by courting "moral hazard" (that is, allies may take risks they would not otherwise accept because the superpower patron bears the true burden of these risks). Also worrisome to retrenchment advocates is that even if the ally does not intend to draw the United States into conflict, alliances may multiply America's enemies; after all, each ally the United States acquires also invites the enmity of all that country's adversaries. In addition, concerns about the reputational costs of failing to honor alliance commitments or the pernicious influence of foreign interest group lobbying might cause US leaders to go to war even when the interests at stake are not American. Finally, fostering the security dependence of allies might also mean that even when they want to intervene, they lack the capability to do so—hence, the United States gets dragged in.

At first glance, entrapment would seem to defy the expectations of the realist theories that retrenchment proponents ostensibly draw from, or indeed any other theory based on the assumptions that states act rationally and their relative power matters. After all, the scenario it posits of a weaker ally pulling the stronger patron into a war not in its interest turns Thucydides on his head, saying, in effect, that the weak do what they can and the strong suffer what they must. The entrapment argument, moreover, holds that the allies are strategically rational players, intelligently exploiting the United States by courting risks at its expense.[35] But the same rationality apparently

---

iv. By "entrapment" Snyder originally intended to encompass the wider array of mechanisms. Tongfi Kim, however, persuasively argues that "entrapment" should refer only to a subset of entanglement, in which a state is dragged into a military conflict purposefully instigated by one of its allies. See Tongfi Kim, "Why Alliances Entangle but Seldom Entrap States," *Security Studies*, Vol. 20, No. 3 (July 2011), pp. 350–377.

does not apply to Washington, which is portrayed by retrenchment proponents as being incapable of acting strategically and easily tricked into acting foolishly. Indeed, at root entrapment arguments propose that alliances are institutions that have potent constraining effects on the United States, causing it to take very costly action against its own best interests. That argument is hard to reconcile with the realist premises underlying retrenchment scholarship, which generally add up to deep skepticism that international institutions strongly constrain states, especially powerful ones.[36]

Scholarship that has appeared in the three decades since the initial work on entrapment has in significant part rescued realism from these contradictions. Rational states might be expected to anticipate the danger of entrapment and seek to protect themselves from it. As it turns out, this is exactly what they do. Tongfi Kim, for example, shows that most alliance agreements are written to protect the allies from entrapment—a problem that is greater for the smaller partner whose bargaining leverage, as realism would expect, is generally dwarfed by that of the great power patron. Given its huge power advantage, entrapment is just not a major problem for the United States, and certainly is not a persuasive rationale for retrenchment. As Kim observes, "Withdrawing from alliance commitments altogether would be a misguided policy, because these commitments alone are not likely to drag the United States into a costly war. Additionally, these commitments enhance US influence on the allies and deterrence against potential enemies. Meanwhile, the United States has more power to entrap its allies, and other states have more reasons to accept entrapment in order to avoid abandonment by the sole super-ally."[37]

This helps to explain why it is hard to find a clear case of the United States being entrapped.[38] Michael Beckley has undertaken the most comprehensive effort so far to find evidence for the broadest notion of entanglement, encompassing all the subtler mechanisms that might draw the United States into a conflict owing to an alliance commitment that is distinct from its national interest. He examined every militarized dispute involving the United States in the post–World War II era, asking simply whether entanglement mechanisms played a role. His conclusion: "Entrapment is rare." Out of 188 disputes, he found entanglement only figured in five major episodes. "Even in these five cases, moreover, the extent of U.S. entanglement is questionable, because there were other important drivers of American involvement, U.S. policymakers carefully limited support for allies, alliances restrained the United States from escalating its involvement, or all of the above."[39] The role that allies sometimes play in restraining escalatory impulses by the United

States is noteworthy given its complete absence from the writings of retrenchment advocates. While advocates of retrenchment worry that allies will drag the United States into unnecessary wars, Beckley finds that actually:

> The historical record shows that allies often help keep U.S. troops at home not only by bearing some of the burden for U.S. wars, but also by encouraging the United States to stay out of wars altogether. Large-scale retrenchment would sacrifice these and other benefits of alliances while doing little to compel U.S. leaders to define national interests modestly or choose military interventions selectively.[40]

Indeed, Beckley, Kim, and other researchers find that the best observable evidence of entrapment are cases that work in the opposite direction—with the United States dog wagging the allied tail, as analysts contend may have occurred in Iraq and Afghanistan.[41] Many US allies contributed to those interventions less from a sense of immediate national interest than from a more long-term calculation about the value of the alliance or as part of a complex quid pro quo with the Americans.[42] For critics of these operations within many of those states, the notion of their country being the tail wagging the American dog would appear fantastical.

More recent scholarship has also ratified Paul Schroeder's analysis of alliances as not just power-aggregating mechanisms but also tools for controlling risks and exerting influence.[43] As noted in chapter 6, empirical studies find strong support for the claim that defensive alliances work to deter war without making allied states more likely to initiate conflict.[44] Much about the United States' experience supplies evidence to support this view. Victor Cha shows how each post–World War II US-East Asian alliance was a "power-play . . . designed to exert maximum control over the smaller ally's actions," where one key aim was "to constrain anticommunist allies in the region that might engage in aggressive behavior against adversaries that could entrap the United States in an unwanted larger war."[45] Recent developments in the US-Taiwan relationship—arguably the most salient entrapment concern for advocates of retrenchment—also constitute a case in point. After repeated cross-strait tensions in the 1990s and early 2000s, US officials became concerned that the policy of strategic ambiguity regarding support for Taiwan was leaving them exposed to the risk of entrapment. The George W. Bush administration adjusted the policy to clarify dual deterrence: deterring China from an unprovoked attack, but also deterring Taiwan from provocative moves toward independence that might give Beijing cause to resort to force.^{v} Although it is impossible to rule out speculation that the United States might get dragged in no matter what, all the observable evidence is consistent with the view that major power patrons can ward against entrapment and use their alliances to control risks.

Distorting US Interests, Part 2: Temptation

Many critics believe that deep engagement generates an endemic temptation toward dangerous global activism. Two interdependent mechanisms—often implicit in the writings of retrenchment advocates—are in play: capabilities and rhetorical entrapment.

First, retrenchment advocates see the mere possession of peerless, globe-girdling military capabilities as leading to a dangerous expansion of US definitions of national interest that then drag the country into expensive wars.[46] In this view, peerless military power creates the temptation to seek total, non-Clausewitzian solutions to security problems, as allegedly occurred in Iraq and Afghanistan.[47] Only a country in possession of such awesome military power and facing no serious geopolitical rival would fail to be satisfied with partial solutions such as containment and instead embark on wild schemes of democracy building in such unlikely places. In addition, critics contend, the United States' outsized military creates a sense of obligation to use it if it might do good, even in cases where no US interests are engaged. As Madeleine Albright famously asked Colin Powell, "What's the point of having this superb military you're always talking about, if we can't use it?"[48] Americans have values and care about humanitarian catastrophes, and they also generally like democracies and would like to help peoples struggling for democracy if it can be done without major costs and risks. As long as their country is so powerful, critics allege, they will be tempted to right the world's wrongs—by the sword if necessary.

Second, by emphasizing the centrality of its own leadership, the United States may entrap itself rhetorically by generating expectations of action that

v. Thomas Christensen recounts that in 2002–2003 and again in 2007–2008 the United States actively opposed Taiwanese moves to unilaterally change the status quo across the strait and actually "coordinated international criticism" of Taiwanese moves, but it did so while criticizing China's military buildup around the strait and taking steps to deepen US defense ties with Taiwan. As Christensen argues, the United States was not entrapped by its security commitment to Taiwan but—on the contrary—used the security commitment, along with careful diplomacy, to restrain and deter both sides. See Thomas J. Christensen, *Worse Than a Monolith: Alliance Politics and Problems of Coercive Diplomacy in Asia* (Princeton, N.J.: Princeton University Press, 2011), pp. 242–255.

it then feels obligated to honor.[49] In almost any crisis, the US president—more often and more insistently than the leaders of China or India or France or any other country—will be asked what he or she intends to do. Having set themselves up as leaders of the international system, US presidents may be prone to periodically issue "red lines," and then, retrenchment advocates worry, credibility concerns may create pressure for action. This mechanism was certainly observable in the case of Syria's civil war and the use of chemical weapons, although a military response was avoided in that instance.

These mechanisms raise three key questions. First, to what extent are they a function of grand strategy? Clearly, grand strategy cannot change US preferences. Americans' concern for the plight of others and their basic pro-democracy disposition will remain whatever grand strategy the country adopts. Hence the salience of the capabilities logic. Undoubtedly, possessing global military intervention capacity expands opportunities to use force. If it were truly to "come home," the United States would be tying itself to the mast like Ulysses, rendering itself incapable of succumbing to temptation. Any defense of deep engagement must acknowledge that it increases the opportunity and thus the logical probability of US use of force compared to a grand strategy of true strategic disengagement. Of course, if the alternative to deep engagement is an over-the-horizon intervention stance (under which US forces would be stationed at sea and/or back in the continental United States but configured to be quickly deployable to a theater), then the temptation risk would persist after retrenchment. Indeed, as noted, even analysts who call for the most decisive form of retrenchment entailing full-scale abrogation of all US alliances still call for retention of a global intervention capacity second to none. As yet, no advocate of retrenchment has outlined a grand strategy and supporting military posture that would eliminate the temptation risk. At best, retrenchment might reduce the temptation risk: a post-retrenchment America will still have the capacity to intervene in far-flung regions of the world and still be governed by people who care about others and can make mistakes.

There are, however, some dynamics in play that are at least partially a function of grand strategic choice. Strong versions of retrenchment would entail fewer or no allies, perhaps more capable remaining allies or nonallied friends, and a lower salience for the official rhetoric of global leadership. These shifts would plausibly engender less temptation, which raises the second question: What might the price of such reduced temptation risks be in terms of new risks? The main risk is that the country may nonetheless decide to intervene after having shed many allies and partners but retained a powerful latent

intervention capacity. A retrenched America would arguably set fewer impru-
dent red lines and feel less pressure to demonstrate leadership. But it would
still be deeply interdependent with a world that it cares about, and American
leaders might come to regret having ruled out involvement in some region
or on some issue. In previous eras it was more feasible to sit out foreign wars,
picking the opportune moment to engage and build up the required capabilities; in contrast, in today's much more interdependent world, that period
of assessment could be massively costly to the United States. As compared
to previous eras, global economic interdependence—and the US link to the
global economy specifically—is now far greater; the financial markets and
global production networks the United States depends on would almost certainly be disrupted by significant wars elsewhere. Environmental interdependence also matters: even a "small" regional nuclear war could disrupt global
temperatures and rainfall patterns, potentially crippling global agriculture
over a sustained period.[50] At least for the foreseeable future, moreover, the
United States will be reliant on importing a large amount of its energy from
other parts of the world. In short, there is no longer a neat dividing line between the United States and what happens "over there."

If the analysis of chapter 5 is right, that a world with a retrenched America
is likely to have considerably more tension and risk of war in its key regions,
then the probability of some major turn of events creating a compelling intervention pull on Washington is likely to increase over what we now observe.
And were that to occur, US policymakers may regret having shed useful
allies, since the resulting intervention would be more expensive and harder
without established access and allies. Of course, access could potentially be
reestablished, but perhaps not on a sufficiently speedy timeline. Moreover, it
is also doubtful that the facilities themselves will be as usefully maintained
by local governments. In turn, although security partnerships can potentially
be reestablished, this would occur with foreign militaries that would have less
experience training and working directly with US forces.

Nevertheless, the upshot is that deep engagement does court more temptation risk than the most comprehensive versions of retrenchment. And that
raises the third question: Empirically, how large is this cost? One case, it turns
out, accounts for the lion's share of the observed temptation/interest-expansion
costs: Iraq. Sixty-seven percent of all the casualties and sixty-four percent of all
the budget costs of all the wars the United States has fought since 1990 were
caused by that war. Twenty-seven percent of the causalities and twenty-six percent of the costs were related to Operation Enduring Freedom in Afghanistan.
All the other interventions—the 1990–1991 Persian Gulf War, the subsequent

airstrike campaigns in Iraq, Somalia, Bosnia, Haiti, Kosovo, Libya, and so on—account for 3% of the casualties and 10% of the costs.[51]

Iraq is the outlier not only in terms of its human and material costs but also in the degree to which the overall burden was shouldered by the United States alone. As Beckley has shown, in the other interventions allies either spent more than the United States on a per capita basis, suffered greater relative casualties, or both. In the 1990–1991 Persian Gulf War, for example, the United States ranked fourth in overall casualties (measured relative to population size) and fourth in total expenditures (relative to GDP). In Bosnia, EU budget outlays and personnel deployments ultimately swamped those of the United States as the Europeans took over postconflict peacebuilding operations. In Kosovo, the United States suffered one combat fatality, the sole US loss in the whole operation, and it ranked sixth in relative monetary contribution. In Afghanistan, the United States is the number one financial contributor (it achieved that status only after the 2010 surge), but its relative combat losses rank fifth.[52] And in Libya, the European powers took on the lion's share of the military mission. In short, the temptation/interest-expansion argument would look much different without Iraq in the picture. There would be no evidence for the United States shouldering a disproportionate share of the burden, and the overall pattern of intervention would look "unrestrained" only in terms of frequency, not cost, with the debate hinging on whether the surge in Afghanistan was recklessly unrestrained.[vi]

An important point to note about the US experience in Iraq is that it was not an expression of deep engagement's core. As Gregory Gause underscores:

> The American decision to invade Iraq in 2003 [was] a major departure from the past pattern of American policy in the Gulf. Before the 2003 war, American foreign policy in the Persian Gulf was relatively simple to understand. Washington wanted to maintain itself as the dominant regional power, because of the oil resources there. Because the United States was the dominant force in the area, "stability" was Washington's Gulf mantra. Interruptions in the status quo, such as the Iranian Revolution and Iraq's invasion of Kuwait, challenged American dominance and, where possible, had to be reversed. But 2003 was something different. . . . The 9/11 attacks changed the

---

vi. The initial operations in Afghanistan were widely supported, including by prominent advocates of retrenchment, many of whom went on to oppose the surge in 2010. Some 40% of total US casualties have occurred since the surge.

perceptions of the major decision-makers in the George W. Bush administration about American interests in the region, devaluing stability as a predominant American concern and substituting for it an ambitious effort to remake both the international and the domestic politics of the region.[53]

A key question is whether continuing the current grand strategy condemns the United States to more such wars. The Cold War experience suggests a negative answer. After the United States suffered a major disaster in Indochina (to be sure, dwarfing Iraq in its human toll), it responded by waging the rest of the Cold War using proxies and highly limited interventions. Nothing changed in the basic structure of the international system, and US military power recovered by the 1980s, yet the United States never again undertook a large expeditionary operation until after the Cold War had ended. All indications are that Iraq has generated a similar effect. If there is an Obama doctrine, Dominic Tierney argues, it can be reduced to "No more Iraqs."[54] Moreover, the president's thinking is reflected in the recent defense strategic guidance, which asserts that "U.S. forces will no longer be sized to conduct large-scale, prolonged stability operations."[55] Those developments in Washington are also part of a wider rejection of the Iraq experience across the American body politic, which political scientist John Mueller dubbed the "Iraq Syndrome."[56]

Net Assessment

Ultimately, retrenchment advocates are right that deep engagement raises temptation risks but wrong when they exaggerate their scale and assume away the risks retrenchment would bring. We have analyzed the optimality of deep engagement from the standpoint of large swaths of scholarship, but do recognize that the United States has periodically chosen to pursue objectives or add missions that go considerably beyond the underlying grand strategy. We conclude that maintaining deep engagement does marginally increase temptation but does not necessitate foreign interventions of the type and scale of Iraq and Afghanistan. As we write this, evidence abounds of strong incentives for the United States to avoid a "deep engagement plus" stance. The Obama administration's disposition to act accordingly is consistent with our analysis. To the degree that Washington responds to incentives we've identified, it should be sustainable.

It is important to understand that impulses that cause expansions beyond deep engagement are in large part reflections of the US polity itself—a decision-making process that responds—imperfectly, to be sure—to the values, emotions and nonstrategic preferences of elites and populace. And neither we nor advocates of retrenchment can wish that reality away. It would doubtless cause any real-world retrenchment to veer from the path the strategy's advocates favor, just as it has done with deep engagement. If America engaged in retrenchment, it would still have people who care about the plight of others, would still be governed by leaders who are human beings with human flaws who can make mistakes, and, it is clear, would still have the capacity to intervene in far-flung regions of the world.

In the end, the core solution to temptation lies at home, not in America's grand strategy abroad. As Beckley concludes in this regard:

> When the United States has overreached militarily, the main cause has not been entangling alliances but rather . . . the tendency of U.S. leaders to define national interests expansively, to exaggerate the magnitude of foreign threats, and to underestimate the costs of military intervention. Developing a disciplined defense policy therefore will require the emergence of prudent leadership, the development (or resurrection) of guidelines governing the use of force, the establishment of domestic institutional constraints on the president's authority to send U.S. forces into battle, or some combination of these. Scrapping alliances, by contrast, would simply unleash the United States to act on its interventionist impulses while leaving it isolated diplomatically and militarily.[57]

Conclusion

Critics of deep engagement point to a number of arguments about the security costs of a leading state seeking the power to shape its strategic environment. Most, however, either do not apply to the United States today or have since been reversed by subsequent research. Whereas past rising powers may have had to worry that an overly ambitious grand strategy might spark counterbalancing, sustaining the already established leadership of the United States does not confront that cost. On the contrary, scholarship that has cumulated over the past twenty years has lent strong support to the expectation that strategic withdrawal would hasten the rate at which capabilities diffuse away from the United States. Entrapment may well be an issue for the smaller nations in an alliance, but theory and evidence indicate the United

States can effectively insulate itself from this cost. And there is little reason to think that the problem of terrorism would go away if the United States eliminated its military presence throughout the world—indeed, as we'll discuss in chapters 9 and 10, there is ample reason to worry that severing security relationships would hamper cooperation on counterterrorism.

The security cost highlighted by retrenchment proponents that survives this analysis is temptation. The ability to use military capabilities to try to save lives or stave off humanitarian disasters is almost certainly greater for a country with scores of allies and basing rights than for one with no such assets. But our analysis showed that the overall temptation cost associated with deep engagement is far lower than widely understood for a variety of reasons, including that deep engagement does not condemn the United States to future major nation-building operations like Iraq and Afghanistan and that replacement grand strategies of retrenchment do not eliminate the capability to intervene globally.

With few exceptions, analysts advocating retrenchment are either self-proclaimed realists or explicitly ground their strategic assessment in signature works of realist scholarship. This generates the impression that realism yields an unambiguous verdict in favor of retrenchment for a state in the United States' strategic setting, and that US foreign policy since the Cold War's end stands as a massive anomaly for realism. Indeed, to many realist scholars the current grand strategy is so patently suboptimal that its persistence after the Soviet Union's demise can be explained only by domestic political pathologies or the pernicious influence of America's liberal ideology.[vii] The import of chapters 5–8 reverses these implications. We showed that realism itself yields a strongly positive net assessment of the grand strategy's security costs and benefits, and therefore that America's post–Cold War strategic behavior is not a self-evident anomaly for realism; and that explaining this behavior does not necessarily demand delving deep into the peculiarities of American domestic politics or ideology. In the end, the

---

vii. Stephen Walt maintains that "the United States allowed its foreign policy to be distorted by partisan sniping, hijacked by foreign lobbyists and narrow domestic special interests, blinded by lofty but unrealistic rhetoric, and held hostage by irresponsible and xenophobic members of Congress." Stephen M. Walt, "In the National Interest: A Grand New Strategy for American Foreign Policy," *Boston Review*, Vol. 30, No. 1 (February/March 2005), available at: http://bostonreview.net/BR30.1/walt.php. Christopher Layne notes that "more than most, America's foreign policy is the product of . . . ideas. U.S. foreign policy elites have constructed their own myths of empire to justify the United States' hegemonic role." Christopher Layne, "Graceful Decline: The End of *Pax Americana*," *American Conservative*, Vol. 9, No. 5 (May 2010), p. 30.

fundamental choice to retain a grand strategy of deep engagement after the Cold War is just what the preponderance of realist scholarship would expect a power in the United States' position to do in order to advance its security interests. And as we will see in the next two chapters, the case for sustaining deep engagement becomes stronger still when we examine the nonsecurity benefits of the strategy.

9

The Economic and Institutional Logic of Deep Engagement

THE CASE FOR US retrenchment is very narrowly focused on a specific question: Would pulling back improve the United States' security? Retrenchment proponents say yes, but the previous four chapters showed their case against deep engagement overstates its costs and underestimates its security benefits. Perhaps its most important weakness, however, is that its preoccupation with security issues diverts attention from some of deep engagement's most important benefits: sustaining economic globalization and fostering institutionalized cooperation in ways advantageous to US national interests.[1]

Readers not steeped in this literature may wonder how it can be that the case against the United States' grand strategy largely ignores issues that have figured so prominently in US foreign policy for so long. Some retrenchment proponents explicitly frame the question in ways that exclude the nonsecurity benefits of deep engagement. Barry Posen's important contribution, for example, defines grand strategy "as a nation-state's theory about how to produce security for itself," thus excluding any US interest in fostering economic globalization and cooperating within institutions on nonmilitary issues.[2] Most retrenchment proponents do not explain why they exclude the nonsecurity benefits of deep engagement. Analysts advocating retrenchment, with few exceptions, either are self-proclaimed realists or explicitly ground their strategic assessment in signature works of realist scholarship.[3] Given the tendency in much modern realist scholarship to devalue the overall significance of institutions, these analysts may see little reason to examine the link between a globally engaged grand strategy and the international order. In turn, most modern realists do not focus on the global economy, perhaps explaining why retrenchment proponents generally ignore the issue of sustaining economic globalization.

Whatever the cause, neglecting nonsecurity benefits is a major oversight, as this and the next chapter show. This chapter outlines the core theoretical logic of hegemonic order that underlies deep engagement, and chapter 10 focuses on how that helps produce crucial economic benefits for the United States.

Deep engagement is grounded in a logic of hegemonic order with two foundational points. First, the kind of global order we have today—one characterized by extensive global economic linkages and widespread institutionalized cooperation—is more likely to be created and maintained when it is backed by a powerful state (a "hegemon") that provides leadership in support of such an order.[i] Second, the United States did not help foster this order for free; it has extracted benefits for itself, albeit to a circumscribed extent.

Augmenting the Likelihood of Cooperation

The first point is that an economically open, strongly institutionalized order is more likely to emerge and be maintained when a hegemonic state works toward those ends. In contrast to arguments of this kind advanced decades ago—so-called "hegemonic stability theory"—the claim here is probabilistic and general.[4] These cooperative outcomes can occur with or without hegemonic leadership, but such leadership makes them much more likely. In addition, the older scholarship focused on the global economy, whereas here the claim pertains also to the prospects for institutionalized cooperation.

The influence of hegemonic leadership is clear regarding international trade, in which moving away from protectionism at the global level is hardly

---

i. In the literatures on the global economy and institutionalized cooperation, scholars often use the term "hegemon" to refer both to the state with the greatest share of material capabilities in the system as well as to the relation of political dominance over other states that this high level of material power might enable. In other words, a hegemon is often seen as a state that is extremely powerful in terms of both the material capabilities it possesses and influence it has. Our use of the term hegemon here strictly refers to a state that has the largest share of material capabilities in the system; in so doing, we do not make any judgment about the character of influence or the logic of political relationships that exists within the global system. Understood this way, the United States is certainly a hegemon today, as chapter 2 showed.

the natural or default state of affairs. The most recent experience in which the system shifted from being quite closed to being quite open (the decades following World War II) was aided by the fact that the United States was the leading global power and it wanted economic openness and pushed for it. As Robert Keohane explains, "The creation of contemporary international regimes can largely be explained by postwar US policy, implemented through the exercise of American power. . . . The United States was clearly the leading power in the world political economy . . . [and it] actively worked to reduce tariffs and took the lead in pressing for the removal of discriminatory restrictions."[5]

Although Keohane agrees that American hegemonic leadership greatly aided in the creation of the existing economic order, in his landmark study *After Hegemony* he questioned how important it was for continued order maintenance.[6] Yet we can accept this line of argument and still conclude that hegemonic leadership makes the maintenance of an open global economic order much more likely. In part, this is because order maintenance and creation are not wholly separate tasks: maintaining an order still requires institutional creation, because new and/or revised structures are needed to ensure that an order remains current and does not stagnate. As we stressed in a previous analysis, an order will be more likely to be dynamic and adapt to new challenges if there is a hegemon that acts to provide leadership to push for these needed revisions.[7]

Keohane provides an excellent example of how the maintenance and creation of order are linked in the case of the United States' use of its power to update the international monetary system's outdated set of rules in the early 1970s, thereby laying the foundations for the continuation of the financial order:

> The rules of the old regime . . . written largely by the United States in 1944 to protect interests of creditor countries, now made it impossible for the United States to force Germany and Japan to revalue their currencies. . . . Only by breaking the rules explicitly—by suspending convertibility of the dollar into gold—could the United States transform its bargaining position and make its creditors offer concessions of their own. . . . The United States thus had a political incentive to smash the specific rules of the old regime, even if it had an equally powerful desire to maintain the essential principles of liberalism. Once the old rules had been destroyed, other governments had to pay more attention to U.S. wishes insofar as they also wished to retain these principles. For

the United States, increased discord was a precondition for cooperation on American terms. . . . Although the rules of the Bretton Woods
regime were altered in 1971–1973, the principles of multilateralism and
relatively unfettered capital flows were maintained."[8]

What is the underlying point here? It is not that hegemonic leadership is
a necessary condition for the creation or maintenance of the kind of global
order we have now. As noted, Keohane's book showed that maintenance
could potentially occur "after hegemony." Nor, certainly, is the claim that
hegemonic leadership is sufficient to produce these outcomes—clearly, other
conditions must be present. The point is that both order creation and maintenance are more likely with hegemonic leadership. This is not a controversial
argument; the voluminous literatures on institutionalized cooperation and
the global economy contain no analysis that suggests that this probabilistic
claim is wrong.

Yet one would not know this from reading these literatures, which in
recent decades have tended to either ignore or downplay the significance of
hegemonic leadership.[9] However, this appears to be nothing more than an ar-
tifact of the particular way these literatures were constructed. For one thing,
the most recent wave of institutionalist analyses has largely set aside issues
pertaining to power and thereby neglected to examine how a dominant hegemonic state interacts with the institutional order.[10] And most scholars in
this literature also neglect the linkages between security issues, on the one
hand, and institutionalized cooperation on nonsecurity issues, on the other
hand—a link whose importance will become apparent in chapter 10. In turn,
most of the analyses that do actually examine hegemonic leadership end up
appearing not to accord it much significance; yet this is only because they
typically focus on showing that a deterministic version of hegemonic stability
theory is wrong.

The most important analyst here is Keohane, who in *After Hegemony* focused on the question of whether an existing order could possibly be maintained even absent hegemonic leadership. Such a focus made sense given the
prominence of deterministic versions of hegemonic stability theory at that
time; his conclusion that "post-hegemonic cooperation is also possible" was
an important correction to a line of theorizing that was then very important
and prominent.[11] Whether this deterministic framing of hegemonic stability theory is due to the way it was conceived by its original formulators or is
caused by later caricatures by its critics—or some combination—is hard to
tell and is not necessary to analyze here.[12] For now, the key takeaway is that

this overall framing of the theory meant that the literature on hegemony and cooperation was generally directed away from discussing whether hegemonic leadership makes the continuation of the current global order more likely. In a 2012 analysis, Keohane articulated his understanding of this issue after reviewing a series of core points "relevant to the future of the U.S. global role that can now be said with confidence."

> Leadership is indeed essential in order to promote cooperation, which is in turn necessary to solve global problems ranging from war to climate change. . . . We know that in the absence of leadership, world politics suffers from collective action problems, as each state tries to shift the burdens of adjustment to change onto others. . . . We know that leadership is exercised most effectively by creating multilateral institutions that enable states to share responsibilities and burdens. . . . We know that leadership is costly and states other than the leader have incentives to shirk their responsibilities. . . . [And] we know that. . . only the United States has the material capacity and political unity to exercise consistent global leadership.[13]

Some might see a disjuncture between this recent conclusion and Keohane's earlier analysis in *After Hegemony*. Yet Keohane did not previously maintain that hegemony was unimportant for sustaining the order; rather, he merely argued that it is relatively "*less* important for the continuation of cooperation, once begun, than for its creation."[14] In today's world—in which scholars have rejected the old deterministic version of hegemonic stability theory and ever more analysts and policymakers question whether there is value to America maintaining a globally engaged role—the question at issue has shifted from "Is post-hegemonic cooperation possible?" to "Is the existing order more likely to be maintained if America continues to play a leadership role?" Keohane's answer to both questions is yes. We know of no theoretical or empirical analysis questioning the validity of this conclusion.

Deep Engagement and Leadership

The United States' ability to exercise leadership of the existing order is a function not just of its economic size but also partly of its forward security position and associated alliances.[15] One notable reason why is that, as the previous two chapters showed, deep engagement reduces the threat of conflict and arms races among key US allies; institutionalized cooperation is less likely to eventuate when there is security instability and more likely to flourish when states are secure and leaders can anticipate stable, continuous relations. In this regard, Keohane stresses that one reason hegemonic leadership is essential to promote cooperation is that "without alliances or other institutions helping provide reassurance, uncertainty generates security dilemmas, with states eyeing one another suspiciously."[16]

Another notable reason why the United States' globally engaged security policy augments its ability to provide hegemonic leadership is that even when interests overlap there are typically a multitude of potential cooperative scenarios to achieve a given end. Generating agreement on a particular cooperative solution can often be elusive. In these situations, the US position typically achieves significant prominence and does so in part due to Washington's role as a global alliance leader, which provides a "focal point" that can spur cooperation. And when interests do not overlap, the bargaining becomes yet tougher: on the table is not just how, but whether cooperation will occur. In these circumstances, Washington's security leverage can help push its allies (which include all but one of the world's largest economies) toward cooperation, either indirectly (by acting as a background condition that implicitly prompts allies to adopt certain positions) or directly (when it uses its assets and bargaining chips in the security realm to induce greater cooperation).[17] In this regard, Joseph Nye stresses: "Even if the direct use of force were banned among a group of countries, military force would still play an important political role. For example, the American military role in deterring threats to allies, or of assuring access to a crucial resource such as oil in the Persian Gulf, means that the provision of protective force can be used in bargaining situations. Sometimes the linkage may be direct; more often it is a factor not mentioned openly but present in the back of statesmen's minds."[18]

The United States' extended system of security commitments also creates a set of institutional relationships that foster enhanced political communication. Alliance institutions are in the first instance about security protection, but they also bind states together and create institutional channels of communication. For example, NATO has facilitated institutional ties and associated institutions that increase the ability of the United States and Europe to talk to each other and do business.[19] Likewise, the bilateral alliances in East Asia also play a communication role beyond narrow security issues, allowing consultations and exchanges to spill over into other policy areas.[20]

Regarding the stability of the global economy, the extensive set of US military commitments and deployments throughout the world helps to promote the "global economic commons." The core way is by helping to ensure that sea lanes and other shipping corridors are kept freely available for commerce.[21] The United States is, of course, not the only global player protecting the global economic commons, but it does play by far the most important role, due to its massive naval superiority. If it were to retrench, protecting the global economic commons would likely be much harder to accomplish. This is partly because cooperating with other nations on these matters would be less likely to occur for the reasons noted above. And it is also partly because access to naval bases throughout the world, which are necessary to accomplish this mission, would likely be curtailed to some degree if the United States pulls back from its security partnerships.[22]

The underlying theoretical takeaway is straightforward: US leadership makes the continuation of the order more likely and its leadership capacity is partly a function of its globally engaged grand strategy. It follows that the current order might not be stable and might be consequentially challenged in a counterfactual world in which the United States retrenched. We cannot know for sure, but the existence of this US hedge against challenges to the order may well be why such challenges are not observed.[23] Unless most of what we know about the relationship between hegemonic leadership and institutionalized cooperation is wrong, retrenchment would put the order's stability at risk. It would take a highly risk-acceptant leader to run a grand experiment to determine whether the global order can continue to remain stable in the absence of US leadership that is enabled by its globally engaged grand strategy.

Deep Engagement and the Benefits of the Economic Order

The second fundamental proposition underlying the logic of the hegemonic order is that the United States has provided leadership for the economic order for nearly seven decades, but it has not offered this service for free: it has extracted benefits for itself. Yet the way the United States has done this—and why it has been able to do it so successfully—has generally been obscured by the way the relevant scholarly literature is constructed.

The existing literature on hegemonic leadership typically differentiates between a hegemon that is "benevolent" from one that is "predatory."[24] In the standard formulation, a predatory hegemon is one that uses its power to structure the system to its own advantage and extract benefits, whereas a benevolent hegemon is one that fosters a global system that benefits other states more than itself.[ii] Analysts such as Gilpin stress that the danger of a hegemon falling prey to the temptation of pursuing a predatory course is that other states will back away from the order: "If other states begin to regard the actions of the hegemon as self-serving and contrary to their own political and economic interests, the hegemonic system will be greatly weakened."[25] At the same time, Gilpin stresses that pursuing a benevolent course will ultimately sow the seeds of the hegemon's demise: he argues that access to the market, technology, and capital of the hegemon will allow other states to close the economic gap with it.[26]

In chapter 7 we showed that many claims advanced by Gilpin, Kennedy, Calleo, and other scholars of that era concerning the ways in which hegemonic leadership sows the seeds of its own demise have not withstood further scholarly scrutiny. Here the issue is that the dichotomy between benevolent and predatory hegemons obscures the key issues in play and prevents us from seeing exactly how the United States has been able to successfully extract benefits from the economic order while also keeping it stable. To see why, it is crucial to understand that the distinction between predatory and benevolent behavior should not be thought of as a dichotomy; rather, it is best to conceive of hegemonic behavior as existing on a continuum between perfectly benevolent at one end and perfectly predatory at the other. In turn, it must be recognized that the hegemon is not locked into one general approach; rather, it can modulate its approach both over time and across different issues depending upon factors such as its relative competitiveness, the structure of the global economy, and the existence of crises.

What this means is that the hegemon has the potential to be predatory to some degree yet without becoming so rapacious as to drive other states to exit from or challenge the order. An excellent systematic analysis which reflects this understanding is Michael Mastanduno's study of how the United States has acted both as a "privilege taker" and a "system maker" during its nearly seven decades of hegemonic leadership of the global economy.[27] He argues that the United States has embraced "system maintenance" responsibilities, albeit not always consistently, but at the same time has also leaned toward a more predatory privilege-taker role at several critical junctures in the post–World War II period when cumulative economic imbalances emerged that

---

ii. With respect to the global economy, this distinction might seem to overlap with the question of whether the hegemon is liberal in the sense of pushing for open markets. Yet open markets can be pursued in different ways, some of which may benefit the hegemon more than other states (the overall effect of pushing for capital market openness, for example, depends upon whether the leading state pursues specific rules that favor its financial institutions).

threatened the underlying stability of the system; in each case, Washington sought to shift the burden of economic adjustment onto other states.

In Mastanduno's view, the United States is thus neither benevolent nor predatory, but is rather a mixture of the two: what it asks of the other key economic actors is not that they subscribe to an order which benefits the United States across the board, but rather that they accede to the need to make adjustments in the United States' favor at particular junctures. For example, Mastanduno notes that in response to growing competitiveness pressures from other states in the 1970s and 1980s, the United States forced "America's trading partners to accept 'voluntary' export restraints (VERs) and orderly marketing arrangements (OMAs) that provided relief to import-competing interests"; moreover, its "Super 301" policy granted "the United States the outrageous privilege of acting simultaneously as the self-appointed prosecutor, jury, and judge in adjudicating what it perceived to be the unfair trading practices of others."[28] Yet he also stresses that during this same period when the United States was increasingly demanding these kinds of concessions from its trading partners, the US market remained "among the most open of major industrial powers" and also that it worked to spur further multilateral opening—first by prompting new rounds of GATT negotiations and then later via efforts to deepen economic openness through pushing for the creation of the World Trade Organization and also through the inclusion of "new issues such as trade in services and intellectual property protection that had never fallen under the purview of GATT."[29]

Mastanduno's overall perspective takes us part of the way toward understanding how the United States has been able to successfully extract economic benefits from the system while also keeping it stable. To gain a more complete picture, it is necessary to factor in three additional points advanced by Carla Norrlof. Like Mastanduno, Norrlof stresses that although the United States has created a system that benefits others, it has also been able to successfully reap many specific benefits for itself.[30]

First, Norrlof stresses that when evaluating the advantages of the order, we have to consider that Washington prizes having enhanced flexibility: having leadership over the order simply gives it more options for dealing with an unknown future. She emphasizes that not all of the American gains from the order

> are quantifiable in monetary terms but come in the form of an unusually wide policy autonomy window, i.e., a longer timer horizon and a greater capacity for risk-taking. Because of the leverage the United States has over other states, it has considerable leeway to pursue

policies that would be suicidal if undertaken by another country. . . . The gain in policy flexibility means it can adjust imbalances using its preferred policy instruments, and that its "policy error" threshold is much higher than for other countries.[31]

To give an example, having the most leverage in the IMF is valuable not only because it has permitted Washington to carve out specific benefits in certain circumstances where it has had clear preferences but also because it means the United States will have more choices, and a better chance of implementing its preferences, if something were to happen to it or to the system that directly or indirectly involves a response by the IMF.

Second, Norrlof underscores that a key reason the United States has been able to pursue order maintenance so successfully is that when cooperating with the economic order is too costly, it has had a greater ability than other states to avail itself of exit options. A common implicit assumption in the literature is that a hegemon will have one general approach to these institutional rules: a benevolent hegemon will follow them and a predatory one will not. But the middle-ground Goldilocks approach is for the United States to set up an order that benefits other states but in which it is in an advantageous position to ignore, bend, or change rules when following them becomes especially onerous.

We noted above an excellent example: how in the early 1970s the United States used its bargaining leverage to favorably alter the rules of the international monetary system when they became too disadvantageous. Norrlof highlights another key example concerning the treatment of unfair trade practices, stressing that "American firms have had a relatively easy time insulating themselves from import competition" because many provisions in the GATT and WTO "were directly imputed from the United States' own legal framework."[32] Her general conclusion regarding the trade realm is that the United States has been more able than other countries to "reap the benefits of open markets without fully internalizing their constraints."[iii]

---

iii. As Norrlof observes, "The ability to negotiate loopholes in various sectors has provided the flexibility to ascertain when and what goods are traded freely, enhancing domestic support for liberalization. . . . Because of these flexibility measures, the United States has been better equipped than other countries to adopt import-competing policies in order to adjust trade deficits that have grown too large. . . . While other countries have resisted free trade as well, they have not been able to flout GATT/WTO principles, in GATT or WTO-consistent ways, as the United States has done. The United States' influence on the trade regime has ensured a high degree of conformity of the trade regime and American trade laws." Carla Norrlof, *America's Global Advantage: US Hegemony and International Cooperation* (Cambridge, UK: Cambridge University Press, 2010), pp. 102–103.

Third, Norrlof stresses that the United States' efforts to structure the order to its benefit are not restricted merely to making changes to cope with adjustment struggles, the focus of Mastanduno's analysis. She emphasizes that the United States generally "reaps unequal gains [from] . . . the current world system";[33] as a result, it is important to factor in what we have elsewhere called "macrolevel structuring": the various long-term structural features of the order the United States helped construct that serve its interests.[34] Significant examples along these lines are the role of the dollar as the leading international currency and the privileged position that the United States holds in the IMF. Because many elements of the system's long-term structure are to Washington's liking, much of what the United States wants is simply more of the same. We discuss macro-level structuring in greater detail later.

Of course, the United States does not constantly benefit from having exit options and flexibility; instead, they are only valuable periodically under those circumstances when the United States needs them. Because of their intermittent importance, it will not be possible to use a continuous measure like the US rate of growth compared to other countries to gauge how much the United States benefits from its leadership of the system, as analysts have sometimes done.[35] Ultimately, what recognizing these points does make clear is that we miss the reality of the US position if we stick with the literature's typical dichotomy between, on the one hand, a predatory hegemon that benefits from the system but can't get others to follow it because it is too self-serving and, on the other hand, a benevolent hegemon that can easily gain followers but is itself harmed by the structure of the system. The United States does not conform to either of these positions, and this is why it has been able to successfully extract significant benefits from the system while also keeping it stable.

Deep Engagement and the Benefits of the Institutional Order

What goes for economic order also applies to the larger institutional order. Here, too, the hegemonic leadership enabled by the United States' grand strategy fosters an institutional order that benefits many states but often especially the United States. The United States has been able to strongly benefit from the institutional order for two principal reasons; the first concerns the efficiency gains of institutionalized cooperation and the second pertains to legitimacy.

Scholars have compellingly shown that states derive benefits from institutionalized cooperation.[36] Sometimes the United States can make itself
better off through a properly structured institution that serves its interests, and other times it can avoid becoming worse off by seeking to resolve
problems that can only be addressed through multilateral solutions.[37]
Significantly, newly emerging dynamics arguably are producing a rise in
the benefits of institutionalized cooperation for the United States. Some of
these problems are transnational and emerge from environmental, health,
and resource dangers and vulnerabilities, such as those concerning health
pandemics. Transnational nonstate groups with various capacities for violence have also become salient in recent decades, including groups involved
in terrorism, piracy, and organized crime. These sorts of nontraditional,
transnational problems can be realistically addressed only through various
types of collective, coordinated action, and the United States is thus going
to find itself needing to work with other states to an increasing degree,
sharing information, building capacities, and responding to crises.[38]

It is typically difficult to generate international cooperation, especially
when dealing with new kinds of issues that require many novel bargains and
newly established procedures of shared responsibilities among a wide range
of countries. Having the US-led network of alliances in place to facilitate cooperation on one issue makes it easier, and more likely, that it will be able to
achieve cooperation rapidly with the same set of partners on different issues.
As one example, consider the intelligence-sharing network within NATO,
which was originally designed to gather information on the threat from the
Soviet Union; once in place, it could be quickly adapted to deal with new unforeseen issues, such as the threat from terrorism.[39] More generally, with the
existing US-led security system in place, the United States is in a stronger position than it would be otherwise to build partnerships, strike bargains, and
promote its interests within institutions. In this regard, the United States
was remarkably successful in the early and mid-2000s in shifting the agenda
of the United Nations to address concerns such as terrorism and proliferation that Washington was particularly concerned about. As one indication of
this, the Secretary-General's High-Level Panel on Threats, Challenges, and
Change endorsed in 2005 a range of US-supported positions on terrorism
and proliferation.[40]

Of course, institutions are not just enabling devices that garner efficiencies; cooperating within them can sometimes be costly, because doing so can
conflict with a state's short-term self-interest. What kind of exit options a
state has—and what kinds of costs it pays for exercising them—therefore

greatly influences the overall calculus of how beneficial it is to pursue institutionalized cooperation. Institutionalist theory posits that a state that avails itself of an exit option opens itself to two kinds of potential costs concerning, respectively, retaliation and reputation.[41] The key question is whether the United States faces these costs to the same degree as other states.

Retaliation by other members of an institution is clearly less of a constraint on the United States than on any other state.[42] The United States is so large on the world stage that it will typically require a great many states acting together in opposition to have a sufficiently strong retaliatory effect. Yet the value of maintaining a favorable relationship with it is typically very high: reducing cooperation with the United States generally carries a very high opportunity cost for other states, especially for states that rely on it for their security. America's globally engaged security strategy greatly enhances its ability to create linkages from security institutions to nonsecurity institutions, allowing it to threaten (perhaps implicitly) reduced cooperation with other states in the security realm if they were to attempt to retaliate against the United States in non-security institutions. In the end, America's global alliance system thus gives it relatively greater latitude to exit from institutional structures than it would otherwise have.

What about reputation costs? The underlying institutionalist argument concerning reputation is straightforward: states that do not comply within institutions "pay a serious price for acting in bad faith and, more generally, for renouncing their commitments. This price comes . . . from the decline in national reputation as a reliable partner."[43] For the United States, the general line of argument thus has a clear implication: failure to hew closely to the existing institutional order is costly because it will undermine America's reputation, thereby placing in jeopardy its continued ability to maintain cooperation in areas where it strongly needs and values institutionalization.[44] Yet as we have shown in detail in a previous analysis, the institutionalist argument for why the United States needs to pursue a highly cooperative approach regarding all parts of the institutional order is premised on a faulty view of how reputations work.[45] Institutionalist theory relies on the assumption that states have a single overall reputation for cooperativeness across all institutions, but this conception does not have empirical support. It is more compelling to view states as having multiple, or segmented, reputations that vary across different issues and institutions. For this reason, the negative repercussions of noncompliance within a given institution are far more bounded than institutionalist scholarship presumes; as we showed, this is especially the case with respect to the United States, which, due to its leadership position in the system, is likely to face fewer linkages across issue areas than other states.[46]

Beyond the efficiency gains of cooperation, the second principal reason why the United States has derived significant benefits from the institutional order is because it has helped to legitimate its actions and role as well as to socialize other actors.[47] Of key importance is that the institutional order that Washington fostered after the Second World War is by far history's most elaborate, encompassing an unprecedented range of issues. Scholars grounded in constructivism (an approach which centers the role of ideas in international relations and emphasizes how key elements of world politics are socially constructed—that is, shaped by the nature of widely shared beliefs, interactions, and other social processes in international relations) stress that international institutions are the embodiment of the taken-for-granted scripts, schemas, habits, and routines through which actors interpret the world and so govern what they view as appropriate behavior.[48] Constructivists recognize that these powers of socialization make modern international institutions especially potent tools of legitimation for the United States: they argue convincingly that the US global position would be far harder to maintain if other states stopped supporting the current institutional status quo in a habitual, routinized way and began to evaluate the order on the basis of constantly updated cost-benefit calculations.[49]

Yet constructivists argue that these legitimation benefits of the order for the United States come at the price of imposing potentially strong constraints on America's behavior: if a hegemon appeals to some set of principles to legitimate its power and establish roles for other states to follow, it is liable to be bound by those principles. For this reason, they stress that the United States must itself act in accordance with the formal and informal rules of the current institutional order, since otherwise it will be undermined.[50] In this view, in seeking to legitimate its power, the United States has thus opened itself up to a very significant constraint.

Although there is some merit to this constructivist line of argument, there are several considerations that individually and collectively weaken it.[51] First, these constructivist treatments generally downplay or neglect that material power can potentially shape standards of legitimacy. Second, the relationship between breaking rules and legitimacy is complex and contingent, opening up avenues for the use of power unbound by rules or simply to rewrite rules. Third, constructivist and closely related international legal scholarship point toward numerous strategies by which a leading state can draw on its power to minimize any legitimacy costs associated with making and breaking rules.

A particularly significant recent example of how the United States can sometimes effectively recraft standards of legitimacy concerns revisions to antiterrorism rules in the early and mid-2000s. Instead of working within the confines of existing rules during this period, the United States sought to reshape them to help ensure that an even wider range of actions that it favored would be seen as legitimate. Most notably, it pushed through UNSC 1373, which endorsed a new general rule legalizing the use of force against states that harbor terrorists and transformed a raft of US-sponsored antiterrorism measures into formal international commitments (it imposed a set of uniform, mandatory counterterrorist obligations on all member states and established a committee to monitor compliance).

Of course, to say that the United States has the ability to make and break rules hardly means that it can do so exactly as it likes. UNSC 1373 was a successful effort at rule revision, but US efforts to rewrite the rules have clearly failed in many other circumstances. And breaking rules certainly does sometimes impose legitimacy costs on America. Constructivists are thus correct to point out that legitimacy does not merely enable but also constrains American power; they simply have overemphasized the latter dynamic relative to the former. Regarding legitimacy dynamics, there is a feedback loop between a globally engaged grand strategy and the maintenance of the United States' privileged position within the system: the United States is more able to both break and create rules (and thereby benefit from legitimation dynamics within the system) in part because its position as the leader of a set of global alliances means that its security partners are less likely to be inclined to punish it for transgressions and are also more likely to be supportive of US efforts to revise the rules of the system.

Conclusion

At the end of the Second World War, the United States made a decision to strongly promote global economic openness. This move marked a decisive break from US practices just a few years before, when American actions, most notably the Smoot-Hawley Tariff, had played a key role in pushing the world toward economic closure during the 1930s. And partly to push forward an open global economy, the United States also broke from its previously conflicted posture toward international institutions to become history's most successful institution builder.

The analysis in this chapter has explicated the underlying theoretical logic for how the United States has been able to leverage its forward security position (and associated alliances) to provide leadership of the global order and to benefit from doing so. Economic globalization has flourished during the post–World War II era. The institutional structure the United States pushed for after 1945 remains in place and has promoted high levels of cooperation in many issue areas of importance for the United States. Washington has hardly been the only state to benefit from these developments. But during the seven decades that the United States has provided leadership for the economic and institutional order, it has been in a position to extract some special gains for itself and has also insulated itself from paying some kinds of costs.

10

Assessing the Economic Benefits of Deep Engagement

TODAY'S GLOBAL ORDER boasts the most extensive economic linkages and institutionalized cooperation in history. In chapter 9, we developed the theoretical logic explaining why such an order would be much harder to sustain without American leadership and why that leadership is partly a function of the United States' forward security position and associated alliances. We also explained why the United States is in a favorable position to extract benefits from this system leadership.

But how specifically does the United States benefit from its global position? A well-established and influential line of scholarly research by the likes of John Ikenberry, Robert Keohane, Erik Voeten, and David Lake details the benefits the United States obtains from the enhanced global cooperation within institutions due to its leadership role.[1] By comparison, the study of how the United States gains economic benefits from its globally engaged grand strategy is in its infancy: some scholars (notably Carla Norrlof, Michael Mastanduno, Michael Beckley, Douglas Stokes, and ourselves) have begun to make the case for how the United States gains in this way, while a few others—most notably Daniel Drezner—have questioned some of those claims. What the field currently lacks is a systematic, detailed analysis of the full range of economic benefits the United States can potentially derive from its pursuit of deep engagement.

In this chapter, we will carefully unpack these benefits, which come in four forms. First, the United States benefits greatly from the stability of economic globalization due to the fact it is the most significant economic player in the system. Second, the United States has not simply promoted an open global economic order but has also structured some of its long-term features to match up with its own particular interests. Third, on occasion the United States has been able to secure better bargains during particular negotiations on specific economic issues due to its globally engaged security policy. And fourth, deep engagement helps to protect the current global order from potentially damaging conflicts, which is very beneficial for the United States.

The Benefits of an Open Global Economic System

Our discussion of the economic wellsprings of American power in chapter 2 stressed the importance of assessing economic data with due regard to the globalized nature of today's world economy. Applying that lesson to assessing the United States' stake in the global economy further underscores its importance, revealing clearly that the United States is globalization's most significant player regarding trade, finance, and production.

Concerning trade, the United States is the world's leading exporter when we measure export shares using value-added calculations (the most appropriate metric for today's global economy, since "much of the value-added in manufactured goods comes from earlier stages of production" prior to the final assembly stage). Calculated this way, the United States' 14.4% global share of exports is almost 50% larger than the next highest state, China.[2] Of course, exposure to trade has significant potential costs. Lacking a strong social safety net, American workers in import-competing sectors who are harmed by global economic competition feel these costs intensely.[3] At the same time, exports support a very large number of US workers. As of 2013, export of goods and services supported an estimated 11.3 million jobs in the United States.[4] And when looking at the United States economy overall, it is clear that trade has significant benefits: a recent Commerce Department estimate is that nearly one-third of US economic growth during the 2009–2014 period was driven by exports.[5] In stark contrast to the pre–World War II era and even until a few decades ago, American economic capacity is thus very dependent upon global trade.

Regarding finance, one indicator—foreign exchange reserves—places China, not the United States, on top. This development notwithstanding, Drezner concludes that the United States remains "the most central actor in the network of global finance, with the United Kingdom a distant second. Indeed, the network centrality of the United States *increased* after 2008."[6] As he shows, the US share of global capital markets is now around twice as high as the next largest state.[7] Employing a network analysis to measure structural financial power, William Winecoff reaches the same conclusion: since 2008, the United States "has increased in prominence according to some measures and remained at the core in others. European financial centers have declined by most measures, while the rest of the countries have remained peripheral. Notably, this includes emerging markets known as the BRICS—Brazil, Russia, India, China, South Africa—which have not increased in prominence."[8] Regarding the dollar specifically, a recent analysis by Benjamin Cohen and Tabitha Benney that employs a systematic methodology for measuring the scope and domain of currencies today concludes: "Contrary to the popular impression of an emerging multipolarity in the global currency system . . . even now, decades after WWII, the greenback remains unique, a truly global money. . . . The euro lags behind considerably; also-rans like the yen, pound sterling, and Swiss franc are at best niche players; and the yuan is so far back in the race that it barely even registers as yet."[i] Looking forward, Oatley and his coauthors conclude that the United States is "firmly ensconced at the center of the global financial system," and there is little reason to expect this to change anytime soon: "The EU's struggles and China's lack of financial development and extant positive feedback effects interact to keep the United States at the center of the global financial system for the foreseeable future."[9]

Of course, American financial exposure is hardly all positive; instabilities associated with the global financial system have sometimes been extremely disruptive and costly in the past two decades. Yet reduced exposure to the global financial system would also have downsides, most notably higher borrowing costs (for both American firms and the US government) and reduced opportunities for US investors.[10] And given that the United States is already so open financially and also that this is unlikely to change, it is beneficial to

---

i. Benjamin Cohen and Tabitha Benney, "What Does the International Currency System Really Look Like?" *Review of International Political Economy*, Vol. 21 (2014), pp. 1014–1041. In his recent analysis of the dollar's role, Eric Helleiner reveals that it was unaffected by the 2008 crisis: "The dollar's share of all foreign exchange reserves, for example, declined only slightly from 64% at the start of the crisis to 62% by the end of 2012. In 2013, the dollar also continued to be used on one side of 87% of all foreign exchange transactions, a figure that was slightly higher than the 85.6% share in 2007. Between 2007 and 2010, there was also a slight increase in the dollar's share of all cross-border bank claims (from 41.9% to 43.7%) and international security issues outstanding (36% to 37.8%)." He underscores that the continuation of the dollar's international preeminence stems "in part from the broader structural power of the United States within the global political economy arising from factors such as its uniquely attractive financial markets, the dependence of foreigners on the United States as an export market, its geopolitical power, its veto power in the IMF, and foreigners' vulnerability to the 'dollar trap.'" Eric Helleiner, *The Status Quo Crisis: Global Financial Governance after the 2014 Meltdown* (New York: Oxford University Press, 2014), p. 90.

have the central role in the financial system because this provides a greater opportunity to design responses to crises as well as to promote global reforms that enhance long-term stability. America's financial centrality also results in a number of consequential long-term benefits, most notably those that flow from having the dollar as the key global currency (a point we discuss further below).

Foreign direct investment (FDI) deserves particular attention. The flow of outward FDI from the United States is the core mechanism that Robert Gilpin highlights as the basis of his argument that the US effort to promote an open global economic system after World War II would ultimately prove harmful to its long-term standing. In his 1975 book *US Power and the Multinational Corporation*, Gilpin stressed that multinational corporations (MNCs) cause the dispersion of advanced technologies and capital from the leading power, thereby allowing rising powers to catch up more quickly.[11] More specifically, he argued that the very high level of FDI outflow from the United States, in combination with a very low FDI inflow, would hasten American relative decline.

Things have greatly changed in the decades since. When Gilpin's book was written, the flow of FDI was largely one-way: out of the United States, with very little coming in. As we noted in chapter 3, the United States continues to be far and away the largest source of FDI: its stock of outward FDI stands at $6.35 trillion, a level more than three times greater than that of the next largest state, the United Kingdom.[12] But unlike during the era when Gilpin was writing, over the past twenty-five years the United States has also been the most popular host destination for inward FDI: from 1990 to 2013, 15.7% of all FDI flowed to America. As a result, the United States' accumulated stock of inward FDI is now huge—just shy of US$5 trillion, an amount more than three times as high as the next largest state, the United Kingdom. When Gilpin formulated his original argument in 1975, the United States FDI ratio was 4.5—that is, its outward FDI was 4.5 times greater than its inward FDI. In the present era, by comparison, the United States has a rough balance in terms of outward and inward FDI: its FDI ratio now stands at 1.29.

The massive presence of MNCs based in the United States produces a series of consequential economic benefits. Summarizing these benefits, a recent Commerce Department report concludes:

> In 2011, value-added by majority owned U.S. affiliates of foreign companies accounted for 4.7 percent of total U.S. private output. These firms employed 5.6 million people in the United States, or 4.1 percent

of private sector employment. These affiliates account for 9.6 percent of U.S. private investment and 15.9 percent of U.S. private research and development spending. . . . Compensation at U.S. affiliates has been consistently higher than the U.S. average over time, and the differential holds for both manufacturing and non-manufacturing jobs.[13]

An additional change since when Gilpin's argument was formulated concerns the role of outward FDI as a source of competitiveness for American firms. When Gilpin analyzed these issues, international production linkages within firms were very weak: foreign affiliates of MNCs tended to be miniature replications of their parent organizations in the home country. Since that time, many US MNCs have moved to extensively employ various new global production strategies designed to reap locational efficiencies. FDI has increasingly become a means for MNCs to access particular factors of production as part of a strategy for organizing production globally in the most efficient manner possible.[14] And US MNCs have been leaders in enhancing their competitiveness via these new global production strategies. Chinese firms, by contrast, have very little experience and skill in this area and have consequently only marginally benefitted in this regard.[15] As chapter 2 reviewed, US MNCs are dominant in far more sectors than those of any other country, and this is especially true in sectors at the technological frontier.

As US multinational corporations have increasingly dispersed their activities across borders, another consequence is that sales of US foreign affiliates have become the key means of serving foreign markets: "Sales through foreign affiliates are more than three times the size of American exports."[16] Furthermore, US foreign affiliates emerged as massive exporters of intermediate goods and components.[17] As Norrlof emphasizes, the very significant income generated by the sales and exporting activities of American foreign affiliates located abroad has significant positive consequences for the United States: "The income from foreign affiliates flows back to the United States as a matter of accounting practice. It shows up on current account as income from direct investment, regardless of whether profits are repatriated to the United States or not. American households, which hold between 80 to 90 percent of US equities, are the principle beneficiaries of the profits generated through the worldwide diffusion and integration of production."[18]

The fact that US foreign affiliates located in other countries are so economically vital in the various ways noted earlier means that the United States has a stake in the continued stability of the countries in which these investments are located. It is thus perhaps not surprising that FDI by US MNCs tends to be located in countries that have a strong security partnership with the United States. More than three quarters of the existing US FDI stock in the top thirty host countries (which collectively account for 85% of all US FDI) is located in states that are either an official ally of the United States or have a long-standing security partnership with Washington.

When we look across the realms of trade, finance, and production, the United States is clearly the most significant player in the global economic system. It consequently benefits greatly from the continued expansion and stability of economic globalization, especially given that, unlike in previous eras, it reaps major gains from FDI.

Macro-Level Structuring of Globalization

The United States also benefits because it has structured some of the long-term features of the global economy along lines that it prefers. Regarding trade, arguably the key constant American preference throughout the Cold War and after is that "global economic activity was to be organized on the basis of multilateralism and non-discrimination, rather than on the basis of exclusionary regional blocs."[19] And concerning global finance, two key constant American preferences are for the dollar to be the key global currency and for the United States to have the leading role in the core global institution that is most responsible for managing capital flows, the International Monetary Fund. Of course, the United States is not simply a status quo actor in the global economy; it has changed its approach to the global economy in various ways.[ii] The point simply is that the United States does have some key long-term preferences it wants to preserve. In turn, political scientists and historians agree that America's alliances with many of the other key economic players have helped it to succeed in this effort.[20]

Because much of what the United States wants from economic globalization is simply more of the same—a continuation of the basic structural arrangements that it established during the Cold War that serve it so

---

ii. Regarding trade, for example, Washington focused during the initial decades of the Cold War on creating an open market for goods, but during the 1970s and 1980s it shifted to carving out more exemptions for itself. In this later period, it also began to focus on pushing openness in the particular sectors, such as services, in which it was most competitive. Concerning the global financial system, the United States centered on maintaining the link between the dollar and gold during the initial decades of the Cold War, but this focus ended in 1971, and the United States later shifted to strongly emphasize reductions in the limits on global capital flows.

well—what is typically ideal from Washington's perspective is for allies and other countries to favor a status quo approach regarding the global economy without the need to directly employ any "blocking power" to produce this outcome. The IMF is an excellent example of this status quo disposition. Although all 188 member countries technically have voting power, the actual voting share is highly concentrated in the hands of the United States and its allies. All major IMF decisions are made by a twenty-four-person board of executive directors, and the United States, France, Germany, Japan, and the United Kingdom are the only states with permanent, individual seats. These G5 countries have immense control due to the particular nature of voting rules in the executive board, and among them, the United States has an especially strong ability to shape these decisions. In this regard, Keshav Poddar's recent comprehensive analysis of IMF loans during the post–Cold War era shows that "the United States exercises unique influence over IMF loan provision, and even in the extreme cases where American economic and strategic interests most dramatically diverge from those of the G5, its allies almost always reconcile to the US position." Overall, he maintains that the "IMF is an example of an international institution which, as currently structured, functions in a way that consistently produces outcomes favorable to American geopolitical interests, both in the short-term and the long-term. America's G5 allies consistently support its agenda in a wide variety of critical cases, and the structural power that the US derives from its de facto leadership of the IMF is therefore tremendously valuable."[21] Key in regarding loans is that US contributions to the fund "are matched more than four-fold by other states, a significant bargain for the United States."[22] What this means, as Randall Stone aptly concludes, is that the IMF functions as "an inexpensive form of foreign aid" for the United States.[23]

As it is, the IMF works well for the United States due to its current structure, and all Washington wants is for that to continue. Were the United States to retrench, it is unlikely that countries such as Germany, Japan, and France would continue to support US preferences regarding loans and other IMF policies as much as they have done historically, given that their economic interests do not always coincide with Washington's. Since the US preference is simply for these countries to continue doing what they have already been doing, the incentive is not to disrupt the existing set of relationships that sustain this status quo.

This same is true when we look beyond support from US allies in particular and consider how America's globally engaged security policy can generally help it to forward its preferred structure of economic globalization even without it engaging in any direct actions to produce this result. Arguably the most prominent example here concerns the benefits the United States receives due to the role of the dollar as the key global currency. Among these benefits is that "the United States gains substantially from valuation adjustments, reinforcing policy autonomy and the gains derived from asymmetry in the structure of borrowing and lending."[24] The key point is that, as Harold James stresses, at present "the dollar's position in the international system does not depend on explicit political pressure."[25]

That said, scholars identify three mechanisms by which the US geopolitical role helps to buttress the long-term role of the dollar. First, the work of a number of analysts forms the basis for the "geopolitical approach" to understanding the dollar's role; as Helleiner and Kirshner summarize it, this perspective stresses that the United States' global military role fosters a sense of greater financial security that bolsters the dollar's long-term status: "The enduring, indeed unprecedented, concentration of hard (military) power in the hands of, and the physical security of, the United States provides confidence in the endurance of the greenback unparalleled (and essentially unattainable) by any other issuer of international money."[26] Second, Kathleen McNamara argues that the US global military role bolsters the likelihood that the dollar will long continue to be the currency that actors converge upon as the " 'natural' dominant currency."[27] Third, Adam Posen emphasizes that because the United States helps to provide for European security, this makes it more likely that the euro countries will refrain from developing a true military global capacity and consequently that "the dollar will continue to benefit from the geopolitical sources of its global role" in ways that the euro countries will not match.[iii] Through these mechanisms, the

---

iii. Adam S. Posen, "Why the Euro Will Not Rival the Dollar," *International Finance*, Vol. 11, No. 1 (May 2008), p. 76. Posen underscores in this regard

the critical role that foreign policy and national security ties play in countries' decisions about exchange rate relationships. . . . Long-term holdings of US dollar assets by foreigners . . . are held for non-financial reasons, at least in part. . . . Other countries' reserve currency holdings and exchange rate management are importantly influenced by security ties, and thus decisions to link to the dollar (and to accumulate dollar reserves for intervention) from Taiwan to Saudi Arabia to Panama depend as much on foreign policy as economics. . . . The European Union, let alone the eurozone itself, is unable or unwilling to offer these systemic or security benefits beyond a very limited area, and thus is fundamentally limited in its ability to attract currency adherents, despite the success of the euro on its own terms as a currency and store of value. . . . Given the limited desire and ability of the eurozone members to project security relationships beyond their immediate neighborhood, there is little incentive for other countries around the world to

US military position in the system contributes to the dollar's status as the key global currency, although it is not the only or even the most important variable in this regard.[28]

Although in an ideal world the structure of the global economy that the United States prefers can be sustained without it having to directly employ any security leverage over its allies, it sometimes does so. The most significant example is the American effort to influence regional integration efforts in Asia during the post–Cold War period. The US was strikingly successful in heading off the emergence of exclusionary economic integration schemes in Asia during the 1990s and 2000s.[29]

Needless to say, not all US attempts to gain support for its conception of globalization by exercising security leverage over its allies are successful. Some analysts hold up the recent experience of the China-led Asian Infrastructure Investment Bank (AIIB) as an example of such a failed leverage attempt. It is true that numerous close US security allies, led by the United Kingdom, prominently disregarded calls from the Obama administration to refrain from joining the AIIB. Yet it is unclear whether the United States directly attempted to exploit allies' security dependence in its ill-fated campaign against the AIIB bank. It would appear the main story was simply China's enhanced economic influence, as evidence from London and other allied capitals indicated that reluctance to jeopardize lucrative deals with Beijing played a role in decisions to defy Washington.[iv] Moreover, there is no indication that the overall structure of the global economy that Washington favors was actually at stake in this case. In the eyes of many prominent analysts and former policymakers—including Fred Bergsten, Robert Zoellick, Madeline Albright, and Joseph Nye—the Obama administration's effort to oppose the AIIB was based on a mistaken premise that it was competitive, rather than

---

shift their pegging, formal but also informal, from the dollar to the euro. (Ibid., pp. 88, 80, 92)

See also Carla Norrlof, *America's Global Advantage: US Hegemony and International Cooperation* (Cambridge, UK: Cambridge University Press, 2010), p. 233.

iv. It should be noted that although China's growth clearly enhances its economic leverage, there are several mitigating factors. As chapter 2 showed, the United States' overall role in the global economy has not declined commensurate with China's rise. Rather, China's increased economic heft has been accompanied by a decline in the relative weight of Japan and the EU. The overall picture is thus more complicated than a simple "China rising, US declining" story. Rather, economically the United States remains remarkably central globally, in some ways looming even larger over its allies, but China's potential economic influence vis-à-vis US allies has grown dramatically.

complementary, with the World Bank.[30] Moreover, as Bergsten concludes, the AIIB is not likely to have "a big impact on global governance or the financial architecture" but is instead likely to have "global implications [that] are quite modest."[31] In this view, the Obama administration should not have tried to pressure its allies, many of whom clearly regarded AIIB as a regionally centered institution that was narrowly focused on infrastructure improvement (for which there is a massive need in Asia that existing institutions clearly cannot satisfy).[32] Had the AIIB actually been a significant threat to the existing global economic order, Washington likely would have been more successful in its lobbying efforts.

It is also clear that whatever leverage the United States attempted regarding the AIIB was compromised by Washington's failure to suggest an alternative. Leverage is likely to be more effective when the United States has a positive alternative to offer: "Do this instead" and not merely "Do not do that." The contrast between the AIIB and the Trans-Pacific Partnership (TPP) is illustrative here. Regarding the TPP, Washington eventually decided that rather than merely trying to block any unfavorable regional integration efforts in Asia, it would instead seek to forward a sweeping agreement for the region that reflected its political and economic priorities. And while Bergsten may go too far when he describes the TPP as "the most important trade agreement in world history in both economic and geopolitical terms," the scope of the agreement and its overall importance for the global economic order are clearly much greater than the AIIB.[33] Significantly, former administration officials stress in interviews that the willingness of allies, especially Japan, to pursue and support the TPP was intimately linked to their desire to strengthen security ties with the United States.[34]

Whether the AIIB case is a harbinger of the emergence of significant future challenges to the current structure of the global economy that run against Washington's interests is unclear. If this does happen, then America's globally engaged security policy is helpful for sustaining its conception of globalization because it serves as a hedge: it is like money in the bank that the United States is in a position to deploy if and when a significant challenge ever emerges and the United States needs to actively round up support from its allies to preserve the status quo.[35] In this vein, Norrlof emphasizes that "because so many countries rely on American security provision, governments are sometimes willing to go the extra mile with economic assistance and adjustments when the United States finds itself in economic trouble."[36]

The role of the US dollar is the most substantively important example of Norrlof's point. Analysts debate whether the dollar's role may soon become threatened.[37] If it does, the leverage flowing from America's globally engaged security policy can be used to put political pressure on its allies to support the dollar. In this regard, Harold James stresses that during the Cold War the United States did use the leverage associated with its security commitments to further the use of the dollar; as he concludes, the United States "instrumentalized security policy in order to persuade countries to hold dollar reserves."[v] In turn, he recognizes that, looking forward, the dollar's reign is likely to last much longer than it otherwise might because of the significant leverage America can employ as "the world's largest concentration of political and military might."[38] Similarly, Helleiner and Kirshner emphasize that "the fact that the United States is the overwhelmingly dominant geopolitical power in the world bodes well for the dollar's enduring international position. Indeed, the British showed how it was possible to bolster their currency's international standing through explicit political bargains with other states. If the United States chose to bolster the dollar's international position through negotiation and by putting pressure on foreign governments, it can draw on unparalleled power resources to do so."[39]

Micro-Level Structuring of Globalization

America's globally engaged security policy can be economically beneficial in a third respect: it can sometimes facilitate "micro-level structuring" of globalization. That is, the United States may secure better bargains during

---

v. Harold James, "The Enduring International Preeminence of the Dollar," in Eric Helleiner and Jonathan Kirshner, eds., *The Future of the Dollar* (Ithaca, N.Y.: Cornell University Press, 2009), p. 29. Exhaustive historical research by Francis Gavin provides strong backing for this assertion. He notes that to garner support of the dollar, "the United States often exerted enormous pressure on countries with payments surpluses to hold their dollars and limit their purchases of American gold. Sometimes incentives were offered. . . . In other cases, overt political pressure was used, as when the United States linked its continuing military presence to the Federal Republic of Germany's reserve management policies." Francis J. Gavin, *Gold, Dollars, and Power: The Politics of International Monetary Relations, 1958–1971* (Chapel Hill, N.C.: Duke University Press, 2004), pp. 30–31. Regarding Germany, Gavin argues that "by linking America's security policies to West Germany monetary cooperation, the United States essentially forced the FRG into accepting a pure dollar standard." Gavin, "Ideas, Power, and the Politics of America's International Monetary Policy during the 1960s," in Jonathan Kirshner, ed., *Monetary Orders* (Ithaca, N.Y.: Cornell University Press, 2002), p. 209. Gavin reports that "similar, less formal reserve management policies were made with other allies, most notably Japan." Ibid, pp. 196–197. See also the discussion of the linkage between US security policies and German support for the dollar in Hubert Zimmermann, *Money and Security: Troops, Monetary Policy, and West Germany's Relations with the United States and Britain, 1950–1971* (Cambridge, UK: Cambridge University Press, 2002), especially pp. 103, 107, 140, and 227.

particular negotiations on specific economic issues than it otherwise would if it did not play the same security role. Many current and former policymakers stress the significance of this leverage.[40] As a concrete example, we highlighted in a previous analysis the US efforts to shape the terms of the US-Korea Free Trade Agreement (KORUS)—which is far and away the United States' largest bilateral preferential trading agreement. As we noted, former American policymakers insist that the Korean desire to cement a stronger security relationship with the United States played an important role regarding both the initiation of the agreement and in allowing it to be successfully concluded on terms beneficial to the United States.[41]

In a subsequent article, Daniel Drezner challenged this conclusion: "If geopolitical favoritism mattered, then the free trade agreement between the United States and South Korea should contain terms that are appreciably more favorable to Washington than those contained in the South Korea-European Union free trade agreement, which was negotiated at the same time."[42] Drezner asserts this is not the case, arguing that the observed differences between the two agreements can be traced to differing economic priorities of the United States and the EU.

Both our previous examination and Drezner's were very preliminary, because they lacked any detailed empirical analysis of the agreements (his conclusions largely rest on one Korean analysis that compared the tariff rates of these two agreements).[43] To adequately compare the agreements, it is necessary to carefully pull them apart and examine all of their dimensions.[44] A recent systematic comparison that meets this standard ultimately finds that "in issues areas or sectors where the EU and US both placed similarly high priority, the United States garnered appreciably better terms on multiple significant issues."[45] This is despite the fact that, contra Drezner, the two agreements were not negotiated at the same time: the underlying terms of the KORUS were established before negotiations with the EU even began; the EU then explicitly set out to secure a deal with at least the same, and hopefully better, terms than Washington had negotiated. Despite this "parity" objective, and despite the fact that the EU is a more significant trading partner with Korea than the United States, EU negotiators ultimately failed to achieve nearly as favorable terms as their American counterparts.[46]

Securing KORUS on favorable terms was very valuable to the United States. An analysis of the agreement by Kozo Kiyota and Robert Stern concludes that the agreement could increase annual US GDP by up to $25 billion per year.[47] As Poddar recounts, the favorable terms the United States secured in KORUS were very concerning to a number of European producers as well as controversial among South Korean legislators and the public, resulting in popular protests. President Lee's strong support for these terms for KORUS also led to a significant reduction in his approval ratings. Notably, he was openly criticized by the main opposition Democratic Party as having given the United States substantial economic concessions in order to garner more assistance from the United States on national security issues.[48] Lee himself confirmed this understanding, underscoring in a 2009 press conference that he decided to make some concessions in KORUS in order to secure a stronger security relationship with the United States in the face of the threat from North Korea.[49]

KORUS shows clearly that the even during the post–Cold War era, the United States still sometimes can and does secure more favorable terms in economic negotiations due to its globally engaged security policy. This kind of microstructuring hardly happens all the time and is far from being the principal economic benefit of deep engagement. But if the United States were to pursue retrenchment, policymakers would ultimately be depriving themselves of the opportunity to benefit from this kind of security leverage in economic negotiations, some of which may well have significant implications for America's long-term economic prospects.

Exactly how often the United States secures better terms in specific economic negotiations due to its globally engaged security policy is impossible to judge. Of key importance in this regard is that the United States may obtain better economic bargains without having to explicitly remind states that they benefit from its security policy, in which case it is unlikely that we will directly see evidence of this dynamic.[50] As Joseph Nye underscores, this is, in fact, the ideal method by which America's security policy and economic negotiations are linked: "The linkage between economics and security is more effective as a strategic reminder in the backs of leaders' minds than as a short-term tactic."[51] Having to explicitly employ security leverage to extract economic concessions from other states is not attractive for many reasons; the United States would be wise to refrain from doing so to an excessive degree in future years to avoid having a draining effect on its legitimacy as the system leader.[52]

The United States is most likely to be tempted to deploy its security leverage in economic negotiations under two conditions: (1) negotiations are in process where the outcome is in doubt and the United States cares significantly about the result and (2) US policymakers assess that they have usable security leverage. Explicitly employing US security leverage is not very likely if the economic negotiations concern an issue of little importance and/or they are proceeding swimmingly or have little chance of reaching fruition.

Nor is such leverage very likely to be used if Washington assesses that it does not, in fact, have much ability to link its security policy to the ongoing negotiations because of the nature of its relationship with the other country (or countries) in question.

It is important to recognize that there may be little direct evidence of when the United States does directly employ security leverage, because the parties involved will likely not want this to be revealed. Michael Mastanduno concludes in this regard that "the United States and its international economic collaborators have engaged in a series of tacit political deals which preserve the special privileges of the United States."[53] For example, David Spiro builds a very convincing case that the United States and the Saudis reached a secret deal in the 1970s in which the United States would provide for Saudi security and the Saudis, in turn, would support the dollar.[54] However, Spiro was not able to secure direct confirmation that this deal was ever struck aside from an interview with a former ambassador which "confirmed that the United States promised Saudi Arabia a security umbrella in return for placement of Saudi capital in US coffers."[55] The bottom line is that it may not be until many decades later when all archives are released that a full array of direct evidence will be available of how the United States has directly exploited its globally engaged security policy during particular economic negotiations.

The archives are now sufficiently available regarding US policy toward its allies in the 1950s and 1960s for historians to document this kind of leverage in action. In particular, Francis Gavin shows in his exhaustive study of declassified documents that Washington actively used its military presence and security commitments to exert immense pressure during negotiations with Germany, Japan, and other allies to prod them to support various policies that helped the United States economically—notably by holding surplus dollars rather than converting them into gold, by increasing military procurements from American suppliers, and by offsetting the costs of US troops stationed overseas.[56]

Protecting the Global Order from Conflict

Deep engagement helps to keep the global order stable by reducing the likelihood of the kinds of conflicts that would greatly disrupt it. Retrenchment proponents have so far neglected the argument that we, Keohane, and others have advanced that by lowering the likelihood of conflict, US hegemonic leadership helps to promote and foster institutionalized cooperation.[57] But they do recognize the significance of economic globalization and appreciate that the United States greatly benefits from it; indeed, it is precisely for this reason that it is a misnomer to label these analysts as isolationists. What some of them question is the degree to which conflict would lead to long-term economic disruptions that would harm the United States. Specifically, on the basis of an extensive theoretical analysis and a careful case study of the experience of World War I, Gholz and Press stress that because markets are flexible, the United States would likely suffer little over the long-term from even a major war in Europe or Asia provided that the United States remained studiously neutral.[58]

Gholz's and Press's study is the most persuasive challenge yet to the claim that deep engagement benefits the United States by reducing the likelihood of conflict in key regions. It is especially revealing regarding the fact that wars are not merely costly but can also potentially provide economic opportunities for neutral countries. Yet there are four reasons to doubt their conclusion that the United States can step aside from its security presence in Europe and Asia without incurring economic risks. The first is that one of the key conditions they specify for a neutral country weathering a war relatively unscathed—that it is a major creditor with a large trade surplus—manifestly does not apply to the United States today.[vi]

Second, their conclusion that the United States would not suffer much economically from a war in Europe or Asia assumes that it could in fact stand aside and watch such a conflict without becoming concerned to the point that it eventually would get involved. Were this to happen after the United States had left a region, then even Gholz and Press recognize that the war would likely be very costly for the United States economically—undoubtedly more so than if the United States had never left in the first place.[59]

Third, their analysis does not factor in some of the key qualitative globalization shifts that have occurred since World War I that would make a war more economically costly for the United States. This deficiency clearly shows up with respect to their treatment of the globalization of finance, in which the focus of their analysis centers on the interest rates paid on international borrowing.[60] Yet this is only one element of the globalization of finance: the United States is

---

vi. At the time when they wrote their article, both conditions they identified for a neutral country weathering a major power war held for the United States, and they concluded that "the U.S. economy is ideally suited to adjust to foreign economic disruptions." Eugene Gholz and Daryl G. Press, "The Effects of Wars on Neutral Countries: Why It Doesn't Pay to Preserve the Peace," *Security Studies*, Vol. 10, No. 4 (Summer 2001), pp. 1–57, p. 3.

now globalized to a very substantial extent via other forms of global financial linkages, notably global currency trading, cross-border investments in stock markets, and linkages between financial institutions (both private and public) in forms other than borrowing. After the onset of two major global financial crises in a roughly ten-year period, it is evident that global financial markets are not very stable. A war in Asia or Europe could well spook the markets and lead to a financial crisis that would take a very long time to correct itself. And if this were to occur, the notion that the United States could somehow undertake policies to insulate itself from such a crisis is a chimera, given the degree to which the United States is strongly enmeshed within financial globalization.

Gholz and Press's portrayal of the globalization of production and trade suffers from the same problem. Their analysis of these elements of globalization is based on three notions: (1) the main way US firms serve global markets is through trade, (2) arms-length trade—that is, trade among unrelated firms—dominates global commerce, and (3) the one international production activity that MNCs engage in is FDI. Although all of these conditions held at the time their World War I case occurred, none of them hold today.[61] Regarding serving foreign markets, the sales of US MNC foreign affiliates now dwarf exports from the United States. Arms-length trade, in turn, no longer dominates global commerce as it did during the World War I period: much trade, perhaps as much as half, is now intra-firm (that is, it consists of transfers across borders within the confines of a single firm). Finally, international production activity is now about much more than simply FDI. FDI only reflects the globalization of production to a partial degree because MNCs engage in a variety of other production strategies that serve to disperse their production activities geographically, including international outsourcing and inter-firm alliances.[62]

Given these qualitative changes in the globalization of trade and production, what is the bottom line? Gholz and Press assume that there is a neat economic dividing line between the United States and other countries. In their World War I case the United States was in a position to safely produce goods on its territory and then ship them to war zones "over there." If a war erupted now in Europe or Asia, then the activities of US firms would be deeply enmeshed within the war zone itself due to intra-firm linkages with their foreign affiliates based there and through the various kinds of extra-firm linkages with other firms from the region. Of course, with enough effort, US firms eventually might be able to insulate themselves from the conflict, but the point is that this would be extremely costly and difficult. The challenging nature of this task is simply very different than it was a century ago. As

Stephen Kobrin underscores, we now live in a world where "unraveling the very complex networks of production would be considerably more costly and difficult" than was the case in the first part of the 20th century, when the costs of such a shift were "still marginal and incremental."[63]

Fourth, the Gholz and Press analysis can be questioned regarding its assumptions about the significance of short-term and long-term economic costs. They argue that while a war would likely have a very significant negative economic adjustment cost in the short term, over the long term the United States could do well. Yet it is easy to say that in the long term, things will be fine. Short-term economic shocks are still painful and still matter. Moreover, a short-term shock will not necessarily be easily overcome: it may produce a new long-term dynamic that results in foregone economic gains. If policymakers do not respond with appropriate policies after a war-induced short-term economic shock, then what might have been a short recession could easily become a very long one. Perhaps more importantly, Gholz and Press assume that the long-term prospects of economic globalization will not be affected by a war in Europe or Asia. But we have never had anything like the current structure of economic globalization, and it could potentially be ripped apart and be very hard to put back together after a conflict; this would be especially likely if the political foundations of economic globalization were compromised by the conflict or if firms that undertook a very costly effort to disentangle themselves from a war-prone region did not fully re-engage after the war or took a very long time to do so.[vii]

Ultimately, Gholz and Press make many valuable points and do help undercut the notion that wars are only costly economically, a position many analysts adopt. But, at best, they show that the economic costs of a war in Asia or Europe for the United States are simply not as high as one would expect if markets were less flexible. They do not undermine the notion that the onset of such a conflict would be very costly even to a studiously neutral United States today.

Guarding Against Economically Disruptive Oil Shocks in the Middle East

Beyond Asia and Europe, the US presence in the Middle East is also relevant to the stability of the international order. As Keohane emphasizes, access to

---

vii. MNCs might not quickly adjust after a major security shock—they might overreact and withdraw their production activities in a region to an excessive extent due to a loss in confidence in the safety of the international business environment there.

oil at stable prices is one of the core elements of the global order that the United States constructed after World War II.[64] US security commitments in the region aim to reduce the likelihood of disruptive oil-market shocks. This interest predated the United States' transition from oil exporter to major importer and, in the view of many analysts, will continue even in light of dramatically increased US production as a result of the shale revolution.[65] In an important study, Gholz and Press agree that the United States retains an interest in guarding against major oil shocks.[66] But they argue that the United States can and should retrench in the region by cutting back on its broader range of missions and focusing narrowly on "protecting the prize." From the perspective of deep engagement, guarding against oil market shocks is one benefit of its presence in the region on top of a suite of other security objectives—such as nonproliferation—that were delineated in chapter 6. For Gholz and Press, in contrast, the oil market stability interest is *the* chief purpose of US engagement in the region, and limiting its role to that one mission would allow the United States to end its security partnerships in the region and shift to an "over the horizon" military posture.

Their analysis of the Middle East makes many valuable points, but their overall conclusion—that the United States can pull back from the Middle East because oil markets can and will "successfully adapt"—underestimates the substantial economic risks such a move would incur. Throughout their theoretical and empirical analysis, Gholz and Press's focus is on the overall level of oil supply and not on oil prices, yet it is the latter that is crucial to economic growth. In their view, even a war- or crisis-induced oil price spike lasting as long as 1.5 years would still qualify as being a successful market adaptation provided that the oil supply readjusted within a few months.[67] Yet such a price surge is long enough to potentially cause a substantial disruption for the United States and the global economy, which is ultimately what matters. If the nature of the oil price change triggers a US recession and/or some kind of major disturbance in the global economy, then the fact that the oil supply might quickly readjust is scant comfort. Economists have found that oil price shocks have been a key cause of many US recessions over the past several decades, and some of these oil shocks in turn can be linked to wars.[68] Of key importance here is that wars, security tensions, and crises in the Middle East have the potential to have an outsized influence on oil prices beyond simply the effect that they have on the overall level of supply; panic and fear clearly do matter for oil prices.[69]

It is also important to bear in mind that even if oil markets were completely flexible and responsive, various scenarios might eventuate that would require the use of the United States military in response. Gholz and Press agree that at least two of these (reversing an effort at conquest and keeping the Strait of Hormuz open) could require the reintroduction of ground troops to the region—a costly scenario for a post-retrenchment United States.[70] Gholz and Press assume that US ground forces will always be able to achieve easy access to the region at will no matter what kind of security relationships Washington has and also that the bases it leaves behind will be adequately maintained. But as we discussed in chapter 5, there are strong reasons to doubt that the United States will be able to reestablish sufficient access to the bases it would need in the region after it has abandoned its security partnerships there; moreover, to be fully useful, the bases must be maintained by US personnel.

Conclusion

Theoretical logic and empirical evidence show that the United States derives many economic benefits from deep engagement. While this key finding is consistent with a new wave of scholarship on the economic implications of the United States' leading position and globally engaged grand strategy, its full import can only be appreciated when we examine the full range of interactions between the security and economic realms. Of course, many states besides the United States also gain economically from the economic order deep engagement supports. But four kinds of benefits discussed in this chapter add up to a particularly significant long-term positive economic flow for the United States. The cumulative loss to the United States over time if that flow were to be reduced is a critical weakness in the case for retrenchment.

11

Conclusion

TODAY'S GLOBAL ORDER reflects the unique position of the United States as the sole superpower that alone among states has the capability to sustain a worldwide network of alliances and organize major politico-military operations in multiple key regions. A rising tide of opinion emanating from universities, think tanks, government agencies, and foreign capitals claims that this key buttress of the strategic setting has eroded and is about to crumble, paving the way for a new order reflecting a transformed power relationship. More than any other factor—including Russia's new assertiveness in Europe and the Middle East—this narrative is driven by China's rise. Take China out of the picture, and it is doubtful that talk of a system-altering power shift would have reached anywhere near the proportions it assumed in the years after 2008.

In chapters 2 and 3 of this book we developed a set of concepts and measures tailored to understanding America's position in the system and the significance of China's rise. We found that the global strategic setting has moved from 1 + X—one superpower plus a number of great powers—to 1 + 1 + X, with the United States set to long remain the sole superpower followed by China as an emerging potential superpower that stands in a class by itself apart from great powers such as Russia and Japan. Its spectacular economic rise notwithstanding, China has a long way to go before it will be in a position to develop, let alone procure and be able to use effectively, the broad-spectrum military capabilities required to match or negate the United States' superpower position. Economic heft alone does not portend system change to the extent that it did in the middle of the last century. It is much harder today to translate raw economic output into other elements of state capability, especially military capacity: modern weapons systems and their associated infrastructure are orders of magnitude harder to develop and learn to use effectively than their mid-20th-century predecessors. The size of the US military advantage is also much bigger than the analogous gaps in previous eras. Moreover, China ultimately confronts a higher bar for peer competitor status than earlier challengers from a relatively lower position of indigenous technological capacity did. Put simply, this is not your grandfather's power transition.

The conceptual framework we developed in this book does not force us to downplay or exaggerate change, as we showed was the case with the popular concept of polarity, which fosters "either/or" debates about whether the system is unipolar, bipolar, or multipolar. The shift from 1 + X to 1 + 1 + X does not mean that the single superpower system is on the cusp of structural change or that the United States has fallen so far that it will be compelled to abandon its grand strategy. However, it does generate new pressures on the United States to face the tradeoffs inherent in its strategic choices.

The remaining chapters in the book focused on those choices. We established that there are three broad grand strategic options: concentrating on sustaining the globe-shaping deep engagement grand strategy the United States has pursued in various forms for seven decades; pursuing a more ambitious "deep engagement plus" approach that also places a premium on spreading US values and adds new missions as well as obligations; or beginning to seriously disengage strategically from the world via retrenchment. Our analysis revealed that the cost/benefit ratio for sustaining deep engagement is positive. The balance of what scholars know about the workings of international politics yields a strongly favorable verdict on sustaining deep engagement and high expected costs and risks of major strategic disengagement. Changing power relationships (notably increasing Chinese capability, augmented Russian military power, and declining relative capabilities of US allies) create strong incentives for reinforcing this fundamentally defensive global posture and strong incentives to avoid a more expansive "deep engagement plus" stance that assumes new foreign policy obligations or seeks revisions of the existing international system.

Deep Engagement and Nonstate Threats

In a world periodically gripped by fear of terrorism, deep engagement, with its focus on managing the rise of major states and sustaining state-based

alliances and interstate cooperation in the global economy and other do-
mains, may seem antiquated and beside the point, but it is anything but. As
we noted in the introduction, the grand strategy has been embedded in the
global status quo for so long that it often assumes a taken-for-granted quality. It is only by thinking carefully through the counterfactual about what
the world would be like without a deeply engaged United States that the
strategy's implications for nonstate challenges can be appreciated. By undertaking that task, this book has made clear that, far from being a distraction
from an earlier era, deep engagement is a crucial bulwark of counterterrorism strategy.

We have shown that the grand strategy yields a net gain in security that is
favorable to US national interests and a major increase in opportunities for
interstate cooperation. Both of these outcomes are hugely consequential for
addressing terrorism and other forms of nonstate violence. A more violent
and unstable interstate setting would arguably increase the incentives, opportunities, and capabilities of terrorist organizations. Even if the terrorist
challenge did not increase, the task of effectively addressing it would be im-
measurably harder and more complicated if the United States simultaneously
had to grapple with a much more challenging and threatening interstate strategic setting than the one it faces today. By helping to keep that world at bay,
deep engagement's security alliances are an important part of counterterrorism strategy. Moreover, the clear verdict of scholarship is that those alliances
enable far more, and far more efficient, intergovernmental cooperation in the
fight against terrorism than would occur in a less institutionalized setting
without a clear leading state.

The grand strategy would only contradict rather than complement the
struggle against terrorism if it could be shown to exacerbate terrorism or
cause terrorists to direct their attention to the United States. In chapter 8 we
demonstrated that this objection is unwarranted: there is no evidence that
deep engagement's forward-leaning military posture in Asia and Europe generates anti-US terrorism. And in the Persian Gulf deep engagement does not
require a major onshore military posture of the type most worrying to some
terrorism specialists. Moreover, because critics of deep engagement still wish
to retain the ability to undertake massive military interventions in the region
if necessary, the military postures they recommend do not diverge from deep
engagement as much as it may seem. There is no theoretical or empirical basis
for concluding that differences of this scale would affect the disposition of
actors like al-Qaeda and ISIS/ISIL toward the United States.

Potential Pitfalls

We assessed the strategic setting and used theory and evidence to adduce the optimal policy response. But we freely acknowledge that it is a lot easier for scholars to describe optimal strategies than for policymakers to implement them. While we cannot scrutinize every potential bump on the road from concept to practice, the analysis in the preceding pages addresses in depth the most salient ways in which deep engagement might go off the rails. One need look no further than Iraq to see that not all US efforts to shape the global environment are successful. In the preceding chapters we analyzed the many potential pitfalls that might befall the United States if it opts to sustain deep engagement. We found that critics of the grand strategy overstate most of these, but two stand out: temptation and escalation risk.

The possibility that pursuing a deeply engaged grand strategy will increase both the opportunity and the temptation to engage in military actions is arguably the number one argument in favor of retrenchment. We noted in chapter 8 that there are many indications that the US experience in Iraq and Afghanistan has lowered the likelihood of similar large-scale counterinsurgency and nation-building projects in the future. But that reticence may well not extend to US military actions below this level, such as those it conducted in Kosovo and Libya. Retrenchment proponents are right that the continued pursuit of deep engagement does make such operations more likely than if America retrenched. To be sure, under any grand strategy the United States would remain a powerful actor with the ability to use force in a wide variety of settings and thus a state others would still look to for help when things go wrong in various regions. A hypothetical post-retrenchment America would not only still have the capacity to intervene in far-flung regions of the world, but it would also still contain many people who care about the plight of others and would still be governed by leaders who are human beings with human flaws, human emotions, and the human propensity to make mistakes.

Though retrenchment would certainly not eliminate temptation risk, it would reduce it. All else being equal, it is easier to argue that an intervention is necessary for a grand strategy that features global leadership and a worldwide system of alliances than it would be for one that eschewed both. The increased temptation risk of deep engagement feeds directly into the challenge of determining the edge of the grand strategy's essential commitments, which we discussed in chapter 4. Some potential interventions or added missions may strike observers as being necessary to the strategy. Crucially missing in the debate so far have been clear criteria for distinguishing essential commitments from nonessential ones. Chapter 4 derived from the grand strategy's logic and the history of its execution just such criteria, and they would have excluded nation building in Iraq in 2003, just as they exclude various proposed expansions of security guarantees—for example, to Ukraine in 2016.

Put simply, if new missions put essential ones at risk, our findings say that the game is not worth the candle. Most potential new commitments or operations are outside the logic of deep engagement. This means that whether or not they succeed on their own terms (in saving lives, promoting democratization, thwarting humanitarian abuses, promoting stability, stemming refugee flows, or what have you), they will not change the calculus of deterrence and reassurance that lies at the heart of deep engagement. Perceived success in Kosovo did not solve all of NATO's problems; perceived failure in Libya did not ruin NATO or render it uncredible. The credibility of commitments to allies is not in question in every potential conflict involving non-allies in regions outside the core.

As we showed in chapter 5, the same focus on the conservative, status quo essence of deep engagement opens up paths for avoiding the second potential pitfall, escalation risk. It would truly be a "tragedy of great power politics" if American efforts to stabilize key regions actually generated more insecurity. But we showed that in each key region there are military postures that meet the test of buttressing the grand strategy and thus serving America's key interests without courting undue escalation risks or forfeiting opportunities to cooperate with key powers like Russia and China. We discussed in detail what such a posture would look like in East Asia—where the escalation risk is most significant—and also outlined the key features of a similar response in the generally more favorable strategic setting of Europe.

Of course, even if the United States is able to successfully make adjustments, the continuation of deep engagement will still produce frustrations and challenges. It is simply harder to implement the strategy than it was in the halcyon 1990s, requiring much greater attention to the classical great power issues of deterrence and the avoidance of conflict spirals. The 1990s featured a Russia in free fall, with its state institutions barely able to make coherent policy and a China in the very early stages of its rise. With all the other major powers as allies, it was easy for the United States to sustain its alliances as hedges and focus its attention elsewhere. The possibility that alliance commitments might get very expensive or that US force-posture decisions might spark dangers of escalation seemed distant. Indeed, in the case of NATO, the argument was that the alliance had to "go out of area" in search of global humanitarian missions or "go out of business." The United States now faces more acute trade-offs between the key defensive interests and missions that define deep engagement and additional, optional foreign policy aims it might like to pursue. Facing these trade-offs might call for wrenching decisions to limit military support for the democratic or other aspirations of some political communities whose plight Americans find sympathetic. All of these complications might prompt the thought that this global role has simply become too hard or frustrating; that pulling back would perhaps lead to a much simpler and manageable world, or at least a less exasperating one.

This objection is not wrong; it is just biased. It is biased by the fact that deep engagement is part of the status quo, and so it is natural to focus on the challenges it brings. And despite our best efforts, that bias against deep engagement infects this book. We have devoted immense efforts to discussing all the potential problems that lie between deep engagement in theory and its actual implementation. No such discussion occurs with respect to retrenchment: proponents of pulling back do not devote commensurate efforts to assessing in detail the pitfalls that might complicate the journey of their preferred strategy from the analyst's keyboard to implementation by leaders, diplomats, and soldiers in the real world. In part this is the natural result of the fact that deep engagement is part of the world we observe, and so all of its warts and scars are readily apparent. Retrenchment remains a pristine ideal, and it takes some imagination to work through the ways in which it might end up looking less attractive in reality than it does to an ever increasing number of analysts and policymakers as well as a large swath of the public.

The Devil We Know

Ultimately, the United States' globe-girdling grand strategy is the devil we know, and a world with a disengaged United States is the devil we don't know. Retrenchment would in essence entail a massive experiment: How would the world work without a globally engaged America? That raises a critical question: What are the things that proponents of disengagement must presume will go right in order for their recommended strategic posture to really be less costly and less risky than deep engagement? Retrenchment proponents do not answer in any detail. This silence is telling, for their most penetrating criticisms of deep engagement are not about the cost/benefit ratio of sustaining the grand strategy itself but are instead about the temptations of moving beyond it or responding to its challenges in a suboptimally escalatory manner. Any effort to pull back from the world would also present the United States with temptations and potential challenges of implementation; it is just harder to call them to mind because we have no relevant recent experience with this kind of foreign policy stance.

Disengagement faces the same key potential pitfall as deep engagement: the temptation to overdo it. Just as deep engagement courts pressure from those who push for Washington to do too much, disengagement courts pressure from those who might want to do too little. And just as there are deep traditions and attitudes within the American body politic that periodically push policies that lie outside deep engagement's logic, so too are there political forces and traditions that might push for policies outside the logic of the kind of strategic disengagement that retrenchment proponents advocate. Deep engagement's critics in the academy are not isolationists. They favor decoupling the United States' military commitments from Eurasia, but not pulling back from an embrace of economic globalization. But in the real world the political movement that might be attracted to retrenchment might not be so discriminating; the foreign policy pronouncements of Donald Trump on the campaign trail have made this evidently clear: on top of the same basic batch of new security policies that retrenchment proponents favor, he adds greatly augmented protectionism and immigration restrictions—which they have not advocated.

The bottom line is that there is ample evidence today of powerfully inward-looking attitudes and preferences in the American body politic, and it is not hard to imagine where they might want to push a United States that had opted to pull back from the world. And if the United States did dramatically pull back, fixing the resulting mess might get very expensive indeed. As we noted in chapter 7, once the United States sheds allies, access, and military infrastructure abroad and at home, the costs of re-engaging in some key region, should it become necessary, escalate dramatically. And should the United States pull back from seeking to manage the world economy, should it decide again as it did in the 1930s to try to wall itself off from the vicissitude of global commerce, the damage might not be reparable. If it could be repaired, it would likely take an extremely long time; consider that it was not until the 1970s that global trade flows exceeded the level that existed just prior to America's imposition of the Smoot-Hawley Tariff in 1930.

It is all too easy to think of other ways retrenchment might be taken in directions unforeseen by its advocates, but even if it were implemented perfectly, it rests on what many might see as optimistic assumptions about the robustness of the current, and largely favorable, global order. Most important are the expectations that any disruptions to the order from the shock of a

US pullback would be minor, borne mainly by others, and ultimately less costly to the United States than sustaining deep engagement. In other words, retrenchment proponents assume either that today's economic and institutional order does not need to be backstopped by US deep engagement or, to the degree that it does, that it is just not important enough to the United Stated to warrant the cost of a deeply engaged grand strategy.

This book has shown that the weight of scholarship casts strong doubt on those assumptions. Ending the US leadership role would put the institutional order—necessary for managing the global economy as well as other transnational issues—at risk. Withdrawing US security guarantees would raise security tensions in regions, potentially generating conflict that could harm US economic interests and ultimately its security as well. A newly insecure and leaderless world would be much more prone to nuclear proliferation. To their credit, a number of retrenchment proponents acknowledge these risks, just as we have acknowledged deep engagement's potential pitfalls. The chief response of these analysts is that these risks are most likely to be borne by other states, and so the costs they might impose on the United States are likely to be less than the costs of sustaining deep engagement.

To take that bet, one must believe that the United States is well insulated from potential disruptions abroad. This book shows that the odds on that bet are unfavorable across a range of issues. Retrenchment proponents discount some of these, like cooperation in international institutions, but they clearly agree that economic well-being is a basic US interest. And grand strategic retrenchment would be a wager on the proposition that economic globalization would not be disrupted by any regional security competition or war that emerged as a result of US withdrawal or that, if it is disrupted, US firms and investors can avoid being significantly harmed by any turbulence in the markets. Eugene Gholz and Daryl Press are the only retrenchment proponents who examine the global economy in any depth, and they have a noteworthy faith in economic globalization simultaneously being remarkably resilient and yet also highly adaptable. They argue that US firms and investors will be able to adapt, and that economic costs from any turbulence in the markets will be lower than the costs of deep engagement. Although they do not say why they expect this to be the case, they appear to presume cooperation on the global economy will continue relatively unhindered without a single leading state that can use alliance relationships to help broker favorable bargains. Finally, they predict that global oil markets will remain efficient and oil prices will always quickly stabilize if a conflict emerges in a major oil-producing region.

Retrenchment thus depends in some measure on a belief that markets are resilient in the face of major geopolitical shocks, or that if they are not and market failures erupt, the United States would either be able to safely ride out the storm or quickly reengage before any widespread damage to its interests occurred. In our view, such confidence is misplaced. The United States once had ample breathing room because it was largely insulated from what happened overseas, but this is no longer the case; as we showed in chapter 10, the United States is now not just deeply intertwined with the global economy but is far and away the most important player in this economic system.

This basic difference in assumptions about how well-insulated the United States can be from troubles abroad goes for international security as well as the global economy. Arguably the clearest difference in the arguments swirling around the choice between deep engagement and retrenchment concerns nuclear proliferation. Advocates of pulling back agree with us that there will be many more nuclear states if the United States disengages from the world, but they disagree with our assessment that this will be counterproductive for US interests. The reason is that arguments for retrenchment exude one or both of two kinds of "nuclear optimism": that nuclear spread will promote peace because states are rational and nuclear deterrence works reliably, or that the costs of any deterrence failure that might occur will be borne by others, not the United States.

We provided strong arguments and copious evidence against these optimistic assessments. As the number of nuclear states rises, so too does the risk of nuclear war and the risk of nuclear leakage to undeterrable nonstate actors. Decoupling the United States from its alliance commitments not only removes the security provision that arguably keeps a number of states from seeking nuclear weapons now; it vitiates the leverage the United States possesses for sanctions and other disincentives to would-be proliferators. And it is hard to be confident in the United States' ability to ride out a nuclear deterrence failure somewhere abroad. Even a "small" regional nuclear war would likely produce a crisis in the global economy and disrupt the global environment in various ways, among other downsides.

Time for the Grandest Strategic Experiment in History?

No book, certainly not this one, can pretend to be the last word on its subject. There remains a lot of work to be done to understand fully the shifts underway in the distribution of power and their implications for US grand strategy. The measures we used to try to capture the changing distribution of capabilities are comprehensive, but flaws remain. More research is crucial on issues such as technological capacity, as are better indicators of the organizational and institutional wellsprings of state capabilities. And additional work needs to be done to fine-tune our assessments of the costs and benefits of the core deep engagement grand strategy; in particular, more regionally focused research is needed that is directly geared to addressing the question of what would happen if America pulled back.

As we noted in the introduction, ours is an analysis conducted at the more general level of global power and grand strategy. We contend that this kind of study is necessary, especially as the United States confronts major questions about what role it should have in the world. But such a study cannot answer every question about what to do tomorrow in every region. It cannot yield the precise parameters of each weapon system or military plan. It does not divulge the specific terms Washington must seek in each key negotiation. What it does do is reach definitive answers to the questions we posed at the outset. The United States is and will long remain the only state that can choose a globally engaged grand strategy. It is not now nor will it soon be in such dire international straits as to warrant what would constitute the greatest grand strategic experiment in history: to abandon that strategy and see how the world works with a disengaged America. To make the case for such a gamble, we would need evidence that the current strategy cannot be sustained and that the United States' global position is in crisis. This book has demonstrated the opposite: America's global position remains firmly ensconced, the global order remains largely favorable, and the right choice is to sustain the deep engagement grand strategy that helped to produce and continues to sustain that order.

Notes

CHAPTER I

1. See Stephen M. Walt, "Alliance Formation and the World Balance of Power," *International Security*, Vol. 9, No. 4 (Spring 1985), pp. 3–43; John R. Oneal, "Measuring the Material Base of the East-West Balance of Power," *International Interactions*, Vol. 15, No. 2 (January 1989), pp. 177–196; and William C. Wohlforth, *The Elusive Balance: Power and Perceptions During the Cold War* (Ithaca, N.Y.: Cornell University Press, 1993).

2. Washington warned that America should have "as little political connection as possible" with foreign nations: "Europe has a set of primary interests, which to us have none, or a very remote relation. Hence she must be engaged in frequent controversies the causes of which are essentially foreign to our concerns. Hence, therefore, it must be unwise in us to implicate ourselves, by artificial ties, in the ordinary vicissitudes of her politics, or the ordinary combinations and collisions of her friendships or enmities." George Washington, "Farewell Address," September 1796.

3. We agree with Joseph Nye that "deep engagement" is the best descriptor of Cold War and post–Cold War US grand strategy. Joseph Nye, "East Asian Security: The Case for Deep Engagement," *Foreign Affairs*, Vol. 74, No. 4 (July/August 1995), pp. 90–102.

4. G. John Ikenberry, "America's Imperial Ambition," *Foreign Affairs*, Vol. 81, No. 5 (September/October 2002), pp. 44–60.

5. Stephen G. Brooks and William C. Wohlforth, *World Out of Balance: International Relations and the Challenge of American Primacy* (Princeton, N.J.: Princeton University Press, 2008).

6. Fareed Zakaria, *The Post-American World* (New York: W. W. Norton, 2009); Parag Khanna, *The Second World: How Emerging Powers Are Redefining Global Competition in the Twenty-First Century* (New York: Random House, 2009);

National Intelligence Council, *Global Trends 2025: A Transformed World* (Washington, D.C.: US Government Printing Office, 2008); Ian Bremmer, *Every Nation for Itself: Winners and Losers in a G-Zero World* (New York: Penguin, 2012); Charles Kupchan, *No One's World: The West, the Rising Rest, and the Coming Global Turn* (Oxford, 2012); and Amitav Acharya, *The End of American World Order* (New York: Polity, 2014).

7. On the frequency of the Germany-China analogy, see Steven M. Ward, "Status Immobility and Systemic Revisionism in Rising Great Powers," PhD dissertation, Georgetown University, 2012.

8. The most notable early call for retrenchment is Eugene Gholz, Daryl G. Press, and Harvey M. Sapolsky, "Come Home, America: The Strategy of Restraint in the Face of Temptation," *International Security*, Vol. 21, No. 4 (Spring 1997), pp. 5–48.

9. Barry R. Posen, *Restraint: A New Foundation for U.S. Grand Strategy* (Ithaca, N.Y.: Cornell University Press, 2014); Barry R. Posen, "The Case for Restraint," *American Interest*, Vol. 3, No. 1 (November/December 2007), pp. 7–17; Barry R. Posen, "A Grand Strategy of Restraint," in Michèle A. Flournoy and Shawn Brimley, eds., *Finding Our Way: Debating American Grand Strategy* (Washington, D.C.: Center for a New American Security, 2008), pp. 81–102; Barry R. Posen, "Stability and Change in U.S. Grand Strategy," *Orbis*, Vol. 51, No. 4 (October 2007), pp. 561–567; Barry R. Posen, testimony given before the Oversight and Investigations Subcommittee of the House Armed Services Committee, *A New U.S. Grand Strategy*, 110th Cong., 2d sess., July 15, 2008; Stephen M. Walt, *Taming American Power: The Global Response to U.S. Primacy* (New York: W. W. Norton, 2006); Stephen M. Walt, "In the National Interest: A Grand New Strategy for American Foreign Policy," *Boston Review*, Vol. 30, No. 1 (February/March 2005), http://bostonreview.net/BR30.1/walt.php; Stephen M. Walt, "A New Grand Strategy for the War on Terrorism," paper presented at the National Policy Forum on Terrorism, Security, and America's Purpose, Capitol Hilton Hotel, Washington, D.C., September 6–7, 2005; John J. Mearsheimer, "Imperial by Design," *National Interest*, No. 111 (January/February 2011), pp. 16–34; John J. Mearsheimer, "Pull Those Boots Off the Ground," *Newsweek*, December 31, 2008, http://www.newsweek.com/id/177380; John J. Mearsheimer and Stephen M. Walt, *The Israel Lobby and U.S. Foreign Policy* (New York: Farrar, Straus and Giroux, 2008); Eugene Gholz and Daryl G. Press, "The Effects of Wars on Neutral Countries: Why It Doesn't Pay to Preserve the Peace," *Security Studies*, Vol. 10, No. 4 (Summer 2001), pp. 1–57; Gholz, Press, and Sapolsky, "Come Home, America"; Eugene Gholz and Daryl Press, "Footprints in the Sand," *American Interest*, Vol. 5, No. 4 (March/April 2010), pp. 59–67; Eugene Gholz, Daryl G. Press, and Benjamin Valentino, "Time to Offshore Our Troops," *New York Times*, December 12, 2006; Eugene Gholz and Daryl G. Press, "Protecting 'The Prize': Oil and the U.S. National Interest," *Security Studies*, Vol. 19, No. 3 (August 2010), pp. 453–485; Benjamin H. Friedman, Eugene Gholz, Daryl G. Press, and Harvey Sapolsky, "Restraining Order: For Strategic Modesty," *World Affairs*, Fall

2009, pp. 84–94; Paul K. MacDonald and Joseph M. Parent, "Graceful Decline? The Surprising Success of Great Power Retrenchment," *International Security*, Vol. 35, No. 4 (Spring 2011), pp. 7–44; Christopher A. Preble, *Power Problem: How American Military Dominance Makes Us Less Safe, Less Prosperous, and Less Free* (Ithaca, N.Y.: Cornell University Press, 2009); Christopher Layne, "America's Middle East Strategy after Iraq: The Moment for Offshore Balancing Has Arrived," *Review of International Studies*, Vol. 35, No. 1 (January 2009), pp. 5–25; Charles V. Peña, "A Smaller Military to Fight the War on Terror," *Orbis*, Vol. 50, No. 2 (Spring 2006), pp. 289–306; Christopher Layne, *The Peace of Illusions: American Grand Strategy from 1940 to the Present* (Ithaca, N.Y.: Cornell University Press, 2006); Christopher Layne, "Offshore Balancing Revisited," *Washington Quarterly*, Vol. 25, No. 2 (Spring 2002), pp. 233–48; Christopher Layne, "From Preponderance to Offshore Balancing: America's Future Grand Strategy," *International Security*, Vol. 22, No. 1 (Summer 1997), pp. 86–124; Christopher Layne, "Less Is More: Minimal Realism in East Asia," *National Interest*, No. 43 (Spring 1996), pp. 64–77; Benjamin Schwarz and Christopher Layne, "A New Grand Strategy," *Atlantic Monthly*, January 2002, pp. 36–42; Richard K. Betts, *American Force: Dangers, Delusions, and Dilemmas in National Security* (New York: Columbia University Press, 2012); Robert A. Pape, "It's the Occupation, Stupid," *Foreign Policy*, October 18, 2010, http://www.foreignpolicy.com/articles/2010/10/18/it_s_the_occupation_stupid; Robert A. Pape, "Empire Falls," *National Interest*, No. 99 (January/February 2009), pp. 21–34; Robert A. Pape and James K. Feldman, *Cutting the Fuse: The Explosion of Global Suicide Terrorism and How to Stop It* (Chicago: University of Chicago Press, 2010); and Robert A. Pape, *Dying to Win: The Strategic Logic of Suicide Terrorism* (New York: Random House, 2005).

10. For example, Tom Coburn advocated reducing the number of US personnel stationed in Asia and Europe by one-third, which he posits will save $69.5 billion over ten years. Elisabeth Bumiller and Thom Shanker, "Panetta to Offer Strategy for Cutting Military Budget," *New York Times*, January 2, 2012.

11. For example, former US representative Barney Frank recently maintained, "The reality of America's tough budgetary outlook leads me to insist that our wealthy Asian and European allies stop essentially free riding on American taxpayers. . . . Maintaining in Asia and Europe the military capability necessary to counter the Chinese and Russian threats should not remain almost exclusively America's responsibility—as it now effectively is. . . . Our NATO allies should be given a clear deadline. . . . Three years from now is plenty of time for the Europeans to become militarily self-sufficient—i.e., for them to learn to do without us." Barney Frank, "It's Time to Rearm Germany and Japan," *Politico*, October 21, 2015, available at http://www.politico.com/magazine/story/2015/10/its-time-to-rearm-germany-and-japan-213279#ixzz3pjHByi1I. In another example, Representative Jared Polis (a liberal Colorado Democrat) argued on the House floor in 2012: "At a time when we must seriously consider cuts to our budget and balancing our budget,

we should not continue to subsidize the defense of wealthy European nations against a Soviet threat that ceased to exist two decades ago." Quoted in Emmarie Huetteman, "Despite Cuts, U.S. Army Prepares for Threats in Europe," *New York Times*, October 18, 2015, available at http://www.nytimes.com/2015/10/19/world/europe/despite-cuts-us-army-readies-for-threats-in-europe.html?_r=1.

12. Pew Research Center, "Public Sees U.S. Power Declining as Support for Global Engagement Slips." *America's Place in the World 2013* (Washington, D.C.: Pew Research Center, December 2013), http://www.people-press.org/2013/12/03/public-sees-u-s-power-declining-as-support-for-global-engagement-slips/.

13. Ibid.

14. Pew Research Center, "In Shift from Bush Era, More Conservatives Say 'Come Home, America,'" (Washington, D.C.: Pew Research Center, June 2011), http://pewresearch.org/pubs/2027/foreign-policy-conservative-republicans-isolationism-afghanistan-libya?utm_source=feedburner&utm_medium=-feed&utm_campaign=Feed%3A+pewresearch%2Fall+%28PewResearch.org+%7C+All,+Feeds%29.

15. Randall L. Schweller, *Maxwell's Demon and the Golden Apple: Global Discord in the New Millennium* (Baltimore, M.D.: Johns Hopkins University Press, 2014), p. 8.

16. Pew Research Center, "In Shift from Bush Era, More Conservatives Say 'Come Home, America.'"

17. "Remarks by the President at the United States Military Academy Commencement Ceremony," speech given at West Point, New York, May 28, 2014, http://www.whitehouse.gov/the-press-office/2014/05/28/remarks-president-united-states-military-academy-commencement-ceremony.

18. Hillary Clinton, "America's Pacific Century," *Foreign Policy*, October 2011, available at: http://foreignpolicy.com/2011/10/11/americas-pacific-century/.

19. Most retrenchment proponents do not have any direct analysis of the potential benefits of deep engagement associated with economic globalization or international institutions; see, for example, Posen, *Restraint*; Layne, "From Preponderance to Offshore Balancing"; Pape, "Empire Falls"; and Mearsheimer, "Imperial by Design." With respect to liberal institutions, their direct criticisms of the current grand strategy almost always center specifically on democracy promotion efforts; see, for example, Posen, "Stability and Change in U.S. Grand Strategy." Perhaps reflecting the underlying realist perspective, which devalues the overall significance of institutions, these analysts have relatively little to say directly about why the United States should refrain from taking efforts to foster the set of international institutions that comprise the current order; hence, their criticism of this element of the current US grand strategy is largely implicit. Regarding the significance of the economic benefits that may flow from deep engagement, Gholz and Press are notable outliers within this literature, since they do carefully address some of the key issues at stake; that being said, they explicitly critique

their relevance; see Gholz and Press, "The Effects of Wars on Neutral Countries"; and Gholz and Press, "Protecting 'The Prize.'"

CHAPTER 2

1. See Jacek Kugler and Marina Arbetman, "Choosing Among Measures of Power: A Review of the Empirical Record," in Richard J. Stoll and Michael D. Ward, eds., *Power in World Politics* (Boulder, Colo.: Lynne Rienner, 1989).

2. Stephen G. Brooks and William C. Wohlforth, *World Out of Balance: International Relations and the Challenge of American Primacy* (Princeton, N.J.: Princeton University Press, 2008), pp. 12–13, 27–35, 40–44; Stephen G. Brooks and William C. Wohlforth, "American Primacy in Perspective," *Foreign Affairs*, Vol. 81, No. 4 (July/August 2002), pp. 21–23; William C. Wohlforth, "The Stability of a Unipolar World," *International Security*, Vol. 24, No. 1 (Summer 1999), pp. 10–18; Wohlforth, "Measuring Power—and the Power of Theories," in John A. Vasquez and Colin Elman, eds., *Realism and the Balancing of Power: A New Debate* (Englewood Cliffs, N.J.: Prentice-Hall, 2002); and William C. Wohlforth, "How Not to Evaluate Theories," *International Studies Quarterly* (March 2012), p. 219–222.

3. Ashley J. Tellis, Janice Bially, Christopher Layne, and Melissa McPherson, *Measuring National Power in the Postindustrial Age* (Santa Monica, Calif.: RAND, 2000).

4. Brooks and Wohlforth, *World Out of Balance*, p. 29.

5. See Richard Bitzinger, Michael Raska, Collin Koh Swee Lean, and Kelvin Wong Ka Weng, "Locating China's Place in the Global Defense Economy," in Tai Ming Cheung, ed., *Forging China's Military Might: A New Framework for Assessing Innovation* (Baltimore: Johns Hopkins University Press, 2014), p. 202.

6. Charles Glaser, "Why Unipolarity Doesn't Matter (Much)," *Cambridge Review of International Affairs*, Vol. 24, No. 2 (2011), p. 135, footnote 4; Barry Posen, "From Unipolarity to Multipolarity: Transition in Sight?" in G. John Ikenberry, Michael Mastanduno, and William Wohlforth, eds., *International Relations Theory and the Consequences of Unipolarity* (New York: Cambridge University Press, 2012), p. 320.

7. Brooks and Wohlforth, "American Primacy in Perspective," p. 22; see also the discussion in Wohlforth, "The Stability of a Unipolar World," p. 18.

8. A notable example in this regard concerns nuclear attack submarines (SSNs): Chinese SSNs are relatively noisy, whereas US SSNs have "already reached absolute levels of silencing." Owen Cote, "Assessing the Undersea Balance between the U.S. and China" (MIT SSP Working Paper, February 2011), p. 28, available at: http://web.mit.edu/ssp/publications/working_papers/Undersea%20Balance%20WP11-1.pdf. See also the discussion in Ronald O'Rourke, "China Naval Modernization: Implications for U.S. Navy Capabilities: Background and Issues for Congress," Congressional Research Service Report, June 1, 2015, pp. 11–12.

9. David Wertime, "It's Official: China Is Becoming a New Innovation Powerhouse," *Foreign Policy*, February 6, 2014, available at: http://www.foreignpolicy.com/articles/2014/02/06/its_official_china_is_becoming_a_new_innovation_powerhouse.

10. This is something we failed to do in the past. We previously used eight measures of technological capacity, and, in so doing, we mixed together measures of technological outputs with measures of technological inputs; see Brooks and Wohlforth, *World Out of Balance*, p. 33, Table 2.3.

11. Wertime, "It's Official," p. 1.

12. MNC efforts to "slice up the value chain" through a greater intra-firm international division of the production process as well as via a higher reliance on international outsourcing have been very significant in technological industries for two reasons: (1) these are industries that "involve production stages—design, component, production, final assembly—that are physically separable," and (2) "the production stages exhibit different factor intensities," which gives firms strong incentives to exploit differences in factor costs across countries." Gordon Hanson, Raymond Mataloni, and Mathew Slaughter, "Expansion Strategies of U.S. Multinational Firms" (NBER Working Paper no. 8433, 2001), p. 20. For a general overview of these new MNC production strategies, see Stephen G. Brooks, *Producing Security: Multinational Corporations, Globalization, and the Changing Calculus of Conflict* (Princeton, N.J.: Princeton University Press, 2005), ch. 2.

13. Organisation for Economic Co-operation and Development, *China in Focus: Lessons and Challenges* (Paris: OECD, 2002), p. 73.

14. Organisation for Economic Co-operation and Development, Directorate for Science, Technology and Innovation, *OECD Science, Technology and Industry Outlook 2014* (Paris, November 2014), available at http://www.oecd.org/sti/oecd-science-technology-and-industry-outlook-19991428.htm.

15. United Nations University International Human Dimensions Programme on Global Environmental Change and United Nations Environment Programme, *Inclusive Wealth Report 2012: Measuring Progress toward Sustainability* (Cambridge, UK: Cambridge University Press, 2012), p. 16.

16. National Science Foundation, "R&D: National Trends and Comparisons," *Science and Engineering Indicators 2012*, chapter 4, p. 3, available at: http://www.nsf.gov/statistics/seind12/c4/c4s8.htm.

17. This ICT infrastructure index provides an overall country score on a 0–100 scale on the basis of combined performance: (a) five measures of ICT access, (b) three measures of ICT use, (c) an index that measures the government's online services, and (d) the UN's e-participation index. This ICT infrastructure index also ranks the 142 examined countries on this dimension. For a full description of the ICT index, see Cornell, INSEAD, and World Intellectual Property Organization, *The Global Innovation Index 2013*, p. 368, available at: http://www.globalinnovationindex.org/content.aspx?page=gii-full-report-2013#pdfopener.

18. Daniele Archibugi, Mario Denni, and Andrea Filippetti, "The Technological Capabilities of Nations: The State of the Art of Synthetic Indicators," *Technological Forecasting and Social Change*, Vol. 76, No. 7 (September 2009), pp. 917–931.

19. Susan Strange, "What Is Economic Power, and Who Has It?" *International Journal*, Vol. 30 (1975), pp. 207–224.

20. See the discussion in Brooks and Wohlforth, *World Out of Balance*, pp. 40–42. See also William C. Wohlforth, "How Not to Evaluate Theories," *International Studies Quarterly*, Vol. 56, No. 2 (March 2012), p. 219, which quotes an IMF official as stressing that "the IMF considers that GDP in PPP terms is not the most appropriate measure for comparing the relative size of countries to the global economy, because PPP price levels are influenced by non-traded services, which are more relevant domestically than globally. The fund believes that GDP at market rates is a more relevant comparison."

21. These percentages differ from Table 2.6 above because for a time series one has to choose a single base year for the exchange rate conversion.

22. See, for example, Barry Eichengreen, Donghyun Park, and Kwanho Shin, "Growth Slowdowns Redux: New Evidence on the Middle-Income Trap" (NBER Working Paper No. 18673, January 2013), available at: http://www.nber.org/papers/w18673, and Homi Kharas and Harinder Kohli, "What Is the Middle Income Trap, Why Do Countries Fall into It, and How Can It Be Avoided?" *Global Journal of Emerging Market Economies*, Vol. 3, No. 3 (2011), pp. 281–289.

23. World Bank and Development Research Center of the State Council, the People's Republic of China, *China 2030: Building a Modern, Harmonious, and Creative Society* (Washington, D.C.: World Bank, 2013), p. 12.

24. See, for example, Eichengreen, Park, and Shin, "Growth Slowdowns Redux," and Barry Eichengreen, Donghyun Park, and Kwanho Shin, "When Fast-Growing Economies Slow Down: International Evidence and Implications for China," *Asian Economic Papers*, Vol. 11, No. 1 (2012), pp. 42–87.

25. Dollar emphasizes that there "are three factors at work here. First, there are diminishing returns to capital so that $1,000 of investment does not have as much growth impact as it did previously. Second, in a market economy, agents respond to that by investing less (the empirical tendency for the investment rate to fall). Third, these economies benefited from opportunities to borrow more advanced technology from developed economies. As development proceeds, those catch-up opportunities are inevitably reduced." David Dollar, "China's Rebalancing: Lessons from East Asian Economic History" (Brooking Institution Working Paper, October 2013, pp. 11–12), available at: http://www.brookings.edu/research/papers/2013/10/02-china-economic-lessons-dollar.

26. Lant Pritchett and Lawrence Summers, "Asiaphoria Meets Regression to the Mean" (NBER Working Paper No. 20573, October 2014), available at: http://www.nber.org/papers/w20573.

27. Jamil Anderlini, "Justin Lin Criticises China Growth Pessimists," *Financial Times*, July 29, 2013, available at: http://www.ft.com/intl/cms/s/0/3e62c9de-f83e-11e2-b4c4-00144feabdc0.html#axzz3MkxsfC7j.

28. World Bank and Development Research Center of the State Council, the People's Republic of China, *China 2030*, p. 9.

29. In its comprehensive recent report on China' economic future, the World Bank outlines a series of domestic reforms that the Chinese government should undertake to shift the country's structure to make it conducive to attaining high-income status, including: reforming and restructuring state-owned enterprises and banks; developing the private sector; promoting competition; deepening reforms in land, labor, and financial markets; adopting new policies regarding environmental protection; encouraging firms to engage in product and process innovation through their R&D and by participating in global R&D networks; promoting social security for all Chinese citizens; and ensuring local governments have adequate financing to meet their rising responsibilities. The World Bank and Development Research Center of the State Council, the People's Republic of China, *China 2030*. David Dollar outlines a somewhat different list of needed reforms: state-enterprise reform; a rebalancing of the economy away from investment and exports and toward consumption; increased public expenditure on health and education; "changes in the system of inter-governmental finances that ensure that local governments have the revenue that they need to provide the required services"; opening up to more foreign investment, especially in the service sector; reforms of the *hukuo* system of residency registration, which limits rural-urban migration; inducing greater household consumption; and changing the incentives for local governments to make them more likely to, and capable of, implementing needed reforms. Dollar, "China's Rebalancing," pp. 22–24.

30. In this regard, Jackson and Howe explain that "demographic aging is about as close as social science ever comes to a certain forecast. Every demographer agrees that it is happening and that, absent a global catastrophe—a colliding comet or a deadly super virus—it will continue to gather momentum." Richard Jackson and Neil Howe, *The Graying of the Great Powers: Demography and Geopolitics in the 21st Century* (Washington, D.C.: CSIS, 2008), p. 3.

31. Nicholas Eberstadt, "Asia-Pacific Demographics in 2010–2040: Implications for Strategic Balance," in Ashley Tellis, Andrew Marble, and Travis Tanner, eds., *Asia's Rising Power and America's Continued Purpose* (Seattle: National Bureau of Asian Research, 2010), p. 248.

32. Fang Cai, "The Coming Demographic Impact on China's Growth: The Age Factor in the Middle-Income Trap," *Asian Economic Papers*, Vol. 11, No. 1 (2012), pp. 95–111.

33. World Bank and Development Research Center of the State Council, the People's Republic of China, *China 2030*, p. 16. Eberstadt emphasizes that by 2040 "China's projected population of senior citizens 65 years and older would be far higher than

that of the United States or Europe today—indeed, possibly higher than any level yet recorded for a national population." Eberstadt, "Asia-Pacific Demographics," p. 246.

34. A notable recent pessimistic assessment about US economic growth prospects is Lawrence Summers, "U.S. Economic Prospects: Secular Stagnation, Hysteresis, and the Zero Lower Bound," *Business Economics*, Vol. 49, No. 2 (2014), pp. 65–73.

35. See, for example, Jackson and Howe, *Graying of the Great Powers*; Mark Haas, "A Geriatric Peace? The Future of U.S. Power in a World of Aging Populations," *International Security*, Vol. 32, No. 1, pp. 112–147; Martin C. Libicki, Howard J. Shatz, and Julie E. Taylor, *Global Demographic Change and Its Implications for Military Power* (Santa Monica, Calif.: RAND, 2011); Susan Yoshihara and Douglas A. Syva, eds., *Population Decline and the Remaking of Great Power Politics* (Washington, D.C.: Potomac, 2012); Jennifer Dabbs Sciubba, *The Future Faces of War: Population and National Security* (Santa Barbara, Calif.: Praeger, 2011); Wenke Apt, *Germany's New Security Demographics: Military Recruitment in the Era of Population Aging* (Dordrecht, Netherlands: Springer, 2014).

36. Diane Coyle, *GDP: A Brief but Affectionate History* (Princeton, N.J.: Princeton University Press, 2014), p. 121.

37. Ibid., p. 122.

38. Joseph E. Stiglitz, Amartya Sen, and Jean-Paul Fitoussi, *Report by the Commission on the Measurement of Economic Performance and Social Progress*, 2009, available at: http://www.insee.fr/fr/publications-et-services/dossiers_web/stiglitz/doc-commission/RAPPORT_anglais.pdf. See also, for example, United Nations University International Human Dimensions Programme on Global Environmental Change and United Nations Environment Programme, *Inclusive Wealth Report 2012*.

39. Michael Mandel, "Beyond Goods and Services: The (Unmeasured) Rise of the Data-Driven Economy," Progressive Policy Institute, October 2012, p. 2, available at: http://www.progressivepolicy.org/wp-content/uploads/2012/10/10.2012-Mandel_Beyond-Goods-and-Services_The-Unmeasured-Rise-of-the-Data-Driven-Economy.pdf.

40. Erik Brynjolfsson and Adam Saunders, "What the GDP Gets Wrong (Why Managers Should Care)," *MIT Sloan Management Review*, Vol. 51, No. 1 (Fall 2009), pp. 95–96.

41. Mandel, "Beyond Goods and Services," p. 2.

42. As quoted in Zachary Karabell, *The Leading Indicators: A Short History of the Numbers that Rule our World* (New York: Simon and Schuster, 2014), p. 223.

43. Organisation for Economic Co-operation and Development and World Trade Organization, "Trade in Value-Added: Concepts, Methodologies and Challenges," p. 1, available at: http://www.oecd.org/sti/ind/49894138.pdf.

44. Karabell, *The Leading Indicators*, p. 166.

45. World Trade Organization, "Globalization of Industrial Production Chains and Measurement of Trade in Value Added," October 2010, p. 3, available at: https://

www.wto.org/english/forums_e/public_forum11_e/globalization_industrial_
production.pdf.

46. Kenneth L. Kraemer, Greg Linden, and Jason Dedrick, "Capturing Value in
    Global Networks: Apple's iPad and iPhone," July 2011, pp. 2, 6, available at: http://
    pcic.merage.uci.edu/papers/2011/value_ipad_iphone.pdf.

47. Sean Starrs, "American Economic Power Hasn't Declined—It Globalized!
    Summoning the Data and Taking Globalization Seriously," *International Studies
    Quarterly*, Vol. 57 (December 2013), p. 817.

48. For a detailed discussion of why MNCs geographically disperse their production
    activities, see Brooks, *Producing Security*, ch. 2.

49. Starrs, "American Economic Power," p. 820.

50. Organisation for Economic Co-operation and Development, *China in Focus*,
    pp. 76–77.

51. Starrs, "American Economic Power," p. 824.

52. Ibid., p. 824.

53. Ibid., p. 825.

54. Zachary Karabell, "(Mis)leading Indicators: Why Our Economic Numbers
    Distort Reality," *Foreign Affairs*, Vol. 93, No. 2 (March/April 2014), pp. 90–101.

55. Joseph Kahn and Jim Yardley, "As China Roars, Pollution Reaches Deadly
    Extremes," *New York Times*, August 26, 2007, available at: http://www.nytimes.
    com/2007/08/26/world/asia/26china.html?pagewanted=all&_r=0.

56. 2014 Environmental Performance Index, available at: https://issuu.com/yaleepi/
    docs/2014_epi_report (consulted March 22, 2014).

57. Kahn and Yardley, "As China Roars."

58. "Pollution Costs Equal 10% of China's GDP," *China Daily*, June 6, 2006, available
    at: http://www.chinadaily.com.cn/china/2006-06/06/content_609350.htm.

59. "A Great Wall of Waste," *Economist*, August 19, 2004, available at: http://www.
    economist.com/node/3104453.

60. World Bank and State Environmental Protection Administration of China, *Cost
    of Pollution in China: Economic Estimates of Physical Damages* (Washington,
    D.C.: World Bank, 2007), p. xvii, available at: http://siteresources.worldbank.
    org/INTEAPREGTOPENVIRONMENT/Resources/China_Cost_of_
    Pollution.pdf.

61. United Nations University International Human Dimensions Programme on
    Global Environmental Change and United Nations Environment Programme,
    Inclusive Wealth Report 2014: Measuring Progress toward Sustainability
    (Cambridge, UK: Cambridge University Pres, 2014), p. 15.

62. Economist, "The Real Wealth of Nations: A New Report Comes Up with a Better
    Way to Size Up Wealth," *Economist*, June 30, 2012. It notes further that GDP "is
    a measure of income, not wealth. It values a flow of goods and services, not a stock
    of assets. . . . Happily, the United Nations this month published balance-sheets
    for 20 nations [that] included . . . [the] stock of natural, human, and physical

assets. . . . By putting a dollar value on everything from bauxite to brainpower, the UN's exercise makes all three kinds of capital comparable and commensurable."

63. This quote is drawn from a description of the merits of the inclusive wealth measure presented at http://inclusivewealthindex.org/inclusive-wealth/#the-better-indicator. See also the discussion in United Nations University International Human Dimensions Programme on Global Environmental Change and United Nations Environment Programme, *Inclusive Wealth Report 2014*.

64. United Nations University International Human Dimensions Programme on Global Environmental Change and United Nations Environment Programme, *Inclusive Wealth Report 2014*, pp. 220, 226.

65. We thank Jonathan Markowitz for a series of helpful conversations on this issue.

CHAPTER 3

1. Tai Ming Cheung, "Modernizing the People's Liberation Army: Aims and Implications," *Handbook of China's International Relations*, 2010, p. 115.

2. Barry Posen, "Command of the Commons: The Military Foundation of U.S. Hegemony," *International Security*, Vol. 28, No. 1 (Summer 2003), pp. 5–46.

3. Ibid., p. 10.

4. Gary Gereffi, Vivek Wadhwa, Ben Rissing, and Ryan Ong, "Getting the Numbers Right: International Engineering Education in the United States, China, and India," *Journal of Engineering Education*, Vol. 97, No. 1 (January 2008), p. 19.

5. Gary Gereffi, Vivek Wadhwa, Ben Rissing, and Ryan Ong, "Where the Engineers Are," *Issues in Science and Technology*, Spring 2007, p. 74. They underscore (p. 75) that "only a few elite universities, such as Tsinghua and Fudan, had been allowed to lower enrollment rates after they noted serious quality problems as a result of increases they had made. The vast majority of Chinese universities complied with government directives to increase enrollment."

6. World Bank and Development Research Center of the State Council, the People's Republic of China, *China 2030: Building a Modern, Harmonious, and Creative Society* (Washington, D.C.: World Bank, 2013), p. 176.

7. McKinsey & Company, *The Emerging Global Labor Market: The Supply of Offshore Talent in Services*, June 2005, p. 23, San Francisco, CA, available at: http://www.mckinsey.com/insights/employment_and_growth/the_emerging_global_labor_market_supply_of_offshore_talent.

8. Gereffi et al., "Where the Engineers Are," p. 75.

9. World Bank and Development Research Center of the State Council, the People's Republic of China, *China 2030*, pp. 35–36.

10. See, for example, Richard Suttmeir and Xiangkui Yao, "China's IP Transition: Rethinking Intellectual Property Rights in a Rising China," National Bureau of Asian Research, July 2011, available at: http://www.nbr.org/publications/element.aspx?id=520.

11. Mauro Gilli, "The Struggle for Military-Technological Superiority: Complexity Systems Integration and the Technological Challenges of Imitation," PhD dissertation, Northwestern University, 2015, ch. 3.

12. Cheung, *Forging China's Military Might*, p. 276; Cheung, *Fortifying China: The Struggle to Build a Modern Defense Economy* (Ithaca, N.Y.: Cornell University Press, 2009).

13. Stockholm International Peace Research Institute, "Military Expenditure Database," available at: http://www.sipri.org/research/armaments/milex (consulted August 2, 2015).

14. For the US figure, see Stockholm International Peace Research Institute, "Trends in World Military Expenditure, 2014," available at: http://books.sipri.org/files/FS/SIPRIFS1504.pdf. On the estimate of China's military R&D, see Richard Bitzinger, Michael Raska, Collin Koh Swee Lean, and Kelvin Wong Ka Weng, "Locating China's Place in the Global Defense Economy," in Tai Ming Cheung, ed., *Forging China's Military Might: A New Framework for Assessing Innovation* (Baltimore: Johns Hopkins University Press, 2014), p. 202.

15. Author's interview with William Murray, conducted July 9, 2015, at the US Naval War College, Newport, RI. For a thorough assessment of the large qualitative gap between US and Chinese SSNs, see Owen Cote, "Assessing the Undersea Balance between the U.S. and China," MIT SSP Working Paper, February 2011, p. 28, available at: http://web.mit.edu/ssp/publications/working_papers/Undersea%20Balance%20WP11-1.pdf. See also the chart systematically comparing the acoustic quietness of current Chinese and Russian SSNs in Ronald O'Rourke, "China Naval Modernization: Implications for U.S. Navy Capabilities—Background and Issues for Congress," CRS Report, June 1, 2015, available at: https://www.fas.org/sgp/crs/row/RL33153.pdf.

16. Posen, "Command of the Commons," p. 10.

17. Bitzinger et al., "Locating China's Place in the Global Defense Economy," p. 172. See also Tai Ming Cheung's recent review of China's defense production capacity, which concludes that "the Chinese defense industry presently lacks the necessary scientific and technological capabilities" to be able to "develop sophisticated . . . weapons that are able to match those of the United States and other advanced rivals." Tai Ming Cheung, ed., *Forging China's Military Might*, p. 277.

18. As quoted in Christina Larson, "With a Stealth Fighter, China Points to Advances in Its Arms Industry," *New York Times*, November 11, 2014.

19. Gabe Collins and Andrew Erickson, "Is China About to Get Its Military Jet Engine Program off the Ground?" *China Wall Street Journal*, May 14, 2012, available at: http://blogs.wsj.com/chinarealtime/2012/05/14/is-china-about-to-get-its-military-jet-engine-program-off-the-ground/.

20. Jesse Sloman and Lauren Dickey, "Why China's Air Force Needs Russia's SU-35," *The Diplomat*, June 1, 2015, available at: http://thediplomat.com/2015/06/why-chinas-air-force-needs-the-su-35/.

21. See Peter Dombrowski and Eugene Gholz, *Buying Military Transformation: Technological Innovation in the Defense Industry* (New York: Columbia University Press, 2006), ch. 6; Harvey Sapolsky, "Inventing Systems Integration," in Andrea Prencipe, Andrew Davies, and Michael Hobday, eds., *The Business of Systems Integration* (New York: Oxford University Press, 2003), pp. 15–34; and Eugene Gholz, "Globalization, Systems Integration, and the Future of Great Power War," *Security Studies*, Vol. 16, No. 4 (2007), 615–636.

22. Collins and Erickson, "Is China About to Get Its Military Jet Engine Program off the Ground?"

23. We thank Riqiang Wu for a series of very helpful conversations on the issues raised here.

24. Daryl Press, "The Myth of Air Power in the Persian Gulf War and the Future of Warfare," *International Security*, Vol. 26, No. 2 (2001), p. 37.

25. Daryl Press, "Lessons from Ground Combat in the Gulf: The Impact of Technology and Training," *International Security*, Vol. 22, No. 2 (1997), p. 37.

26. Tactics and training were clearly also crucial, but technological superiority was a significant source of Israel's superiority. See, for example, Matthew M. Hurley, "The BEKAA Valley Air Battle, June 1982: Lessons Mislearned?" *Airpower Journal*, Winter 1989, available at: http://www.airpower.maxwell.af.mil/air-chronicles/apj/apj89/win89/hurley.html.

27. As quoted in Larson, "With a Stealth Fighter, China Points to Advances in Its Arms Industry."

28. Sloman and Dickey, "Why China's Air Force Needs Russia's SU-35."

29. We thank Mauro Gilli and Andrea Gilli for a helpful conversation on this issue.

30. We thank Riqiang Wu, Tai Ming Cheung, and Daryl Press for helpful conversations on this issue.

31. Brooks, *Producing Security*, p. 235.

32. As US Representative Mike Rogers recently put it, "When they steal it, they leap ahead"; see Dugald McConnell and Brian Todd, "Report: China Gained U.S. Weapons Secrets Using Cyberespionage," CNN, May 29, 2013, available at: http://www.cnn.com/2013/05/28/world/asia/china-cyberespionage/.

33. Gilli, "The Struggle for Military-Technological Superiority," ch. 1. For an analysis that shows that Soviet efforts to engage in reverse engineering became increasingly less effective as the complexity of Western military technology increased, see Brooks, *Producing Security*, pp. 121–122.

34. Brooks, *Producing Security*, pp. 76–78 and ch. 5.

35. See Bitzinger et al., "Locating China's Place in the Global Defense Economy," and Tai Ming Cheung, *Fortifying China* (pp. 245–246) who stresses that

> a crucial success factor for Japanese and Korean firms in their catch-up efforts was their early importation of foreign technologies and knowledge that they were able to copy and improve upon. This channel is not readily accessible to the Chinese defense economy because of foreign restrictions, especially from

Western countries, on defense-related technology transfers. The Chinese defense economy has had some success in overcoming these barriers through the forging of close technological ties with Russia, but this lack of access to Western technologies and knowledge remains a serious structural obstacle. Moreover, the Chinese defense economy has been traditionally reluctant to open up its doors to foreign investment or joint-venture projects. Under this close, vertically integrated model, the prospects for achieving major gains in technological catching up by the defense economy may be limited.

36. As Brooks summarized,

There is general recognition that the production of a massive weapons system such as the B-2 bomber requires thousands of parts and components in its production. But weapons systems far smaller in scale and cost are also highly complex. A 1992 Commerce Department study . . . undertook an exhaustive examination of the supply chain for three weapons systems—the HARM missile, the Mark-48 ADCAP torpedo, and the Verdin communication system—that were chosen as "representative weapons used by the US Navy." A stunning finding emerged: for just these three weapon systems, a total of "15,000 companies were identified at the subcontractor level, with 11,638 companies still serving as active suppliers to the prime contractors for the three weapons systems" (6,818 for the HARM missile, 1,483 for the Verdin, and 3,336 for the Mark-48 torpedo)."

Brooks, *Producing Security*, p. 78.

37. Posen, "Command of the Commons," p. 10.

38. Ibid.

39. Brooks, *Producing Security*, p. 238.

40. As quoted in Andrew Erickson and Michael Chase, "Informatization and the Chinese People's Liberation Army Navy," in Phillip C. Saunders, Christopher Yung, Michael Swaine, and Andrew Nien-Dzu Yang, eds., *The Chinese Navy: Expanding Capabilities, Evolving Roles* (Washington, DC: National Defense University Press, 2011), p. 263.

41. Andrea Gilli and Mauro Gilli, "The Diffusion of Drone Warfare? Industrial, Organizational and Infrastructural Constraints: Military Innovations and the Ecosystem Challenge," *Security Studies*, Vol. 25, No. 1 (Winter 2016), pp. 50–84.

42. Andrew Erickson and Michael Chase, "Information Technology and China's Naval Modernization," *Joint Forces Quarterly*, Vol. 50, No. 3 (2008), pp. 24–30. See also the discussion of the critical importance of delegation and flexibility for using advanced systems in Dombrowski and Gholz, *Buying Military Transformation*, pp. 17–18.

43. In this regard, a recent assessment by the People's Liberation Army Navy concludes: "At present, the simulation devices used by naval units in their military training on the whole cannot satisfy the actual military training needs and still lag behind the development of armaments. The insufficiency of simulation training devices has become a major 'bottleneck' that restrains efforts to build fighting

capacity in naval units." As quoted in Erickson and Chase, "Informatization and the Chinese People's Liberation Army Navy," p. 263.

44. Cheung, *Forging China's Military Might*, p. 1.

45. As Cote notes in a careful review, quiet US submarines can still "operate freely in Chinese coastal waters," and given the inherent difficulty of antisubmarine warfare (ASW) in shallow waters combined with China's very poor ASW capacity— and the great difficulty and lengthy amount of time it would take for China to fundamentally upgrade this capacity—this situation is unlikely to change for an extremely long time; Cote, "Assessing the Undersea Balance," p. 3.

46. An excellent recent analysis is Evan Braden Montgomery, "Contested Primacy in the Western Pacific: China's Rise and the Future of U.S. Power Projection," *International Security*, Vol. 38, No. 4 (Spring 2014), 115–149.

47. Gilli, "The Struggle for Military-Technological Superiority," ch. 3.

48. Cheung, "Modernizing the People's Liberation Army," p. 124.

49. Bitzinger et al., "Locating China's Place in the Global Defense Economy," p. 172.

50. Ibid., p. 184.

51. Yan Xuetong, "A Bipolar World Is More Likely than A Unipolar or Multipolar One," *China-US Focus*, April 20, 2015, available at: http://www.chinausfocus.com/foreign-policy/a-bipolar-world-is-more-likely-than-a-unipolar-or-multipolar-one/#sthash.A4ZC7TiS.dpuf.

52. Since 1990, articles about unipolarity have appeared at four times the rate that papers on bipolarity did in the Cold War era. And although there are at least nine books wholly devoted to unipolarity, there are none solely about bipolarity. Article data from Thomson Reuters Web of Science, http://ipscience.thomsonreuters.com/product/web-of-science/; book count is authors' estimate.

53. National Intelligence Council, *Global Trends 2030: Alternate Worlds* (Washington, D.C.: Office of the Director of National Intelligence, 2012), p. x, available at: http://globaltrends2030.files.wordpress.com/2012/11/global-trends-2030-november2012.pdf.

54. "Vladimir Putin Warns Sanctions on Russia Will Backfire on West," *Telegraph*, May 23, 2014, available at: http://www.telegraph.co.uk/news/worldnews/europe/russia/10851908/Vladimir-Putin-warns-sanctions-on-Russia-will-backfire-on-West.html.

55. Jane Perlez, "Leader Asserts China's Growing Importance on Global Stage," *New York Times*, November 30, 2014, available at: http://www.nytimes.com/2014/12/01/world/asia/leader-asserts-chinas-growing-role-on-global-stage.html?_r=0.

56. Barry Buzan, *The United States and the Great Powers: World Politics in the Twenty-First Century* (Cambridge, UK: Polity, 2004), p. 45.

57. In addition to Kenneth N. Waltz, *Theory of International Politics* (Reading, Mass.: Addison-Wesley, 1979), see especially Morton A. Kaplan, *System and Process in International Politics* (New York: ECPR, 1957); Karl W. Deutsch and J. David

Singer, "Multipolar Power Systems and International Stability," *World Politics*, Vol. 16, No. 3 (April 1964), pp. 390–406; Randall L. Schweller, "Tripolarity and the Second World War," *International Studies Quarterly*, Vol. 37, No. 1 (March 1993), pp. 73–103; Edward D. Mansfield, "Concentration, Polarity, and the Distribution of Power," *International Studies Quarterly*, Vol. 37, No. 1 (March 1993), pp. 105–128; and Ted Hopf, "Polarity, the Offense Defense Balance, and War," *American Political Science Review*, Vol. 85, No. 2 (June 1991), pp. 475–493. For a comprehensive discussion of the polarity literature, see Buzan, *The United States and the Great Powers*.

58. Stephen Brooks and William Wohlforth, "The Rise and Fall of the Great Powers in the Twenty-First Century: China's Rise and the Fate of America's Global Position," *International Security*, Vol. 40, No. 3 (Winter 2015/16), pp. 7–53.

59. Kenneth N. Waltz, "The Origins of War in Neorealist Theory," in Robert I. Rotberg and Theodore K. Rabb, eds., *The Origin and Prevention of Major Wars* (Cambridge, UK: Cambridge University Press, 1989), p. 52.

60. Nuno P. Monteiro, *Theory of Unipolar Politics* (New York: Cambridge University Press, 2014). Another prominent example is John Mearsheimer; for him, the threshold for being a great power is so low (a great power state need only be able to put up a "serious fight" against the leading state) that the unipolarity concept can shed no light on any question having to do with changes in international politics since 1991; the world was multipolar then, in his view, and remains so today (John Mearsheimer, *The Tragedy of Great Power Politics*. [New York: W. W. Norton, 2001]). In our own previous work, we argued that "an international system is unipolar if it contains one state whose share of capabilities places it in a class by itself compared to all other states"; the system would still seem unipolar by this definition, although this is ultimately unclear, since we did not specify how much of a shift away from a lopsided concentration of power must occur before it is no longer reasonable to categorize the system this way (Brooks and Wohlforth, *World Out of Balance*). For further discussion of the limitations of these and other structural definitions of unipolarity for assessing system change today, see Brooks and Wohlforth, "The Rise and Fall of the Great Powers in the Twenty-First Century."

61. Joseph Nye, *The Paradox of American Power: Why the World's Only Superpower Can't Go It Alone* (New York: Oxford University Press, 2002), p. 39. Nye also goes on to delineate a third chessboard (transnational relations), but it does not concern the relative distribution of power among states. In taking this "multiple chessboards" approach, Nye was in distinguished company: Henry Kissinger analyzed the US position as of the early 1970s in much the same terms, as had numerous scholars before him. See the discussion in William C. Wohlforth, *The Elusive Balance: Power and Perceptions during the Cold War* (Ithaca, N.Y.: Cornell University Press, 1993), pp. 211–213, and the critical review of this literature in Waltz, *Theory of International Politics*, ch. 7.

62. Fareed Zakaria, "How Long Will America Lead the World?" *Newsweek*, June 12, 2006.

63. Barry Posen, for example, argues that China's economic growth means that "unipolarity is on the wane and multipolarity is in sight." Barry R. Posen, "From Unipolarity to Multipolarity: Transition in Sight?" in G. John Ikenberry, Michael Mastanduno, and William Wohlforth, eds., *International Relations Theory and the Consequences of Unipolarity* (Cambridge, Mass.: Cambridge University Press, 2011), p. 317. Posen's claim is that one element—raw economic output—effectively is state capability. Given his assumption that economic capacity can be quickly translated into military power, Posen ultimately does not acknowledge a separate military dimension (except in the short term). His is merely the most explicit example of an assumption many other scholars who herald unipolarity's end implicitly adopt by pointing to China's economic ascent; see, for example, Christopher Layne, "The Unipolar Exit: Beyond the *Pax Americana*," *Cambridge Review of International Affairs*, Vol. 24, No. 2 (June 2011), pp. 149–164. This line of argument, that China's economic rise has made it, or is about to make it, into another "superpower," also shows up in many treatments by journalists, pundits, and policymakers; see, for example, Ted Fishman, *China, Inc.: How the Rise of the Next Superpower Challenges America and the World* (New York: Scribner, 2006).

64. See, for example, Charles Kupchan, *The End of the American Era: U.S. Foreign Policy and the Geopolitics of the Twenty-First Century* (New York: Knopf, 2002); and Mark Leonard, *Why Europe Will Run the 21st Century* (New York: Public Affairs, 2005). It should be noted that even if we set aside questions involving the degree to which the EU has successfully aggregated economic decision-making in areas other than trade, increased coherence in economic matters by no means necessarily translates into general strategic heft in the overall foreign policy realm. For the EU to emerge as a global foreign policy player on a level with the United States, its members would need to forsake their sovereign authority to make national security decisions in order to delegate foreign policy to a real collective decision-making authority; moreover, they would need to ramp up defense spending and/or combine their production and deployment of military hardware in a manner that allows for the development of military forces that are truly capable of undertaking a significant global role. The likelihood of these things happening was already vanishingly low before the financial crisis of 2008 and the ensuing great recession and associated divisions that soon emerged within the EU.

65. Joseph Nye, "The Myth of Isolationist America," *Project Syndicate*, February 10, 2014, available at: http://www.project-syndicate.org/commentary/joseph-s—nye-refutes-the-increasingly-widespread-view-that-the-us-is-turning-inward. Elsewhere, Nye also argues, "Whereas Germany in 1914 was pressing hard on Britain's heels (and had surpassed it in terms of industrial strength), the US remains decades ahead of China in overall military, economic, and soft-power resources."

Joseph S. Nye, "1914 Revisited?" Belfer Center for Science and International Affairs, January 13, 2014, available at: http://belfercenter.ksg.harvard.edu/publication/23812/1914_revisited.html.

66. National Intelligence Council, *Global Trends 2030*, p. x.

67. National Intelligence Council, *Global Trends 2025: A Transformed World* (Washington, D.C.: Government Printing Office, 2008), pp. 1, 81.

68. This definition reflects the behavioral understanding of power as the ability to achieve desired outcomes. See David Baldwin, *Paradoxes of Power* (New York: Basil Blackwell, 1989), ch. 1.

69. See, for example, Timothy Ash, "Stagger On, Weary Titan," *Guardian*, August 25, 2005, and Richard Haass, "The End of the Unipolar Era," *Los Angeles Times*, July 18, 2005, available at: http://www.cfr.org/world/end-unipolar-era/p8258.

70. Robert Pape, "Soft Balancing Against the United States," *International Security*, Vol. 30, No. 1 (Summer 2005), p. 11. In the same vein but even more expansively, Samuel Huntington defines unipolarity as a system containing one state that can "effectively resolve all important international issues alone, and no combination of other states would have the power to prevent it from doing so." Huntington, "The Lonely Superpower", *Foreign Affairs*, Vol. 78, No. 2 (March/April 1999), p. 35.

71. See, for example, Jagdish Bhagwati, *The Wind of the Hundred Days: How Washington Mismanaged Globalization* (Cambridge, Mass.: MIT Press, 2001).

72. Here, we agree with Waltz, *Theory of International Politics*.

73. For a useful discussion of the need to distinguish the current concentration of power capacity in the hands of the United States from the amount of influence it has in the system, see David Wilkinson, who terms today's system as being one of "unipolarity without hegemony," in which "the preponderant capability of a single state is not matched by a predominant influence." David Wilkinson, "Unipolarity without Hegemony," *International Studies Review*, Vol. 1, No. 2 (Summer 1999), p. 143.

74. The coming post-American, multipolar world is envisioned in bestsellers by the likes of Fareed Zakaria and Parag Khanna, as well as in forecasts by the National Intelligence Council and numerous prominent private-sector analysts from Goldman Sachs to the Eurasia Group. See Fareed Zakaria, *The Post-American World* (New York: W. W. Norton, 2009); Parag Khanna, *The Second World: How Emerging Powers Are Redefining Global Competition in the Twenty-First Century* (New York: Random House, 2009); National Intelligence Council, *Global Trends 2025*; and Ian Bremmer, *Every Nation for Itself: Winners and Losers in a G-Zero World* (New York: Penguin, 2012). Prominent scholarly treatments include Christopher Layne, "This Time It's Real: The End of Unipolarity and the *Pax Americana*," *International Studies Quarterly*, Vol. 56, No. 1 (March 2012), pp. 203–213; Amitav Acharya, *The End of American World Order* (New York: Polity, 2014); and Posen, "From Unipolarity to Multipolarity."

75. See, in particular, Thomas Christensen, *The China Challenge: Shaping the Choices of a Rising power* (New York: Norton, 2014), and David Shambaugh, *China Goes Global: The Partial Power* (New York: Oxford, 2013).

76. David Baldwin, "The Concept of Security," *Review of International Studies*, Vol. 23 (1997), p. 6.

77. We borrow the terminology but not the other parts of Buzan's framework, which melds behavior and capabilities and also adopts an overly blunt approach to measuring capabilities.

78. Buzan, *The United States and the Great Powers*, p. 69. Although some might take issue with his coding, particularly concerning the EU, the overall usefulness of his 1 + X framework does not depend on it.

79. Buzan, *The United States and the Great Powers*, p. 69. As we discuss elsewhere, attempts to eschew the superpower category run into a number of conundrums; see Brooks and Wohlforth, "The Rise and Fall of the Great Powers in the Twenty-First Century."

80. Buzan, *The United States and the Great Powers*, p. 72.

81. In our own 2008 analysis of this question, we argued that the United States' weight in the scales of world power allowed it the freedom to choose between the pursuit of a grand strategy of "engagement" (which we defined as a policy in which the "US should maintain the security role and military profile that it had prior to 9/11, wary of any significant expansion") or "offshore balancing" (which we defined as a policy in which the United States "should sharply reduce its security commitments and military deployments overseas, pulling toward its own borders"). For similar assessments, see Charles Glaser, "Why Unipolarity Doesn't Matter (Much)," *Cambridge Review of International Affairs*, Vol. 24, No. 2 (June 2011), pp. 135–147, and Jeffrey Legro, "The Mix That Makes Unipolarity: Hegemonic Purpose and International Constraints," *Cambridge Review of International Affairs*, Vol. 24, No. 2 (June 2011), pp. 185–199.

82. For example, Christopher Layne argues in "The Unipolar Exit" that America's "strategic commitments exceed the resources available to support them" (p. 153).

CHAPTER 4

1. See, for example, Robert J. Art, *A Grand Strategy for America* (Ithaca, N.Y.: Cornell University Press, 2003); Richard K. Betts, *American Force: Dangers, Delusions, and Dilemmas in National Security* (New York: Columbia University Press, 2011); Terry L. Diebel, *Foreign Affairs Strategy: Logic for American Statecraft* (Cambridge, UK: Cambridge University Press, 2007); John Lewis Gaddis, "What Is Grand Strategy?" Keynote address at the Conference American Grand Strategy after War at Duke University, Durham, North Carolina, February 26, 2009; Hal Brands, *What Good Is Grand Strategy? Power and Purpose in American Statecraft from Harry S. Truman to George W. Bush* (Ithaca, N.Y.: Cornell University Press, 2014).

2. See Brands, *What Good Is Grand Strategy?* p. 3; and Gaddis, "What Is Grand Strategy?" p. 7.

3. John Lewis Gaddis, *Strategies of Containment: A Critical Appraisal of American National Security Policy during the Cold War* (New York: Oxford University Press, 2005); Melvyn P. Leffler, *A Preponderance of Power: National Security, the*

Truman Administration, and the Cold War (Stanford, Calif.: Stanford University Press, 1992); Brands, *What Good Is Grand Strategy?*; and G. John Ikenberry, *After Victory: Institutions, Strategic Restraint, and the Rebuilding of Order after Major Wars* (Princeton, N.J.: Princeton University Press, 2000).

4. From the early 19th century on, the United States accorded high priority to shaping the security environment in its region by keeping other great powers out of the Americas. With the foundation of the Organization of American States in 1948, Washington acquired formal security alliances with over thirty partners in this hemisphere. Owing to a variety of factors—most notably the absence of local great powers and geographical isolation from the major power centers of Eurasia—these security commitments have not assumed the salience and costs associated with the other regions. As a result, they do not figure centrally in the grand strategy debate.

5. Gaddis, *Strategies of Containment.*

6. Leffler, *A Preponderance of Power*, and Brands, *What Good Is Grand Strategy?*

7. Marc Trachtenberg, *A Constructed Peace: The Making of the European Settlement, 1945–1963* (Princeton, N.J.: Princeton University Press, 1999).

8. See, especially, Victor D. Cha, *Alignment Despite Antagonism: The United States-Korea-Japan Security Triangle* (Stanford, Calif.: Stanford University Press, 1999), and *Powerplay: The Origins of the American Alliance System in Asia's Regional Security Architecture* (Princeton, N.J.: Princeton University Press, forthcoming).

9. Some may object that the George W. Bush administration did seek to back away from the third objective (supporting the institutional order), but this seeming exception actually proves the rule. The shift was strictly limited in scope: it primarily affected security institutions such as the United Nations and did not concern economic institutions such as the International Monetary Fund or the World Trade Organization. Moreover, this shift was decisively reversed in Bush's second term. In this regard, Thomas Christensen makes the case that Bush's second term was "multilateral to a fault" and was one of the most multilateral in US history. See the interview with Christensen in Sarah E. Kreps, *Coalitions of Convenience: United States Military Interventions after the Cold War* (New York: Oxford University Press, 2011), p. 42. Dwight Eisenhower chafed against the core commitment to Europe's defense, but was unable to alter it. See Trachtenberg, *A Constructed Peace.*

10. Providing security, filling in a feared "security vacuum," locking in the new democracies, reducing potential ethno-national conflict among them, and hedging against a potential Russian threat all figured in arguments for expansion. Domestic political considerations and sentiment are also sometimes accorded supporting roles. See James M. Goldgeier, *Not Whether but When: The U.S. Decision to Enlarge NATO* (Washington, D.C.: Brookings Institution Press, 1999); George W. Grayson, *Strange Bedfellows: NATO Marches East* (Lanham, Md.: University Press of America, 1999); and Ronald D. Asmus, *Opening NATO's Door: How the Alliance Remade Itself for a New Era* (New York: Columbia University Press, 2002).

11. Gaddis, "What Is Grand Strategy?" quoted in Jeffrey W. Taliaferro, Norrin M. Ripsman, and Steven E. Lobell, eds., *The Challenge of Grand Strategy: The Great Powers and the Broken Balance between the World Wars* (New York: Cambridge University Press, 2012), p. 14. Elsewhere, Gaddis proposes more restrictive definitions that would deny continuity between Cold War containment and post–Cold War US foreign policy.

12. Colin Dueck, *Reluctant Crusaders: Power, Culture, and Change in American Grand Strategy* (Princeton, N.J.: Princeton University Press, 2006), p. 114; Stephen M. Walt, "More or Less: The Debate on U.S. Grand Strategy," *Foreign Policy*, Vol. 92, No. 1 (January 2013), available at: http://walt.foreignpolicy.com/posts/2013/01/02/more_or_less_the_debate_on_us_grand_strategy.

13. Walt, "More or Less."

14. Dueck, *Reluctant Crusaders*; Stephen M. Walt, "In the National Interest: A Grand New Strategy for American Foreign Policy," *Boston Review*, Vol. 30, No. 1 (February/March 2005), available at: http://bostonreview.net/BR30.1/walt.php; and Christopher Layne, "Graceful Decline: The End of *Pax Americana*," *American Conservative*, Vol. 9, No. 5 (May 2010), pp. 30–33.

15. The functional benefits included a reduction of transaction costs, establishment of credible commitments, facilitation of collective action, creation of focal points, and monitoring. For a theoretical discussion of many of these kinds of benefits associated with institutionalization, see Robert Keohane, *After Hegemony* (Princeton, N.J.: Princeton University Press, 1984).

16. See Brooks and Wohlforth, *World Out of Balance,* chs. 6 and 7.

17. Brands, *What Good Is Grand Strategy?* p. 3.

18. Most notably, see Eugene Gholz, Daryl G. Press, and Harvey M. Sapolsky, "Come Home, America: The Strategy of Restraint in the Face of Temptation," *International Security*, Vol. 21, No. 4 (Spring 1997), pp. 5–48.

19. Thomas Wright, "Should America Power Down?" *American Interest*, August 14, 2015, available at: http://www.the-american-interest.com/2015/08/14/should-america-power-down/. See also Ionut C. Popescu, "Is It Time for Retrenchment? The Big Debate on American Grand Strategy," in Peter Feaver, ed., *Strategic Retrenchment and Renewal in the American Experience* (Carlisle Barracks, Penn.: United States Army War College, 2014).

20. National Intelligence Council, *Global Trends 2030: Alternative Worlds* (Washington, D.C.: National Intelligence Council, 2012); Cindy Williams, "Preserving National Strength in a Period of Fiscal Restraint," in Jeremi Suri and Benjamin Valentino, eds., *Sustainable Security: Rethinking American National Security Strategy*, (Oxford: Oxford University Press, forthcoming 2016); David W. Barno, Nora Bensahel, and Travis Sharp, *Hard Choices: Responsible Defense in an Age of Austerity* (Washington, D.C.: Center for a New American Security, 2011); Pew Research Center, "Public Sees U.S. Power Declining as Support for Global Engagement Slips," *America's Place in the World 2013* (Washington, D.C.:

Pew Research Center, 2013), available at: http://www.people-press.org/2013/12/03/public-sees-u-s-power-declining-as-support-for-global-engagement-slips/.

21. For a brilliant dissection of these traditions and a forceful argument for a third "core plus" tradition, "conservative internationalism," see Henry R. Nau, *Conservative Internationalism: Armed Diplomacy under Jefferson, Polk, Truman, and Reagan* (Princeton, N.J.: Princeton University Press, 2013).

22. Barry R. Posen, "The Case for Restraint," *American Interest*, Vol. 3, No. 1 (November/December 2007), pp. 7–17; G. John Ikenberry, *Liberal Leviathan: The Origins, Crisis and Transformation of the American World Order* (Princeton, N.J.: Princeton University Press, 2011); and Dueck, *Reluctant Crusaders*.

23. Dueck, *Reluctant Crusaders*, p. 119. See also Tony Smith, *America's Mission: The United States and the Worldwide Struggle for Democracy in the Twentieth Century* (Princeton, N.J.: Princeton University Press, 1994; rev. ed., 2012). Jonathan Monten, "The Roots of the Bush Doctrine: Power, Nationalism, and Democracy Promotion in U.S. Strategy," *International Security*, Vol. 29, No. 4 (2005), pp. 112–156; Stephen Sestanovich, *Maximalist: America in the World from Truman to Obama* (New York: Random House, 2015).

24. Posen, *Restraint*, p. 6.

25. For example, both Colin Dueck and Henry Nau interpret the Obama administration's efforts to extricate the United States from nation building in the Middle East and other transformational projects in order to concentrate resources in East Asia as retrenchment. We see the same policies as efforts to buttress the grand strategy. See Colin Dueck, *The Obama Doctrine* (New York: Oxford University Press, 2015), and Henry Nau, "How Restraint Leads to War: The Real Danger of the Iran Deal," *Commentary*, September 2015, pp. 13–21.

26. Steven Simon and Jonathan Stevenson, "The End of Pax Americana: Why Washington's Middle East Pullback Makes Sense," *Foreign Affairs*, Vol. 94, No. 6 (November/December 2015), p. 2.

27. Richard Betts, "Pick Your Battles: Ending America's Era of Permanent War," *Foreign Affairs*, Vol. 93, No. 6 (November/December 2014), p. 23.

28. As noted in chapter 1, retrenchment advocates' criticisms of US leadership of the global liberal order are much less well developed than their arguments for trimming its overseas military presence and commitments.

CHAPTER 5

1. George Bush and Brent Scowcroft, *A World Transformed: The Collapse of the Soviet Empire, The Unification of Germany, Tiananmen Square, The Gulf War* (New York: Knopf, 1998), pp. 230–231.

2. Lawrence Freedman, *Deterrence* (Cambridge, Mass.: Polity, 2004), p. 30.

3. Helga Haftendorn, Robert O. Keohane, and Celeste A. Wallander, *Imperfect Unions: Security Institutions over Time and Space* (Oxford: Clarendon, 1999).

4. Glen H. Snyder, *Alliance Politics* (Ithaca, N.Y.: Cornell University Press, 1997), and William C. Wohlforth, Richard Little, Stuart J. Kaufman, et. al., "Testing Balance-of-Power Theory in World History," *European Journal of International Relations*, Vol. 13, No. 6 (June 2007), pp. 155–185.

5. See, for example, Celeste A. Wallander, *Mortal Friends, Best Enemies: German-Russian Cooperation after the Cold War* (Ithaca, N.Y.: Cornell University Press, 1999).

6. Michael J. Lostumbo, Michael J. McNerney, Eric Peltz, et al., *Overseas Basing of U.S. Military Forces: An Assessment of Relative Costs and Strategic Benefits* (Santa Monica, Calif.: RAND Corporation, 2013).

7. A number of strong arguments on this score are presented in Robert Kagan, *The World America Made* (Random House: Vintage, 2013). Here we address a more limited set of claims in much more detail and do so by explicitly employing international relations theories and accumulated relevant research findings.

8. For reviews, see Patrick Morgan, *Deterrence Now* (Cambridge, UK: Cambridge University Press, 2003); Freedman, *Deterrence*; Elli Lieberman, *Reconceptualizing Deterrence: Nudging Toward Rationality in the Middle East* (New York: Routledge, 2013); Amir Lupovic, "The Emerging Fourth Wave of Deterrence Theory: Toward a New Research Agenda," *International Studies Quarterly*, Vol. 53, No. 2 (September 2010), pp. 705–732; Paul K. Huth, "Deterrence and International Conflict," *Annual Review of Political Science*, Vol. 2 (1999), pp. 25–48; Frank C. Zagare, "Deterrence Is Dead. Long Live Deterrence," *Conflict Management and Peace Science*, Vol. 23, No. 2 (2006), pp. 115–120.

9. Theory expects the conventional balance to matter. See Huth, "Deterrence and International Conflict," and John J. Mearsheimer, *Conventional Deterrence* (Ithaca, N.Y.: Cornell University Press, 1983). There is less consensus on the nuclear balance; many take an "existential" approach, though some argue that this matters too. See Vipin Narang, "What Does It Take to Deter? Regional Power Nuclear Postures and International Conflict," *Journal of Conflict Resolution*, Vol. 57, No. 3 (June 2013), pp. 478–508; Narang, *Nuclear Strategy in the Modern Era: Regional Powers and International Conflict* (Princeton, N.J.: Princeton University Press, 2014); and Kier Lieber and Daryl Press, "Nuclear Weapons and International Politics," book manuscript.

10. Vesna Danilovic, "The Sources of Threat Credibility in Extended Deterrence," *Journal of Conflict Resolution*, Vol. 45, No. 3 (June 2001), pp. 341–369.

11. Thomas Schelling, *Arms and Influence* (New Haven, Conn.: Yale University Press, 1966).

12. Geoffrey Blainey, *The Causes of War* (New York: Free Press, 1988); Mearsheimer, *Conventional Deterrence*; Paul Huth, *Extended Deterrence and the Prevention of War* (New Haven, Conn.: Yale University Press, 1988); Huth, "Deterrence and International Conflict"; Bruce Bueno de Mesquita, James Morrow, and Ethan Zorick, "Capabilities, Perception and Escalation," *American Political Science Review*, Vol. 91, No. 1 (March 1997), pp. 15–27.

13. This claim is increasingly contested; see Jack L. Snyder and Erica Borghard, "The Cost of Empty Threats: A Penny, Not a Pound," *American Political Science Review*, Vol. 105, No. 3 (August 2011), pp. 437–456; Marc Trachtenberg, "Audience Costs: An Historical Analysis," *Security Studies*, Vol. 21, No. 1 (2012), pp. 3–42; and the debate in the special section on audience costs in *Security Studies*, Vol. 21, No. 3.

14. Patrick M. Morgan, *Deterrence Now* (Cambridge, UK: Cambridge University Press, 2003), ch. 3; T. V. Paul, Patrick M. Morgan, and James J. Wirtz, eds., *Complex Deterrence: Strategy in the Global Age* (Chicago: University of Chicago Press, 2009); Robert Powell, *Nuclear Deterrence Theory: The Search for Credibility* (Cambridge, UK: Cambridge University Press, 1990); Frank C. Zagare and D. Marc Kilgour, *Perfect Deterrence* (Cambridge, UK: Cambridge University Press, 2000). Note that it is capabilities interacting with interest, not capabilities alone, that find support in more recent models.

15. Matthew Fuhrmann and Todd Sechser, "Signaling Alliance Commitments: Hand-Tying and Sunk Costs in Extended Nuclear Deterrence," *American Journal of Political Science*, Vol. 58, No. 4 (October 2014), pp. 1–17.

16. Schelling, *Arms and Influence*, pp. 69–75, 100. See also the discussion in Freedman, *Deterrence*, ch. 7.

17. Todd Sechser and Matthew Fuhrmann, "Crisis Bargaining and Nuclear Blackmail," *International Organization*, Vol. 67, No. 1 (Winter 2013), pp. 173–195. See also James D. Fearon, "Signaling versus the Balance of Power and Interests: An Empirical Test of a Crisis Bargaining Model," *Journal of Conflict Resolution*, Vol. 38, No. 2 (June 1994), pp. 236–269, and Paul K. Huth, "The Extended Deterrent Value of Nuclear Weapons," *Journal of Conflict Resolution*, Vol. 34, No. 2 (June 1990), pp. 270–290.

18. See Todd S. Sechser, "Militarized Compellent Threats, 1918–2001," *Conflict Management and Peace Studies*, Vol. 28, No. 4 (Fall 2011), pp. 377–401.

19. Robert J. Art, "Coercive Diplomacy: What Do We Know?" in Robert J. Art and Patrick M. Cronin, eds., *The United States and Coercive Diplomacy* (Washington, D.C.: US Institute of Peace, 2003), pp. 359–420, and Barry R. Posen, "Military Responses to Refugee Disasters," *International Security*, Vol. 21, No. 1 (Summer 1996), pp. 72–111.

20. See Daniel Kahneman, *Thinking Fast and Slow* (New York: Farrar, Straus and Giroux, 2011).

21. Gary Schaub, "Deterrence, Compellence, and Prospect Theory," *Political Psychology*, Vol. 25, No. 3 (June 2004), pp. 389–411. Note that all the arguments for why compellence/coercion is harder than deterrence, including Schelling's, depart from the strict rational choice assumptions governing most current modeling. Formal models may therefore be unable to generate this result.

22. See, for example, Eugene Gholz, Daryl G. Press, and Harvey M. Sapolsky, "Come Home, America: The Strategy of Restraint in the Face of Temptation," *International Security*, Vol. 21, No. 4 (Spring 1997), pp. 5–48, and Christopher

Layne, *The Peace of Illusions: American Grand Strategy from 1940 to the Present* (Ithaca, N.Y.: Cornell University Press, 2007).

23. John J. Mearsheimer, *The Tragedy of Great Power Politics* (New York: W. W. Norton, 2001), pp. 360–402, and Mearsheimer, "The Future of the American Pacifier," *Foreign Affairs*, Vol. 80, No. 5 (September/October 2001), pp. 46–61.

24. Mearsheimer, *The Tragedy of Great Power Politics*, p. 380.

25. On defensive realism, see Stephen Brooks, "Dueling Realisms," *International Organization*, Vol. 51, No. 3 (Summer 1997), pp. 445–477; Jeffrey Taliaferro, "Security Seeking under Anarchy: Defensive Realism Revisited," *International Security*, Vol. 25, No. 3 (Winter 2000/1), pp. 128–161; Charles Glaser, *Rational Theory of International Politics* (Princeton, N.J.: Princeton University Press, 2010); Stephen Van Evera, *Causes of War: Power and the Roots of Conflict* (Ithaca, N.Y.: Cornell University Press, 2001); and Shiping Tang, *A Theory of Security Strategy for Our Time: Defensive Realism* (New York: Palgrave Macmillan, 2010).

26. For this debate, see Michael E. Brown et al., eds., *Offense, Defense, and War* (Cambridge, Mass.: MIT Press, 2004).

27. In part due to defense dominance and the relative ease of distinguishing offensive from defense military postures, Steven Van Evera argued that post–Cold War Europe was "primed for peace," though he held that an active US military presence was still needed for a transitional period of unspecified duration. Stephen Van Evera, "Primed for Peace: Europe after the Cold War," *International Security*, Vol. 15, No. 3 (Winter 1990/91), pp. 7–57.

28. Randall Schweller, "Neorealism's Status-Quo Bias: What Security Dilemma?" *Security Studies*, Vol. 5, No. 3 (Spring 1996), pp. 90–121.

29. See, for example, Richard Ned Lebow, *Why Nations Fight: The Past and Future of War* (Cambridge, UK: Cambridge University Press, 2010); Deborah Larson, T. V. Paul, and William C. Wohlforth, eds., *Status and World Order* (Cambridge, UK: Cambridge University Press, 2014); William C. Wohlforth, "Unipolarity, Status Competition, and Great Power War," *World Politics*, Vol. 61, No. 1 (January 2009), pp. 28–57; Jonathan Renshon, "Status Deficits and War," unpublished manuscript; and Thomas Volgy, Renato Corbetta, Keith Grant, and Ryan Baird, eds., *Major Powers and the Quest for Status in International Politics* (New York: Palgrave Macmillan, 2011).

30. Glaser, *Rational Theory of International Politics*, p. 215.

31. Ibid., p. 213.

32. Ibid., p. 231.

CHAPTER 6

1. See, for example, Richard Ned Lebow, *Between Peace and War: The Nature of International Crisis* (Baltimore: Johns Hopkins University Press, 1981); Lebow

and Janice Gross Stein, "Deterrence: The Elusive Dependent Variable," *World Politics*, Vol. 42 (April 1990), pp. 336–369; and Lebow, Robert Jervis, and Janice Gross Stein, *Psychology and Deterrence* (Baltimore: Johns Hopkins University Press, 1985).

2. Jesse Johnson and Brett Ashley Leeds, "Defense Pacts: A Prescription for Peace?" *Foreign Policy Analysis*, Vol. 7, No. 1 (January 2011), pp. 45–65; Brett Ashley Leeds, "Do Alliances Deter Aggression? The Influence of Military Alliances on the Initiation of Militarized Interstate Disputes," *American Journal of Political Science*, Vol. 47, No. 3 (July 2003), pp. 427–439.

3. Matthew Fuhrmann and Todd S. Sechser, "Signaling Alliance Commitments: Hand-Tying and Sunk Costs in Extended Nuclear Deterrence," *American Journal of Political Science*, Vol. 58, No. 4 (2014), p. 2.

4. Paul Huth, *Extended Deterrence and the Prevention of War* (New Haven, Conn.: Yale University Press, 1988); Huth, "Extended Deterrence and the Outbreak of War," *American Political Science Review*, Vol. 82, No. 2 (June 1988), pp. 423–443; Paul Huth and Bruce Russett, "General Deterrence Between Enduring Rivals," *American Political Science Review*, Vol. 87, No. 1 (March 1993), pp. 61–73. But see more recent research suggesting that nuclear superiority matters: Matthew Kroenig, "Nuclear Superiority and the Balance of Resolve," *International Organization*, Vol. 67, No. 1 (January 2013), pp. 141–171.

5. Huth, "Extended Deterrence and the Outbreak of War," and Vesna Danilovic, "The Sources of Threat Credibility in Extended Deterrence," *Journal of Conflict Resolution*, Vol. 45, No. 3 (2001), pp. 341–369.

6. Patrick M. Morgan, *Deterrence Now* (Cambridge, UK: Cambridge University Press, 2003), ch. 4.

7. Lawrence Freedman, *Strategic Coercion: Concepts and Cases* (Oxford: Oxford University Press, 1988); Robert J. Art and Patrick M. Cronin, *The United States and Coercive Diplomacy* (Washington, D.C.: United States Institute of Peace Press, 2003); Gordon Craig and Alexander George, *Force and Statecraft* (Oxford: Oxford University Press, 1990); Alexander L. George and Richard Smoke, *Limits of Coercive Diplomacy* (Boulder, Colo.: Westview, 1994).

8. Matthew Kroenig, *Exporting the Bomb: Technology Transfer and the Spread of Nuclear Weapons* (Ithaca, N.Y.: Cornell University Press, 2010), p. 3.

9. See, for example, Scott D. Sagan, *The Limits of Safety: Organizations, Accidents, and Nuclear Weapons* (Princeton, N.J.: Princeton University Press, 1993).

10. See Scott D. Sagan, "The Causes of Nuclear Weapons Proliferation," *Annual Review of Political Science*, Vol. 14 (2011), pp. 225–244, and James McAllister, ed., "What We Talk about When We Talk about Nuclear Weapons," *H-Diplo/International Security Studies Forum*, No. 2 (June 15, 2014), available at: http://issforum.org/ISSF/PDF/ISSF-Forum-2.pdf.

11. Philipp C. Bleek and Eric Lorber, "Security Guarantees and Allied Nuclear Proliferation," *Journal of Conflict Resolution*, Vol. 58, No. 3 (April 2014), pp.

429–454; Philipp C. Bleek, "Why Do States Proliferate? Quantitative Analysis of the Exploration, Pursuit, and Acquisition of Nuclear Weapons," in William Potter and Gaukhar Mukhatzhanova, eds., *Forecasting Proliferation in the 21st Century: The Role of Theory* (Stanford, Calif.: Stanford University Press, 2010). Bleek and Lorber's finding contradicts some earlier studies, for example, Sonali Singh and Christopher R. Way, "The Correlates of Nuclear Proliferation: A Quantitative Test," *Journal of Conflict Resolution*, Vol. 48, No. 6 (December 2004), pp. 859–885, and Dong-Joo Jo and Erik Gartzke, "Determinants of Nuclear Weapons Proliferation," *Journal of Conflict Resolution*, Vol. 51, No. 1 (February 2007), pp. 167–194.

12. Kroenig, *Exporting the Bomb.*

13. Etel Solingen, *Nuclear Logics: Contrasting Paths in East Asia and the Middle East* (Princeton, N.J.: Princeton University Press, 2007), pp. 12–14; T. V. Paul, *Power versus Prudence: Why Nations Forgo Nuclear Weapons* (Montreal: McGill-Queen's University Press, 2000), pp. 153–154; Jacques E. C. Hymans, *The Psychology of Nuclear Proliferation* (Cambridge, UK: Cambridge University Press, 2006).

14. Jeffrey W. Knopf, ed., *Security Assurances and Nuclear Nonproliferation* (Stanford, Calif.: Stanford University Press, 2012); John D. Wilshusen, "Do U.S. Security Commitments Discourage Nuclear Proliferation?" MA thesis, Naval Postgraduate School, 1997. Alexandre Debs and Nuno Monteiro test a purely rational-security-based theory of proliferation with over thirty case studies and find strong support for the counterproliferation effects of US alliances; see Alexandre Debs and Nuno Monteiro, *Nuclear Politics: The Strategic Logic of Proliferation* (Cambridge, UK: Cambridge University Press, forthcoming). From a completely different domestic-politics perspective, Solingen, *Nuclear Logics*, concludes that

> U.S. alliances with Japan and South Korea and commitments to Taiwan ... provide an important explanatory layer for these countries' nuclear abstention. Yet understanding their relative receptivity to persuasive and coercive aspects of the U.S. alliance requires us to delve into their domestic politics. Nuclear weapons would have seriously undermined favored strategies of economic growth and regional and global access. The choice for alliance *itself* was the product of domestic models that favored it over other options, trumping internal demands for nuclear weapons and generating receptivity to hegemonic inducements.

15. Alexandre Debs and Nuno Monteiro, "The Strategic Logic of Nuclear Proliferation," Yale University typescript, June 1 2014.

16. Alexander Lanoszka, "Protection States Trust? Major Power Patronage, Nuclear Behavior, and Alliance Dynamics," PhD dissertation, Princeton University, 2014.

17. Philipp C. Bleek and Eric Lorber, "Friends Don't Let Friends Proliferate: Credibility, Security Assurances, and Allied Nuclear Proliferation," policy memo for Project on Strategic Stability Evaluation and the International Studies Association Annual Meeting, February 28, 2013; Lanoszka, Protection

States Trust?; Gene Gerzhoy, "Coercive Nonproliferation: Security, Leverage, and Nuclear Reversals," book manuscript, Harvard University, 2014; Knopf, *Security Assurances*.

18. See, for example, John Mueller, *Atomic Obsession: Nuclear Alarmism from Hiroshima to al-Qaeda* (Oxford: Oxford University Press, 2010).

19. Philipp Bleek, "The Nuclear Domino Myth: Why Proliferation Rarely Begets Proliferation," PhD dissertation, Georgetown University, 2010. Note: one reason for the conclusion implied in the title is that many likely proliferators enjoy security guarantees.

20. Alexandre Debs and Nuno Monteiro, "The Strategic Logic of Nuclear Proliferation."

21. Kenneth N. Waltz, "Nuclear Myths and Political Realities," *American Political Science Review*, Vol. 84, No. 3 (September 1990), pp. 731–745, and Kenneth N. Waltz, *The Spread of Nuclear Weapons: More May Be Better*, Adelphi Papers No. 171 (1981). See also Scott D. Sagan and Kenneth N. Waltz, *The Spread of Nuclear Weapons: An Enduring Debate*, 3rd ed. (New York: W. W. Norton, 2012).

22. See Sagan, *The Limits of Safety*, and Sagan and Waltz, *The Spread of Nuclear Weapons*.

23. Campbell Craig, "Debating American Engagement: The Future of U.S. Grand Strategy," *International Security*, Vol. 38, No. 2 (Fall 2013), pp. 181–199.

24. This point is stressed in Matthew Kroenig, "The History of Proliferation Optimism: Does It Have a Future?" *Journal of Strategic Studies*, Vol. 38, Nos. 1–2 (2015), pp. 98–125.

25. Thomas C. Schelling, *Arms and Influence* (New Haven, Conn.: Yale University Press, 2008).

26. Kroenig, "Nuclear Superiority and the Balance of Resolve."

27. Kroenig, "The History of Proliferation Optimism."

28. Vipin Narang, *Nuclear Strategy in the Modern Era: Regional Powers and International Conflict* (Princeton, N.J.: Princeton University Press, 2014), and Kier Lieber and Daryl Press, "Nuclear Weapons and International Politics," book manuscript.

29. K. J. Holsti, *Peace and War: Armed Conflicts and International Order, 1648–1989* (Cambridge, UK: Cambridge University Press, 1991).

30. Lieber and Press, "Nuclear Weapons and International Politics."

31. An "assured retaliation" posture has no effect on conventional conflict. Vipin Narang, "Posturing for Peace? Pakistan's Nuclear Postures and South Asian Stability," *International Security*, Vol. 34, No. 3 (Winter 2010), pp. 38–78; Narang, "What Does It Take to Deter? Regional Power Nuclear Postures and International Conflict," *Journal of Conflict Resolution*, Vol. 57, No. 3 (June 2013), pp. 478–508; Narang, *Nuclear Strategy in the Modern Era*.

32. See Benjamin Miller, *States, Nations and the Great Powers: The Sources of Regional War and Peace* (Cambridge, UK: Cambridge University Press, 2007);

Barry Buzan and Ole Weaver, *Regions and Powers: The Structure of International Security* (Cambridge, UK: Cambridge University Press, 2003); Peter J. Katzenstein, *A World of Regions: Asia and Europe in the American Imperium* (Ithaca, N.Y.: Cornell University Press, 2005); Paul Papayoanou, "Great Powers and Regional Orders: Problems and Prospects," in David A. Lake and Patrick Morgan, eds., *Regional Orders: Building Security in a New World* (University Park, Pa.: University of Pennsylvania Press, 1997); I. William Zartman, "Systems of World Order and Regional Conflict Reduction," in Zartman and Victor A. Kremenyuk, eds., *Cooperative Security: Reducing Third World Wars* (Syracuse, N.Y.: Syracuse University Press, 1995), pp. 3–24.

33. For analyses strongly grounded in realist theory as well as regional expertise, see Thomas J. Christensen, "China, the U.S.-Japan Alliance, and the Security Dilemma in East Asia," *International Security*, Vol. 23, No. 4 (Spring 1999), pp. 49–80; Robert Ross, "The Geography of the Peace: East Asia in the Twenty-First Century," *International Security*, Vol. 23, No. 4 (Spring, 1999), pp. 81–118; Victor Cha, "Complex Patchworks: US Alliances as Part of Asia's Regional Architecture," *Asia Policy*, Vol. 11, No. 1 (2011), pp. 27–50; Michael Mastanduno, "Incomplete Hegemony: The United States and Security Order in Asia," in Muthiah Alagappa, ed., *Asian Security Order: Instrumental and Normative Features* (Stanford, Calif.: Stanford University Press, 2003), pp. 141–170; and Linton Brooks and Mira Rapp-Hooper, "Extended Deterrence, Assurance, and Reassurance in the Pacific Suring the Second Nuclear Age," in Ashley J. Tellis, Abraham M. Denmark, and Travis Tanner, eds., *Strategic Asia 2013–14: Asia in the Second Nuclear Age* (Seattle, Wash.: National Bureau of Asian Research, 2013), pp. 267–301.

34. Interviews with Avery Goldstein, Taylor Fravel, Thomas Christensen, David Kang, Ja Ian Chong, and Feng Zhang, July 2013. For studies that explicitly question the analytical utility of realism but reach broadly similar conclusions on US security provision, see, for example, Evelyn Goh, *The Struggle for Order: Hegemony, Hierarchy, and Transition in Post-Cold War East Asia* (Oxford: Oxford University Press, 2013). For dissent, see Yan Xue Tong, *Ancient Chinese Thought, Modern Chinese Power* (Princeton, N.J.: Princeton University Press, 2011); and David Kang, *China Rising: Peace, Power, and Order in East Asia* (New York: Columbia University Press, 2007).

35. This scholarly assessment matches up with the results of a 2009 Center for Strategic and International Studies survey of over three hundred "strategic elites" in nine Asian countries, which shows strong majorities—including in China—seeing the United States as the "greatest force for peace and stability" in the region. See Bates Gill, Michael Green, Kiyoto Tsuji, and William Watts, *Strategic Views on Asian Regionalism*, Center for Strategic and International Studies, February 2009.

36. Barry R. Posen, *Restraint* (Ithaca, N.Y.: Cornell University Press, 2014), pp. 100–102.

37. Richard J. Samuels and James L. Schoff, "Japan's Nuclear Hedge: Beyond 'Allergy' and Breakout," in Tellis, Denmark, and Tanner, *Strategic Asia 2013–14*, pp. 233–266.

38. On Korea, see especially, Alexander Lanoszka, The Alliance Politics of Nuclear Statecraft, PhD dissertation, Princeton University, 2014, ch. 7.

39. See, for example, Victor D. Cha, *Alignment Despite Antagonism: The United States-Korea-Japan Security Triangle* (Stanford, Calif.: Stanford University Press, 1999); Cha, *Powerplay: The Origins of the American Alliance System in Asia's Regional Security Architecture* (Princeton, N.J.: Princeton University Press, forthcoming); and Thomas Christensen, *Worse than a Monolith: Alliance Politics and Coercive Diplomacy in Asia* (Princeton, N.J.: Princeton University Press, 2011).

40. As Mearsheimer notes, "The United States will have to play a key role in countering China, because its Asian neighbors are not strong enough to do it by themselves." John J. Mearsheimer, "Imperial by Design," *National Interest*, No. 111 (January/February 2011), p. 33. Therefore, unless China stalls, "the United States is likely to act toward China similar to the way it behaved toward the Soviet Union during the Cold War." Mearsheimer, "The Gathering Storm: China's Challenge to US Power in Asia," *Chinese Journal of International Politics*, Vol. 3 (2010), p. 390. See also Sebastian Rosato and John Schuessler, "A Realist Foreign Policy for the United States," *Perspectives on Politics*, Vol. 9, No. 4 (December 2011), p. 813.

41. Skepticism about the need for balancing or deterring China is naturally the dominant view among Chinese scholars of international relations (e.g., Yan Xuetong; Wu Xinbo). But see David Kang, *China Rising: Peace, Power, and Order in East Asia* (New York: Columbia University Press, 2007), and Charles Freeman, *Interesting Times: China, America, and the Shifting Balance of Prestige* (Charlottesville, Va.: Just World Books, 2013). On capabilities, see Posen, *Restraint*; Robert Ross, "The Rise of Chinese Power and the Implications for the Regional Security Order," *Orbis*, Vol. 54, No. 4 (Fall 2010), pp. 525–545; and John J. Mearsheimer, "Can China Rise Peacefully?" *National Interest*, October 25, 2014, available at: http://nationalinterest.org/commentary/can-china-rise-peacefully-10204.

42. Thomas Christensen, *The China Challenge: Shaping the Choices of a Rising Power* (New York: Norton, 2015).

43. Ibid.

44. See, for example, Evan Braden Montgomery, "Contested Primacy in the Western Pacific: China's Rise and the Future of U.S. Power Projection," *International Security*, Vol. 38, No. 4 (Spring 2014), pp. 115–149.

45. See especially Avery Goldstein, "First Things First: The Pressing Danger of Crisis Instability in U.S.-China Relations," *International Security*, Vol. 37, No. 4 (Spring 2013), pp. 49–89, and Adam P. Liff and G. John Ikenberry, "Racing toward Tragedy?: China's Rise, Military Competition in the Asia Pacific, and the Security Dilemma," *International Security*, Vol. 39, No. 2 (Fall 2014), pp. 52–91.

46. Sam LaGrone and Dave Majumdar, "The Future of Air Sea Battle," *USNI News*, October 30, 2013, available at: http://news.usni.org/2013/10/30/future-air-sea-battle. On escalation risks, see especially Goldstein, "First Things First." See also the excellent analysis of the strategy and alternatives to it in Aaron L. Friedberg, *Beyond AirSea Battle: The Debate over U.S. Military Strategy in Asia* (New York: Routledge, 2014).

47. Jeffrey E. Kline and Wayne P. Hughes Jr., "Between Peace and the Air-Sea Battle: A War at Sea Strategy," *Naval War College Review*, Vol. 65, No. 4 (Autumn 2012), pp. 35–41. Of key strategic significance is that these islands are relatively closely grouped together and are all in friendly hands. See, for example, James Holmes, "Defend the First Island Chain," *Proceedings Magazine*, April 2014, available at: http://www.usni.org/magazines/proceedings/2014-04/defend-first-island-chain. As Coté stresses, "The maritime geography in question is at least as favorable as that which the U.S. successfully exploited during the Cold War." Owen Coté, "Assessing the Undersea Balance between the U.S. and China" (MIT SSP Working Paper, February 2011), p. 12, available at: http://web.mit.edu/ssp/publications/working_papers/Undersea%20Balance%20WP11-1.pdf.

48. On using a reverse A2/AD approach regarding China, see, for example, Holmes, "Defend the First Island Chain"; Toshi Yoshihara and James R. Holmes, "Asymmetric Warfare: American Style," *Proceedings Magazine*, April 2012, available at: http://www.usni.org/magazines/proceedings/2012-04/asymmetric-warfare-american-style; Toshi Yoshihara, *Going Anti-Access at Sea: How Japan Can Turn the Tables on China* (Washington, D.C.: Center for a New American Security, September 2014), available at: http://www.cnas.org/sites/default/files/publications-pdf/CNAS%20Maritime2_Yoshihara.pdf; James R. Holmes, "Strategic Features of the South China Sea: A Tough Neighborhood for Hegemons," *Naval War College Review*, Vol. 67, No. 2 (Spring 2014), pp. 30–51; William S. Murray, "Revisiting Taiwan's Defense Strategy," *Naval War College Review*, Vol. 61, No. 3 (Summer 2008), pp. 13–38; James Holmes and Toshi Yoshihara, *Defending the Strait: Taiwan's Naval Strategy in the 21st Century* (Washington, D.C.: Jamestown Foundation, 2011); Jim Thomas, "Why the U.S. Army Needs Missiles: A New Mission to Save the Service," *Foreign Affairs*, Vol. 92, No. 3 (May/June 2013), available at: https://www.foreignaffairs.com/articles/united-states/2013-04-03/why-us-army-needs-missiles; Terrence Kelly, Anthony Atler, Todd Nichols, and Lloyd Thrall, *Employing Land-Based Anti-Ship Missiles in the Western Pacific*, (Santa Monica, Calif.: RAND Corporation, 2013), available at: http://www.rand.org/pubs/technical_reports/TR1321.html; and Michael D. Swaine, *Beyond American Predominance in the Western Pacific: The Need for a Stable U.S.-China Balance of Power* (Washington, D.C.: Carnegie Endowment for International Peace, April 20, 2015), available at: http://carnegieendowment.org/2015/04/20/beyond-american-predominance-in-western-pacific-need-for-stable-u.s.-china-balance-of-power. It should be noted that pursuing reverse A2/

AD has utility for any approach the United States takes in the region, including AirSea Battle.

49. A systematic analysis of the US advantage in the undersea balance is Coté, "Assessing the Undersea Balance between the U.S. and China." See also Lyle Goldstein, "Beijing Confronts Long-Standing Weaknesses in Anti-Submarine Warfare," *China Brief*, July 29, 2011, available at: http://www.jamestown.org/single/?tx_ttnews%5Btt_news%5D=38252&no_cache=1#.ViaO_36rS71.

50. The authors thank Eugene Gholz for helpful conversations on these issues.

51. The authors thank Owen Coté for a helpful conversation on this issue.

52. As Murray writes,

> Taiwan must rethink its defense strategies. Rather than trying to destroy incoming ballistic missiles with costly PAC-3 SAMs, Taiwan should harden key facilities and build redundancies into critical infrastructure and processes so that it could absorb and survive a long-range precision bombardment. Rather than relying on its navy and air force (neither of which is likely to survive such an attack) to destroy an invasion force, Taiwan should concentrate on development of a professional standing army armed with mobile, short range, defensive weapons. To withstand a prolonged blockade, Taiwan should stockpile critical supplies and build infrastructure that would allow it to attend to the needs of its citizens unassisted for an extended period. Finally, Taiwan should eschew destabilizing offensive capabilities. ... Such shifts constitute a "porcupine strategy." ... A porcupine strategy would enhance deterrence, in that a Taipei truly prepared to defend itself would be able to thwart a decapitation attempt— thereby discouraging Beijing from acting militarily.

See Murray, "Revisiting Taiwan's Defense Strategy," pp. 15–16. A complement to the porcupine approach for Taiwan is the maritime strategy outlined in Holmes and Yoshihara, *Defending the Strait*.

53. Yoshihara, *Going Anti-Access at Sea*, pp. 4, 10.

54. Thomas J. Christensen, "Posing Problems without Catching Up: China's Rise and Challenges for U.S. Security Policy," *International Security*, Vol. 25, No. 4, (Spring 2001), pp. 5–40.

55. See NATO, "Wales Summit Declaration," September 5, 2014, available at: http://www.nato.int/cps/en/natohq/official_texts_112964.htm.

56. This consensus encompasses hawkish analysts, including from frontline states in the Baltic region and Central and Eastern Europe. See, for example, Heritage Foundation, *Threats to the Homeland: Europe* (2015), available at: http://index.heritage.org/military/2015/chapter/threats/europe/; Paul Bernstein, *"Putin's Russia and US Defense Strategy,"* Workshop Report, Lawrence Livermore National Laboratory, August 19–20, 2015, LLNL-PROC-678215, available at: https://cgsr.llnl.gov/content/assets/docs/RussiaWorkshopReport.pdf; Center for Strategic and International Studies, *An Assessment of Russian Defense Capabilities and Security Strategy*, available at: http://csis.org/event/assessment-russian-defense-capabilities-

and-security-strategy; Katarzyna Zysk, "Managing Military Change in Russia," in Jo Inge Bekkvold, Ian Bowers, and Michael Raska, eds., *Security, Strategy, and Military Change in the 21st Century: Cross Regional Perspectives* (London: Cass, 2015); Bernstein, *Putin's Russia and US Defense Strategy*; International Institute for Strategic Studies, *Military Balance 2015* (London 2015); and Stockholm International Peace Research Institute, *SIPRI Yearbook 2015* (Stockholm 2015), ch. 6.

57. The IMF forecasts that Russian GDP will decline from 6% to 4% of NATO's by 2020 (and from 11% to 8.5% of European NATO's GDP over the same interval). *IMPF World Economic Outlook*, October 2015. Defense spending increased from 3.5% to 4.5% of GDP from 2008 to 2014. *SIPRI Military Expenditures Database* available at: http://www.sipri.org/research/armaments/milex/milex_database.

58. Timothy Thomas, "Russia's Military Strategy and Ukraine: Indirect, Asymmetric—and Putin-Led," *Journal of Slavic Military Studies*, Vol. 25 (2015), available at: http://fmso.leavenworth.army.mil/documents/Putin%27sRussia/Russia%E2%80%99s%20Military%20Strategy%20and%20Ukraine%20article%20slavic%20mil%20studies.pdf.

59. With slowing economic growth, stressed government finances, and sanctions that compel a more autarkic approach, even the current military plans present economic difficulties. International Institute for Strategic Studies, *Military Balance*, p. 160.

60. Jim Nichol, *Russian Political, Economic, and Security Issues and U.S. Interests*, Congressional Research Service Report for Congress 7-5700, April 29, 2013, available at: http://www.cfr.org/russian-federation/congressional-research-service-russian-political-economic-security-issues-us-interests/p32582. See also International Institute for Strategic Studies, *Military Balance 2014*, pp. 161–162; Michael Kofman and Matthew Rojansky, *A Closer Look at Russia's "Hybrid War"* (Washington, D.C.: Wilson Center, 2015), available at: https://www.wilsoncenter.org/sites/default/files/7-KENNAN%20CABLE-ROJANSKY%20KOFMAN.pdf; and Keir Giles and Andrew Monaghan, *Russian Military Transformation: Goal in Sight?* (Carlisle, Penn.: U.S. Army War College, Strategic Studies Institute, 2014), available at: http://www.strategicstudiesinstitute.army.mil/pubs/display.cfm?pubID=1196.

61. Barry R. Posen, "Ukraine: Part of America's 'Vital Interests'?" *National Interest*, May 12, 2014, available at: http://nationalinterest.org/feature/ukraine-part-americas-vital-interests-10443.

62. See Dmitry Adamsky, *Cross-Domain Coercion: The Current Russian Art of Strategy*, Proliferation Paper No. 54 (Paris: IFRI, 2015); Bernstein, *Putin's Russia and US Defense Strategy*; Zysk, "Managing Military Change in Russia."

63. Bernstein, *Putin's Russia*, p. 8.

64. For a fuller analysis, see William Wohlforth, "The Right Choice for NATO," in Benjamin Valentino and Jeremi Suri, eds., *Sustainable National Security: Assessing U.S. Security Commitments* (New York: Oxford University Press, forthcoming).

65. See, for example, Sarwar Kashmeri, *NATO 2.0: Reboot or Delete?* (Washington, D.C.: Potomac, 2011); Sean Kay, "A New Kind of NATO," *Foreign Policy*, January 11, 2012, available at: http://walt.foreignpolicy.com/posts/2012/01/11/a_new_kind_of_nato; Kay, *America's Search for Security: The Triumph of Idealism and the Return of Realism* (Rowman and Littlefield, 2014); and Jolyon Howorth, *Security and Defence Policy in the European Union* (Houndmills, UK: Palgrave Macmillan, 2014). A minority of analysts argue that abrogating NATO or transforming it into a political alliance (annulling Article 5) would actually strengthen Europe by jump-starting the EU's autonomous capacity. See, for example, Posen, *Restraint*; Andrew Bacevich, "Let Europe Be Europe," *Foreign Policy*, March/April 2010; and David C. Ellis, "U.S. Grand Strategy Following the George W. Bush Presidency," *International Studies Perspectives*, Vol. 10, No. 4 (November 2009), pp. 364–377.

66. See Stanley R. Sloan, *Permanent Alliance: The Transatlantic Bargain from Truman to Obama* (New York: Bloomsbury Academic, 2010).

67. Sten Rynning, "The Geography of the Atlantic Peace: NATO 25 Years after the Fall of the Berlin Wall," *International Affairs*, Vol. 90, No. 6 (2014), pp. 1399–1400.

68. F. Stephen Larrabee, et al., *NATO and the Challenges of Austerity* (Pittsburgh, Penn.: RAND Corporation, 2002); Clara Marina O'Donnell, *The Implications of Military Spending Cuts for NATO's Largest Members* (Washington, D.C.: Brookings Institution, 2012); John R. Deni, *The Future of American Landpower: Does Forward Presence Still Matter?: The Case of the Army in Europe* (Carlisle, Penn.: US Army War College, Strategic Studies Institute, 2012).

69. As of March 2014, 16,500 US troops were deployed onshore in the region, with plans calling for further reductions. Department of Defense, *Total Military Personnel and Dependent End Strength*, Defense Manpower Data Center, available at: https://www.dmdc.osd.mil/appj/dwp/reports.do?category=reports&subCat=milActDutReg. Figures exclude contractors.

70. Joshua Rovner and Caitlin Talmadge, "Hegemony, Force Posture, and the Provision of Public Goods: The Once and Future Role of Outside Powers in Securing Persian Gulf Oil," *Security Studies*, Vol. 23, No. 3, pp. 550–551.

71. Miller, *States, Nations and the Great Powers*, ch. 5.

72. Zartman, "Systems of World Order and Regional Conflict Reduction."

73. See the expert survey reported in Jane K. Cramer and A. Trevor Thrall, eds., *Why Did the United States Invade Iraq?* (New York: Routledge, 2012), ch. 1, and Robert Jervis, "Explaining the War in Iraq," in Cramer and Thrall, *Why Did the United States Invade Iraq?*, pp. 25–48.

74. See, for example, Steven A. Cook, "Don't Fear a Nuclear Arms Race in the Middle East," *Foreign Policy*, April 2, 2012, available at: http://www.foreignpolicy.com/articles/2012/04/02/don_t_fear_a_nuclear_arms_race; Colin H. Kahl, Melissa G. Dalton, and Matthew Irvine, *Atomic Kingdom: If Iran Builds the Bomb, Will Saudi Arabia Be Next?* (Washington, D.C.: Center for a New American Security, 2013); Dalia Dassa Kaye and Frederic M. Wehrey, "A Nuclear Iran: The Reactions

of Neighbours," *Survival*, Vol. 49, No. 2 (2007), pp. 111–128; Gawdat Baghat, "A Nuclear Arms Race in the Middle East: Myth or Reality?" *Mediterranean Quarterly*, Vol. 22, No. 1 (2011), pp. 27–40; Barry Posen, "We Can Live with a Nuclear Iran?" MIT Paper, Massachusetts Institute of Technology, March 2006.

75. F. Gregory Gause III, *The International Politics of the Persian Gulf* (Cambridge, UK: Cambridge University Press, 2010), p. 3.

76. Steven Simon and Jonathan Stevenson, "The End of Pax Americana: Why Washington's Middle East Pullback Makes Sense," *Foreign Affairs*, Vol. 94, No. 6 (November/December 2015), p. 2.

CHAPTER 7

1. For a full list of citations to this literature, see chapter 1, endnote 9.

2. Barry Posen, "Pull Back: The Case for a Less Activist Foreign Policy," *Foreign Affairs*, Vol. 92, No. 1 (January/February 2013), p. 1.

3. Christopher Layne, "The Unipolar Exit: Beyond the *Pax Americana*," *Cambridge Review of International Affairs*, Vol. 24, No. 2 (June 2011), p. 153.

4. Congressional Budget Office, *The Long-Term Budget Outlook: CBO July 2014 Report* (Washington, D.C.: Congressional Budget Office, 2014).

5. Calculated from Office of the Under Secretary of Defense Comptroller, *FY2013 Defense Budget Overview* (Washington, D.C.: U.S. Department of Defense, 2012), available at: http://dcmo.defense.gov/publications/documents/FY2013_Budget_Request_Overview_Book.pdf.

6. Robert M. Gates, "Remarks Delivered by Secretary of Defense Robert M. Gates," speech given at Abilene, Kansas, May 8, 2010, available at: http://www.defense.gov/speeches/speech.aspx?speechid=1467http://www.defense.gov/speeches/speech.aspx?speechid=1467.

7. As stressed in, for example, Barack Obama, "Remarks by the President at the United States Military Academy Commencement Ceremony," May 28, 2014, available at: http://www.whitehouse.gov/the-press-office/2014/05/28/remarks-president-united-states-military-academy-commencement-ceremony; Department of Defense, *2014 Quadrennial Defense Review*, available at: http://www.defense.gov/home/features/2014/0314_sdr/qdr.aspx; and *Defense Strategic Guidance: Sustaining U.S. Global Leadership; Priorities for 21st Century Defense*, available at: http://archive.defense.gov/news/Defense_Strategic_Guidance.pdf.

8. Congressional Budget Office, "Long-Term Implications of the 2016 Future Years Defense Program" (January 14 2016), p. 14, available at: https://www.cbo.gov/publication/51050.

9. Congressional Budget Office, Long-Term Implications of the 2014 Future Years Defense Program, November 2013, available at: https://www.cbo.gov/sites/default/files/113th-congress-2013-2014/reports/44683-FYDP.pdf. See *An Update to the Budget and Economic Outlook: 2014 to 2024* (Washington, D.C.: Congressional

Budget Office, 2014). This is an estimate of base budget spending, excluding supplemental outlays for overseas contingency operations (OCO) and defense-related parts of the budgets for the Departments of Homeland Security, Veterans Affairs, and Energy. (The base DoD outlays for FY 2014 were 2.9% of GDP, or 3.4% if OCO funding is included. In comparison, the average since the end of World War II has been roughly 5.5% of GDP overall, or 5.0% in peacetime.) Note that spending in real terms will still be higher than in the late 1990s. See Theresa Gullo, "The Federal Budget: Outlook and Challenges," Congressional Budget Office, June 2013. The DoD Comptroller projects the total budget (base + OCO/Supplemental) of $573 billion in 2013 dollars in 2017, compared to $384 billion in 1998. Office of the Under Secretary of Defense Comptroller, *Fiscal Year 2013 Budget Request Briefing* (Washington, D.C.: U.S. Department of Defense, 2012), available at: http://comptroller.defense.gov/defbudget/fy2013/FY2013_Budget_Request.pdf.

10. See, for example, Todd Harrison, *Analysis of the FY2015 Defense Budget* (Washington, D.C.: Center for Strategic and Budgetary Assessments, 2014).

11. See, for example, National Defense Panel report, *2014 Quadrennial Defense Review: Ensuring a Strong U.S. Defense for the Future* (Washington, D.C.: U.S. Institute of Peace, 2014).

12. Department of Defense, Office of the Comptroller, *National Defense Budget Estimates for FY 2012* (Washington D.C.: Department of Defense, March 2011).

13. Patrick Mills, Jennifer Kavanaugh, Leila Mahnad, and Steven Worman, *The Costs of Commitment: Cost Analysis of Overseas Air Force Basing* (Santa Monica, Calif.: RAND Corporation, 2013), p. viii. The navy is different because few of its ships are home-ported overseas; most spend the majority of their deployed time overseas. This pattern would not change in any retrenchment scenario, all of which emphasize the navy. (Home-porting ships overseas would save a great deal of money but is politically infeasible.) The most extensive open-source analysis of the costs and benefits of overseas basing is a major congressionally mandated RAND study, which finds that permanent overseas stationing of forces is modestly but measurably more expensive than basing in the United States. The study also shows that surging forces in contingencies or ramping up for them can be very expensive. Michael J. Lostumbo, Michael J. McNerney, Eric Peltz, et al., *Overseas Basing of US Military Forces: An Assessment of Relative Costs and Strategic Benefits* (Santa Monica, Calif.: RAND Corporation, 2013). See also US Congressional Budget Office, *Options for Changing the Army's Overseas Basing* (Washington, D.C.: Congressional Budget Office, 2012).

14. Benjamin H. Friedman and Justin Logan, "Why the U.S. Military Budget Is 'Foolish and Sustainable,'" *Orbis*, Vol. 56, No. 2 (Spring 2012), pp. 186–187.

15. Ibid.

16. See Eugene Gholz and Daryl G. Press, "Protecting 'The Prize,'" *Security Studies*, Vol. 19, No. 3 (August 2010), pp. 453–485.

17. Note that this is a current estimate of a moving target. We use US government estimates of projected spending as a proxy for deep engagement's requirements, and we rely on official statements concerning the adequacy of those funding levels. See Congressional Budget Office, *Long-Term Implications of the 2015 Future Years Defense Program* (Washington, D.C.: Congressional Budget Office, 2014); Office of the Under Secretary of Defense Comptroller, *Green Book for 2014*, (Washington, D.C.: Department of Defense, 2013), available at: http://comptroller.defense.gov/defbudget/fy2014/FY14_Green_Book.pdf; and Theresa Gullo, *The Federal Budget: Outlook and Challenges* (Washington, D.C.: Congressional Budget Office, 2013).

18. Barry R. Posen, *Restraint: A New Foundation for U.S. Grand Strategy* (Ithaca, N.Y.: Cornell University Press, 2014).

19. "Fiscally sustainable" is a complex term, combining assessments of economic questions (relationship between taxes, public debt, and growth/welfare; projection of expected growth and government revenue) and politics (level and nature of taxation the political system can bear; preferences over trade-offs between guns and butter). The conventional view is that the country can sustain the kind of defense spending levels that are now projected at taxation levels consistent with growth; see, for example, Congressional Budget Office, *2011 Long-Term Budget Outlook* (Washington, D.C.: Congressional Budget Office, 2011); Organisation for Economic Co-operation and Development, *OECD Factbook 2011–2012: Economic, Environmental and Social Statistics*, (Washington, D.C.: Organisation for Economic Co-operation and Development, 2011), available at: http://dx.doi.org/10.1787/factbook-2011-en. In contrast, in her analysis of the economic and political elements of sustainability, Cindy Williams argues that only defense outlays at 1.6–2.6% of GDP are sustainable over the long term. Cindy Williams, "Preserving National Strength in a Period of Fiscal Restraint," in Jeremi Suri and Benjamin Valentino, eds., *Sustainable Security: Rethinking American National Security Strategy* (Oxford: Oxford University Press, forthcoming). The most recent White House budget proposal projects defense expenditures at the upper bound of that range by 2023.

20. Figures from both the Stockholm Peace Research Institute (SIPRI) and the US Office of Management and Budget show US defense spending bottoming out at 3% of GDP from 1999 to 2001. See SIPRI Military Expenditure Database, Stockholm International Peace Research Institute, available at: http://www.sipri.org/databases/milex, and Office of Management and Budget, "Composition of Outlays: 1940 to 2017," in *Historical Tables of the Budget of the United States, Fiscal Year 2013* (Washington, D.C.: Office of Management and Budget, 2013), Table 6.1, available at: http://www.whitehouse.gov/omb/budget/Historicals.

21. Robert Gilpin, *War and Change in World Politics* (Cambridge, UK: Cambridge University Press, 1981); Paul Kennedy, *The Rise and Fall of the Great Powers*

(New York: Random House, 1987); and David P. Calleo, *The Imperious Economy* (Cambridge, Mass.: Harvard University Press, 1982). See also James Chace, *Solvency: The Price of Survival* (New York: Random House, 1981).

22. An absolute and more inherently revisionist interpretation of US leadership is employed in Posen, *Restraint*. In the leadership long-cycle tradition of rise-and-decline scholarship, the term is also used to describe economic leadership and/or naval leadership. See William P. Thompson and Rafael Reuveny, *Growth, Trade and Systemic Leadership* (Ann Arbor: University of Michigan Press, 2004), and Karen Rasler and William P. Thompson, *The Great Powers and Global Struggle, 1490–1990* (Lexington: University Press of Kentucky, 1994).

23. Christopher Layne, "This Time It's Real: The End of Unipolarity and the *Pax Americana*," *International Studies Quarterly*, Vol. 56, No. 1 (January 2012), pp. 203–213. See also Christopher Layne, "The Unipolar Exit: Beyond the *Pax Americana*," *Cambridge Review of International Affairs*, Vol. 24, No. 2 (June 2011), p. 153, where he notes: "Simply put, the United States is imperially overstretched."

24. Gilpin, *War and Change in World Politics*, p. 156.

25. Gilpin's discussion of declining rates of growth is roughly consistent with neoclassical growth models in economics pioneered by Robert Solow, and also foreshadows some of the arguments developed in Mancur Olson, *The Rise and Decline of Nations* (New Haven, Conn.: Yale University Press, 1982). Key is that causes of declining growth in Gilpin, Solow, and Olson are all internal to a country's economy, unrelated to its positioning in the international system.

26. Kennedy, *The Rise and Fall of the Great Powers*, and Calleo, *The Imperious Economy*.

27. See, for example, Eugene Gholz, Daryl G. Press, and Harvey M. Sapolsky, "Come Home, America: The Strategy of Restraint in the Face of Temptation," *International Security*, Vol. 21, No. 4 (Spring 1997), pp. 5–48, and Barry R. Posen, "The Case for Restraint," *American Interest*, Vol. 3, No. 1 (November/December 2007), pp. 7–17.

28. See, for example, Michael J. Mueller and H. Sonmez Atesoglu, "Defense Spending, Technological Change, and Economic Growth in the United States," *Defence Economics*, Vol. 4, No. 3 (1993), pp. 259–269.

29. J. Paul Dunne, Ron Smith, and Dirk Willenbockel, "Models of Military Expenditure and Growth: A Critical Review," *Defence and Peace Economics*, Vol. 16, No. 6 (December 2005), pp. 449–461.

30. Gieogio D'Agostino, J. Paul Dunne, and Luca Pieroni, "Assessing the Effects of Military Expenditures on Growth," in Michelle R. Garfinkel and Stergios Skaperdas, eds., *The Oxford Handbook of the Economics of Peace and Conflict* (New York: Oxford University Press, 2012), pp. 388–411. See also Aynur Alptekin and Paul Levine, "Military Expenditure and Economic Growth: A Meta-Analysis" (MPRA Paper No. 28853, February 21, 2011), available at: http://mpra.ub.uni-muenchen.de/28853/, and Betu Dicle and Mehmet F. Dicle, "Military

Spending and GDP Growth: Is There a General Causal Relationship?" *Journal of Comparative Policy Analysis*, Vol. 12, No. 3 (June 2010), pp. 311–345. On the United States, see Uk Heo, "The Relationship between Defense Spending and Economic Growth in the United States," *Political Research Quarterly*, Vol. 63, No. 4 (December 2010), pp. 760–770.

31. Karen A. Rasler and William R. Thompson, *Great Powers and Global Struggle, 1490–1990* (Lexington: University Press of Kentucky, 1995), p. 134.

32. The best case for the possible growth effects of the US security subsidy in the case of Japan is Michael C. Beckley, Yusaku Horiuchi, and Jennifer Miller, "America's Role in the Making of Japan's Economic Miracle," paper presented at the American Political Science Association 2013 Annual Meeting, December 27, 2013, available at: SSRN: http://ssrn.com/abstract=2299948; though the authors cannot distinguish the security subsidy from specific perks the United States offered (many of which were removed by Richard Nixon in the 1970s) and domestic political developments.

33. William R. Thompson, "Systemic Leadership, Evolutionary Processes, and International Relations Theory: The Unipolarity Question," *International Studies Review*, Vol. 8, No. 1 (March 2006), p. 17.

34. Other challenges to the free riding argument include: (1) many allies actually do create credible forces with lower expenditures. See, for example, Jennifer Lind, "Pacifism or Passing the Buck? Testing Theories of Japanese Security Policy," *International Security*, Vol. 29, No. 1 (Summer 2004), pp. 92–121; and (2) lower defense efforts of some allies result not from parasitism (as the theory suggests) but rather from low threat perceptions. See, for example, Martial Foucault and Frédéric Mérand, "The Challenge of Burden Sharing," *International Journal*, Vol. 68, No. 2, pp. 423–429.

35. Carla Norrlof, *America's Global Advantage: U.S. Hegemony and International Cooperation* (Cambridge, UK: Cambridge University Press, 2010), pp. 167–191, and Michael Charles Beckley, "The Unipolar Era: Why American Power Persists and China's Rise Is Limited," PhD dissertation, Columbia University, 2012.

36. Beckley, "The Unipolar Era."

CHAPTER 8

1. Barry R. Posen, "From Unipolarity to Multipolarity: Transition in Sight?" in G. John Ikenberry, Michael M. Mastanduno, and William C. Wohlforth, eds., *International Relations Theory and the Consequences of Unipolarity* (Cambridge, UK: Cambridge University Press, 2001), p. 333, and Barry R. Posen, "The Case for Restraint," *American Interest*, Vol. 3, No. 1 (November/December 2007), p. 13.

2. Richard K. Betts, *American Force: Dangers, Delusions, and Dilemmas in National Security* (New York: Columbia University Press, 2012), p. 278.

3. Posen, "The Case for Restraint," p. 12. See also Posen, "From Unipolarity to Multipolarity," p. 329; Christopher Layne, "From Preponderance to Offshore

Balancing: America's Future Grand Strategy," *International Security*, Vol. 22, No. 1 (Summer 1997), p. 113; and Betts, *American Force*, p. 278.

4. T. V. Paul, James J. Wirtz, and Michel Fortmann, eds., *Balance of Power: Theory and Practice in the 21st Century* (Palo Alto, Calif.: Stanford University Press, 2004).

5. William C. Wohlforth, "The Stability of a Unipolar World," *International Security*, Vol. 24, No. 1 (Summer 1999), pp. 5–41; Wohlforth, "U.S. Strategy in a Unipolar World," in G. John Ikenberry, ed., *America Unrivaled: The Future of the Balance of Power* (Ithaca, N.Y.: Cornell University Press, 2002), pp. 98–118; Stephen G. Brooks and William C. Wohlforth, *World Out of Balance: International Relations and the Challenge of American Primacy* (Princeton, N.J.: Princeton University Press, 2008), pp. 22–59; Stephen Brooks and William Wohlforth, "American Primacy in Perspective," *Foreign Affairs*, Vol. 81, No. 4 (July/August 2002), pp. 20–33; Stephen Brooks and William Wohlforth, "Correspondence: Striking the Balance," *International Security*, Vol. 30, No. 3 (Winter 2005/6), pp. 186–191; Stephen Brooks and William Wohlforth, "Assessing the Balance," *Cambridge Review of International Affairs*, Vol. 24, No. 2 (June 2011), pp. 201–219; Daniel H. Nexon, "The Balance of Power in the Balance," *World Politics*, Vol. 61, No. 2 (April 2009), pp. 330–359; and David W. Blagden, Jack S. Levy, and William R. Thompson, "Correspondence: Sea Powers, Continental Powers, and Balancing Theory," *International Security*, Vol. 36, No. 2 (Fall 2011), pp. 190–202.

6. Evan Braden Montgomery, "Contested Primacy in the Western Pacific: China's Rise and the Future of U.S. Power Projection," *International Security*, Vol. 38, No. 4 (Spring 2014), p. 125.

7. Ibid. To clarify further, Daniel H. Nexon helpfully distinguishes among balance-of-power theory (claiming that concentrations of capabilities in the system generate countervailing pressure to restore equilibrium), theories of power balances (concerning the various causes that might push a system toward balance), and theories of balancing (specifying the conditions under which states adopt policies that might qualify as balancing). Balance-of-power theory captures only the subset of theories of power balances and balancing that feature the pressures created by a concentration of capabilities in the system. There are many other arguments about how balances emerge and why states may adopt policies that might reasonably be dubbed balancing. See Nexon, "The Balance of Power in the Balance," *World Politics*, Vol. 61, No. 2 (April 2009), pp. 330–359.

8. To be sure, technological and organizational barriers to generating some kinds of capabilities were still formidable in the 19th and 20th centuries, requiring up to a generation of concerted effort. See, for example, James R. Holmes and Toshi Yoshihara, "Hardly the First Time," *U.S. Naval Institute Proceedings*, Vol. 139, No. 4 (April 2013), pp. 22–27, and Michael C. Horowitz, *The Diffusion of Military Power: Causes and Consequences for International Politics* (Princeton, N.J.: Princeton University Press, 2010).

9. Montgomery, "Contested Primacy in the Western Pacific," p. 125.

10. Among other implications, this means the United States is still able to impose a "distant" blockade on China. See the helpful discussion in Llewelyn Hughes and Austin Long, "Is There an Oil Weapon? Security Implications of Changes in the Structure of the International Oil Market," *International Security*, Vol. 39, No. 3 (Winter 2014/15), pp. 178–180.

11. Stephen M. Walt, "Alliances in a Unipolar World," *World Politics*, Vol. 61, No. 1 (January 2009), pp. 86–120.

12. G. John Ikenberry, *After Victory: Institutions, Strategic Restraint, and the Rebuilding of Order after Major Wars* (Princeton, N.J.: Princeton University Press, 2000); Ikenberry, *Liberal Leviathan* (Princeton, N.J.: Princeton University Press, 2012). See also Brooks and Wohlforth, *World Out of Balance*, ch. 7, and Randall L. Schweller and Xiaoyu Pu, "After Unipolarity: China's Visions of International Order in an Era of U.S. Decline," *International Security*, Vol. 36, No. 1 (Summer 2011), pp. 41–72.

13. Mark Zachary Taylor, "Toward an International Relations Theory of National Innovation Rates," *Security Studies*, Vol. 21, No. 1 (March 2012), pp. 113–152; Stephanie Neuman, "Power, Influence, and Hierarchy: Defense Industries in a Unipolar World," *Defense and Peace Economics*, Vol. 21, No. 1 (February 2010), pp. 105–134.

14. On the difficulty of defining soft balancing, see Stephen Brooks and William C. Wohlforth, "Hard Times for Soft Balancing," *International Security*, Vol. 30, No. 1 (Summer 2005), pp. 72–108, and Gerard Alexander and Keir A. Lieber, "Waiting for Balancing: Why the World Is Not Pushing Back," *International Security*, Vol. 30, No. 1 (Summer 2005), pp. 109–139.

15. See the discussion in Brooks and Wohlforth, "Hard Times for Soft Balancing," and Alexander and Lieber, "Waiting for Balancing."

16. Michael Charles Beckley, "The Unipolar Era: Why American Power Persists and China's Rise Is Limited," PhD dissertation, Columbia University, 2012.

17. Giacomo Chiozza, *Anti-Americanism and the American World Order* (Baltimore: Johns Hopkins University Press, 2009).

18. Robert Pape, "Soft Balancing against the United States," *International Security*, Vol. 30, No. 1 (Summer 2005), pp. 7–45; Walt, "Alliances in a Unipolar World"; T. V. Paul, "Soft Balancing in the Age of U.S. Primacy," *International Security*, Vol. 30, No. 1 (Summer 2005), pp. 46–71.

19. See Kai He and Huiyun Feng, "If Not Soft Balancing, Then What? Reconsidering Soft Balancing and U.S. Policy toward China," *Security Studies*, Vol. 17, No. 2 (April 2008), pp. 363–395, and G. John Ikenberry, "The Rise of China: Power, Institutions, and the Western Order," in Robert S. Ross and Feng Zhu, eds., *China's Ascent: Power, Security, and the Future of International Politics* (Ithaca, N.Y.: Cornell University Press, 2008), pp. 89–114.

20. Our initial research along these lines is presented in Brooks and Wohlforth, *World Out of Balance*, ch. 7, but subsequent research has deepened and broadened

empirical support for this argument. See, for example, Kai He, *Institutional Balancing in the Asia-Pacific* (New York: Routledge, 2009); John D. Ciorciari, *The Limits of Alignment: Southeast Asia and the Great Powers Since 1975* (Washington, D.C.: Georgetown University Press, 2010); Vidya Nadkarni, *Strategic Partnerships in Asia: Balancing without Alliances* (New York: Routledge, 2010); and Alexandru Grigorescu, "East and Central European Countries and the Iraq War: The Choice between 'Soft Balancing' and 'Soft Bandwagoning,'" *Communist and Post-Communist Studies*, Vol. 41, No. 3 (September 2008), pp. 281–299.

21. The challenges that this tendency presents to potential revisionist powers is discussed in Schweller and Pu, "After Unipolarity."

22. Robert A. Pape, *Dying to Win: The Strategic Logic of Suicide Terrorism* (New York: Random House, 2005); Pape and James K. Feldman, *Cutting the Fuse: The Explosion of Global Suicide Terrorism and How to Stop It* (Chicago: University of Chicago Press, 2010); Robert A. Pape, "It's the Occupation, Stupid," *Foreign Policy*, October 18, 2010, available at: http://www.foreignpolicy.com/articles/2010/10/18/it_s_the_occupation_stupid; Robert A. Pape, "Empire Falls," *National Interest*, No. 99 (January/February 2009), pp. 21–34; Robert Pape, "The Logic of Suicide Terrorism: It's the Occupation, not the Fundamentalism," *American Conservative*, July 18, 2005, available at: http://www.theamericanconservative.com/articles/the-logic-of-suicide-terrorism/. Although Pape's research is most prominent, many other advocates of retrenchment also contend that reducing the terror threat to the US homeland is an expected benefit of pulling back. See, for example, Harvey M. Sapolsky, Benjamin H. Friedman, Eugene Gholz, and Daryl G. Press, "Restraining Order: For Strategic Modesty," *World Affairs* (Fall 2009), pp. 84–94; Eugene Gholz and Daryl Press, "Footprints in the Sand," *American Interest*, Vol. 5, No. 4 (March/April 2010), pp. 59–67; John J. Mearsheimer, "Pull Those Boots off the Ground," *Newsweek*, December 31, 2008; and Christopher Layne, *The Peace of Illusions: American Grand Strategy from 1940 to the Present* (Ithaca, N.Y.: Cornell University Press, 2006).

23. Robert A. Pape and James K. Feldman, *Cutting the Fuse: The Explosion of Global Suicide Terrorism and How to Stop It* (Chicago: University of Chicago Press, 2010), p. 329. Since some of his analyses are coauthored while others are not, for convenience we merely refer to Pape directly.

24. See, for example, Sara Jackson Wade and Dan Reiter, "Does Democracy Matter? Regime Type and Suicide Terrorism," *Journal of Conflict Resolution*, Vol. 51, No. 2 (April 2007), and Scott Ashworth, Joshua Clinton, Adam Meirowitz, and Kristopher Ramsay, "Design, Inference, and the Strategic Logic of Suicide Terrorism," *American Political Science Review*, Vol. 101, No. 2 (May 2008), pp. 269–273.

25. Pape and Feldman, *Cutting the Fuse*, p. 334.

26. See, for example, Pape and Feldman, *Cutting the Fuse*, p. 12. See also Robert A. Pape, "It's the Occupation, Stupid," p. 4, where he notes, "The research

suggests that U.S. interests would be better served through a policy of offshore balancing."

27. See, for example, Pape, "It's the Occupation, Stupid."

28. See Pape and Feldman, *Cutting the Fuse*, p. 186.

29. Key here is the claim that suicide terrorism now occurs in Pakistan because its government was spurred by America to undertake extensive military operations in Pakistan's western tribal regions; see Pape and Feldman, *Cutting the Fuse*, p. 10.

30. Pape, "The Logic of Suicide Terrorism," p. 2.

31. Pape and Feldman, *Cutting the Fuse*, pp. 247–248.

32. See especially Joshua Rovner and Caitlin Talmadge, "Hegemony, Force Posture, and the Provision of Public Goods: The Once and Future Role of Outside Powers in Securing Persian Gulf Oil," *Security Studies*, Vol. 23, No. 3 (2014), pp. 548–581.

33. A total of 16,500 US troops were deployed onshore in the region as of spring 2014; see Department of Defense, *Total Military Personnel and Dependent End Strength*, Defense Manpower Data Center, available at: https://www.dmdc.osd.mil/appj/dwp/reports.do?category=reports&subCat=milActDutReg.

34. Glenn H. Snyder, *Alliance Politics* (Ithaca, N.Y.: Cornell University Press, 1997); Snyder, "The Security Dilemma in Alliance Politics," *World Politics*, Vol. 36, No. 4 (July 1984), pp. 461–495.

35. Arguments from economics about moral hazard solve this problem by (1) stipulating an information asymmetry between the principal (e.g., an insurance agency) and the agent (e.g., a client), where the agent knows more about the risks he or she undertakes than the principal and (2) assuming the existence of a binding legal obligation on the principal to make good on promises of support in times of need. Neither assumption applies to security risks in US alliances.

36. See John Mearsheimer, "The False Promise of International Institutions," *International Security*, Vol. 19, No. 3 (Winter 1994/95), pp. 5–49.

37. Tongfi Kim, "Why Alliances Entangle but Seldom Entrap States," *Security Studies*, Vol. 20, No. 3 (July 2011), p. 355.

38. In addition to Kim, "Why Alliances Entangle but Seldom Entrap States," see especially Michael C. Beckley, "The Myth of Entangling Alliances: Reassessing the Security Risks of U.S. Defense Pacts," *International Security*, Vol. 39, No. 4, (Spring 2015), pp. 7–48. Also relevant are Robert J. Art, *A Grand Strategy for America* (Ithaca, N.Y.: Cornell University Press, 2003), pp. 139, 143–144, 196; Charles L. Glaser, "Why NATO Is Still Best: Future Security Arrangements for Europe," *International Security*, Vol. 18, No. 1 (Summer 1993), pp. 5–50; Richard K. Betts, *American Force: Dangers, Delusions, and Dilemmas in National Security* (New York: Columbia University Press, 2012), ch. 12; and Thomas J. Christensen, *Worse Than a Monolith: Alliance Politics and Problems of Coercive Diplomacy in Asia* (Princeton, N.J.: Princeton University Press, 2011), pp. 242–255.

39. Beckley, "The Myth of Entangling Alliances." In the most important case, Vietnam, Beckley concludes that the key driver was internally conceived US interest in containing communism.

40. Beckley, "The Myth of Entangling Alliances," p. 48.

41. See Kim, "Why Alliances Entangle but Seldom Entrap States." Cases of the related phenomenon of "chain-ganging," in which alliance ties expand wars beyond the real interest of some or all alliance members, are also now far more contested than they were two decades ago. According to new research by a growing cadre of historians and political scientists, even the canonical case of World War I does not qualify. Dominic Tierney, "Does Chain-Ganging Cause the Outbreak of War?" *International Studies Quarterly*, Vol. 55, No. 2 (June 2011), pp. 285–304, and Keir A. Lieber, "The New History of World War I and What It Means for International Relations Theory," *International Security*, Vol. 32, No. 2 (Fall 2007), pp. 155–191.

42. See, for example, Janice Gross Stein and Eugene Lang, *The Unexpected War: Canada in Kandahar* (Toronto: Viking, 2007).

43. Paul W. Schroeder, "Alliances, 1815–1945: Weapons of Power and Tools of Management," in Klaus Knorr, ed., *Historical Dimensions of National Security Problems* (Lawrence: University of Kansas Press, 1975), pp. 227–263, quotes at 227 and 256, respectively. For a theoretical analysis that captures the points made herein about alliances as risk-management tools, see Timothy W. Crawford, *Pivotal Deterrence: Third-Party Statecraft and the Pursuit of Peace* (Ithaca, N.Y.: Cornell University Press, 2003). See Jeremy Pressman, *Warring Friends: Alliance Restraint in International Politics* (Ithaca, N.Y.: Cornell University Press, 2008), which shows that when a great power is willing to throw its weight around, it can reliably restrain smaller allies.

44. Jesse C. Johnson and Brett Ashley Leeds, "Defense Pacts: A Prescription for Peace?" *Foreign Policy Analysis*, Vol. 7, No. 1 (January 2011), pp. 45–65.

45. Victor D. Cha, "Powerplay: Origins of the U.S. Alliance System in Asia," *International Security*, Vol. 34, No. 3 (Winter 2009/10), p. 158. For the full analysis of historical evidence, see Cha, *Powerplay: The Origins of the American Alliance System in Asia's Regional Security Architecture* (Princeton, N.J.: Princeton University Press, forthcoming).

46. See especially Christopher A. Preble, *Power Problem: How American Military Dominance Makes Us Less Safe, Less Prosperous, and Less Free* (Ithaca, N.Y.: Cornell University Press, 2009).

47. See Betts, *American Force*.

48. Michael Dobbs, "With Albright, Clinton Accepts New U.S. Role," *Washington Post*, December 8, 1996, A1.

49. We thank Chris Preble for a helpful conversation on this issue.

50. Owen B. Toon, Alan Robock, Richard P. Turco, et al., "Consequences of Regional-Scale Nuclear Conflicts," *Science*, Vol. 315 (2007), pp. 1224–1225.

51. Casualties as of 2010 calculated from Hannah Fischer, *U.S. Military Casualty Statistics: Operation New Dawn, Operation Iraqi Freedom, and Operation Enduring Freedom* (Washington, D.C.: Congressional Research Service, 2010). Costs are actual budget outlays (not estimated total cost) as of 2011, calculated from Stephen Daggett, *Costs of Major U.S. Wars* (Washington, D.C.: Congressional Research Service, 2010); Jeremiah Gertler, *Operation Odyssey Dawn (Libya): Background and Issues for Congress* (Washington, D.C.: Congressional Research Service, 2011); and Nina M. Serafino, *Military Contingency Funding for Bosnia, Southwest Asia, and Other Operations: Questions and Answers* (Washington, D.C.: Congressional Research Service, 1999), available at: http://stuff.mit.edu/afs/sipb/contrib/wikileaks-crs/wikileaks-crs-reports/98-823.pdf.

52. Data from Beckley, "The Unipolar Era."

53. F. Gregory Gause III, *The International Politics of the Persian Gulf* (Cambridge, UK: Cambridge University Press, 2010), p. 2.

54. Dominic Tierney, *The Obama Doctrine and the Lessons of Iraq* (Philadelphia: Foreign Policy Research Institute, 2012), available at: http://www.fpri.org/enotes/2012/201205.tierney.obama-doctrine-iraq.html. Afghanistan has also shaped Obama's thinking, as David Sanger reports:

> The lessons Mr. Obama has learned in Afghanistan have been crucial to shaping his presidency. Fatigue and frustration with the war have defined the strategies his administration has adopted to guide how America intervenes in the world's messiest conflicts. Out of the experience emerged Mr. Obama's "light footprint" strategy, in which the United States strikes from a distance but does not engage in years-long, enervating occupations. That doctrine shaped the president's thinking about how to deal with the challenges that followed—Libya, Syria and a nuclear Iran."

Sanger, "Charting Obama's Journey to a Shift on Afghanistan," *New York Times*, May 20, 2012.

55. Department of Defense, *Sustaining U.S. Global Leadership: Priorities for 21st Century Defense* (Washington, D.C.: Department of Defense, 2012), p. 6.

56. John Mueller, "The Iraq Syndrome," *Foreign Affairs*, Vol. 84, No. 6 (November/December 2005), pp. 44–54.

57. Beckley, "The Myth of Entangling Alliances," p. 47.

CHAPTER 9

1. The exceptions that prove this rule are Eugene Gholz and Daryl Press, the former of whom has extensively researched economic issues and the pair of whom are the only analysts in the retrenchment literature to extensively address how the global economy factors into the grand strategy debate (although they, like other analysts in this literature, neglect the role of international institutions). Yet as valuable as Gholz and Press's work is, it only addresses some of the relevant arguments: they

examine the link between military conflict and the global economy but do not address the fundamental logic of hegemonic order that underlies deep engagement. See Eugene Gholz and Daryl G. Press, "The Effects of Wars on Neutral Countries: Why It Doesn't Pay to Preserve the Peace," *Security Studies*, Vol. 10, No. 4 (Summer 2001), pp. 1–57, and Eugene Gholz and Daryl G. Press, "Protecting 'The Prize': Oil and the U.S. National Interest," *Security Studies*, Vol. 19, No. 3 (August 2010), pp. 453–485.

2. Barry R. Posen, *Restraint: A New Foundation for U.S. Grand Strategy* (Ithaca, N.Y.: Cornell University Press, 2014), p. 1.

3. See, for example, Christopher Layne, "From Preponderance to Offshore Balancing: America's Future Grand Strategy," *International Security*, Vol. 22, No. 1 (Summer 1997), pp. 86–124; Robert A. Pape, "Empire Falls," *National Interest*, No. 99 (January/February 2009), pp. 21–34; and John J. Mearsheimer, "Imperial by Design," *National Interest*, No. 111 (January/February 2011), pp. 16–34.

4. See especially Robert Gilpin, *The Political Economy of International Relations* (Princeton, N.J.: Princeton University Press, 1987), and Gilpin, *U.S. Power and the Multinational Corporation* (New York: Basic Books, 1975).

5. Robert O. Keohane, *After Hegemony: Cooperation and Discord in the World Political Economy* (Princeton, N.J.: Princeton University Press, 1984), pp. 14, 135. See also G. John Ikenberry, *After Victory: Institutions, Strategic Restraint, and the Rebuilding of Order after Major Wars* (Princeton, N.J.: Princeton University Press, 2000).

6. Keohane, *After Hegemony*, p. 12.

7. See Stephen Brooks and William Wohlforth, "Reshaping the World Order," *Foreign Affairs*, Vol. 88, No. 2 (March/April 2009), pp. 49–63. See the related discussion in Stephen G. Brooks and William C. Wohlforth, *World Out of Balance: International Relations and the Challenge of American Primacy* (Princeton, N.J.: Princeton University Press, 2008), chs. 6 and 7.

8. Keohane, *After Hegemony*, p. 208.

9. See the discussion of these literatures in David Lake, "Leadership, Hegemony, and the International Economy: Naked Emperor or Tattered Monarch with Potential?" *International Studies Quarterly*, Vol. 37 No. 4 (December 1993), pp. 459–489, and Brooks and Wohlforth, *World Out of Balance*, ch. 5.

10. See, for example, Erik Voeten, "Outside Options and the Logic of Security Council Action," *American Political Science Review*, Vol. 95, No. 4 (December 2001), p. 845, who notes that "institutionalists believe that power asymmetries are important, but their consequences are rarely explicitly modeled." As the organizers of a prominent team of scholars seeking to move the institutionalist research program forward stress, the analytical framework that guided their collective research "did not emphasize power" because "the formal literature does not offer compelling results." See Barbara Koremenos, Charles Lipson, and Duncan

Snidal, "Rational Design: Looking Back to Move Forward," *International Organization*, Vol. 55, No. 4 (Autumn 2001), p. 1067; see also the discussion in John Duffield, "The Limits of Rational Design," *International Organization*, Vol. 57, No. 2 (Spring 2003), pp. 417–418, and Barbara Koremenos and Duncan Snidal, "Moving Forward, One Step at a Time," *International Organization*, Vol. 57, No. 2 (Spring 2003), p. 437.

11. Keohane, *After Hegemony*, p. 31. Numerous other analysts such as Snidal also argued in response to hegemonic stability theory that hegemonic leadership is not absolutely necessary for the continuation of economic globalization—that it *could* potentially continue under a variety of potential scenarios even absent a hegemon who was willing to provide leadership of the global economy; see Duncan Snidal, "The Limits of Hegemonic Stability Theory," *International Organization*, Vol. 39, No. 4 (Autumn 1985), pp. 579–614. This general line of critique was powerful, and ultimately led analysts of the global economy to largely turn away from the general issue of how hegemony and the distribution of power influence global economic affairs; see the discussion in Lake, "Leadership, Hegemony, and the International Economy."

12. See the discussion of this issue in Gilpin, *The Political Economy of International Relations*, pp. 86–88. He notes: "Contrary to the overly simplistic characterization of [hegemonic stability] theory by some critics as determinative, the theory holds that the hegemonic political structure is permissive, but does not determine either the nature of commercial policy or the content of economic transactions." Gilpin, *Political Economy*, p. 86. At the same time, he also maintains that "a hegemon is necessary to the existence of a liberal political economy." Gilpin, *Political Economy*, p. 88.

13. Robert O. Keohane, "Hegemony and After: Knowns and Unknowns in the Debate over Decline," *Foreign Affairs*, Vol. 91, No. 4 (July/August 2012), pp. 117–118.

14. Keohane, *After Hegemony*, p. 12 (emphasis added).

15. The next three paragraphs draw significantly from pp. 47–49 of Stephen Brooks, G. John Ikenberry, and William Wohlforth, "Don't Come Home, America: The Case against Retrenchment," *International Security*, Vol. 37, No. 3 (Winter 2012/13), pp. 7–51.

16. Keohane, "Hegemony and After," p. 118.

17. For further discussion of this point along with interviews with former US administration officials that confirm the usefulness of the US alliance system for generating enhanced nonsecurity cooperation, see Brooks, Ikenberry, and Wohlforth, "Don't Come Home, America," pp. 49–50. On how the United States used its provision of security assistance as direct leverage to get its allies to accede to US plans for the management of the global economy, see Francis J. Gavin, *Gold, Dollars, and Power: The Politics of International Monetary Relations, 1958–1971* (Chapel Hill: University of North Carolina Press, 2004); Francis J. Gavin, "Ideas,

Power, and the Politics of America's International Monetary Policy during the 1960s," in Jonathan Kirshner, ed., *Monetary Orders: Ambiguous Economics, Ubiquitous Politics* (Ithaca, N.Y.: Cornell University Press, 2002), pp. 195–217; and Hubert Zimmermann, *Money and Security: Troops, Monetary Policy, and West Germany's Relations with the United States and Britain, 1950–1971* (Cambridge, UK: Cambridge University Press, 2002).

18. Joseph Nye, "The Changing Nature of World Power," *Political Science Quarterly*, Vol. 105, No. 2 (Summer 1990), p. 181.

19. For discussions of the wider social structures that have grown up around the Atlantic security alliance, see G. John Ikenberry, "Democracy, Institutions, and American Restraint," in Ikenberry, ed., *America Unrivaled: The Future of the Balance of Power* (Ithaca, N.Y.: Cornell University Press, 2002), pp. 213–238, and Thomas Risse, "U.S. Power in a Liberal Security Community," in ibid., pp. 260–283.

20. See Thomas Risse-Kappen, *Cooperation among Democracies: The European Influence on U.S. Foreign Policy* (Princeton, N.J.: Princeton University Press, 1997), and Daniel Deudney and G. John Ikenberry, "The Nature and Sources of Liberal International Order," *Review of International Studies*, Vol. 25, No. 2 (April 1999), pp. 179–196.

21. See, for example, Carla Norrlof, *America's Global Advantage: US Hegemony and International Cooperation* (Cambridge, UK: Cambridge University Press, 2010), p. 16, and Richard Maas, "Correspondence: The Profitability of Primacy," *International Security*, Vol. 38, No. 4 (Spring 2014), p. 191. Some analysts overstate the significance of this mission and presume that maintaining key transportation corridors is necessary to prevent an outright disruption of globalization, but Gholz and Press are correct that this is not the case; see Gholz and Press, "Protecting 'The Prize,'" p. 462. Ultimately, maintaining the openness of sea lanes and other shipping corridors is important principally for ensuring that transportation costs remain as low as possible.

22. See the discussion of basing access in chapters 5 and 6.

23. This essentially is the nonsecurity analogue of the argument one of us forwarded in 1999 regarding the security realm: that other states refrain from challenging America's strongly entrenched position because they wish to avoid the focused enmity of the United States; see William C. Wohlforth, "The Stability of a Unipolar World," *International Security*, Vol. 24, No. 1 (Summer 1999), pp. 5–41.

24. See the discussion in Stephen Brooks, "Can We Identify a Benevolent Hegemon?" *Cambridge Review of International Affairs*, Vol. 25, No. 1 (2012), pp. 27–38. Duncan Snidal and Christopher Layne provide two helpful discussions of this distinction in, respectively, the international political economy and security studies literatures; see Snidal, "Limits of Hegemonic Stability Theory," and Christopher

Layne, "The Unipolar Illusion Revisited: The Coming End of the United States' Unipolar Moment," *International Security*, Volume 31, No. 2 (Fall 2006), pp. 7–41. It should be noted that "benign hegemon" is often used as a substitute term for "benevolent hegemon"; the terms are interchangeable, and the latter is employed here simply because it is more firmly established within the international political economy literature. In turn, some scholars use the term "coercive hegemon" rather than "predatory hegemon." While there is not a meaningful difference between how these two terms are employed in the literature, we will use the latter term, since the former carries a connotation of using military force that the latter clearly does not. The use of military force by the hegemon is not the only issue at stake, nor should it be built into the definition.

25. Gilpin, *The Political Economy of International Relations*, p. 73.

26. Robert Gilpin, *U.S. Power and the Multinational Corporation* (New York: Basic Books, 1975); Gilpin, *War and Change in World Politics* (Cambridge, UK: Cambridge University Press, 1981); and Gilpin, *The Political Economy of International Relations*, especially pp. 78, 89.

27. Michael Mastanduno, "System Maker and Privilege Taker: US Power and the International Political Economy," in G. John Ikenberry, Michael Mastanduno, and William C. Wohlforth, eds., *International Relations Theory and the Consequences of Unipolarity* (Cambridge, UK: Cambridge University Press, 2011), pp. 140–177.

28. Mastanduno, "System Maker and Privilege Taker," p. 159.

29. Ibid., pp. 144, 165.

30. Norrlof, *America's Global Advantage*. It should be noted that these three points we discuss here are just some of the arguments that Norrlof advances in her book for why the United States gains significant economic benefits from its hegemonic role. The most notable argument that she advances that we do not highlight in this chapter is that US military hegemony allows it to secure higher foreign financial inflows than it would otherwise be able to. We view the evidence she presents on this score as merely suggestive. In a later correspondence with Daniel Drezner (who criticized her evidence on this point), Norrlof herself underscores the need to examine this issue in greater depth and notes that she will do so in future research; see Carla Norrlof, "Correspondence: The Profitability of Primacy," *International Security*, Vol. 38, No. 4 (Spring 2014), p. 197.

31. Norrlof, *America's Global Advantage*, pp. xi, 5.

32. Ibid., pp. 98–99.

33. Ibid., p. 3.

34. See Brooks, Ikenberry, and Wohlforth, "Don't Come Home, America," pp. 44–45.

35. See, for example, Keohane, *After Hegemony*, p. 45.

36. See, for example, Robert O. Keohane, "Multilateralism: An Agenda for Research," *International Journal*, Vol. 45, No. 4 (Autumn 1990), pp. 731–764.

37. This paragraph draws on material from pp. 46–50 of Brooks, Wohlforth, and Ikenberry, "Don't Come Home, America."

38. See, for example, Robert O. Keohane, *Power and Governance in a Partially Globalized World* (New York: Routledge, 2002), and Bruce Jones, Carlos Pascual, and Stephen John Stedman, *Power and Responsibility: Building International Order in an Era of Transnational Threats* (Washington, D.C.: Brookings Institution Press, 2010).

39. For good accounts of the ways in which NATO has established habits and capacities for cooperation that extend beyond traditional European and Atlantic defense into nontraditional security and other areas, see Daniel Hamilton, Charles Barry, Hans Binnendijk, Stephen Flanagan, Julianne Smith, and James Townsend, *Alliance Reborn: An Atlantic Compact for the 21st Century* (Washington, D.C.: Washington NATO Project, 2009), and Peter Barschdorff, *Facilitating Transatlantic Cooperation after the Cold War* (Hamburg: LIT Verlag, 2001).

40. United Nations, *A More Secure World: Our Shared Responsibility*, Report of the Secretary-General's High-Level Panel on Threats, Challenges and Change (New York: United Nations, 2004).

41. Keohane, *After Hegemony*.

42. The next two paragraphs draw extensively from ch. 5 of Brooks and Wohlforth, *World Out of Balance*.

43. Charles Lipson, "Why Are Some International Agreements Informal?" *International Organization*, Vol. 45, No. 4 (Autumn 1991), p. 511.

44. See Lisa L. Martin, "Multilateral Organizations after the U.S.-Iraq War," in Irwin Abrams and Gungwu Wang, eds., *The Iraq War and its Consequences: Thoughts of Nobel Laureates and Eminent Scholars* (Singapore: World Scientific Publishing Company, 2003).

45. See Brooks and Wohlforth, *World Out of Balance*, 158–169; see also George W. Downs and Michael A. Jones, "Reputation, Compliance, and International Law," *The Journal of Legal Studies*, Vol. 31, No. S1 (January 2002), pp. S95–S114.

46. As one example, there is no evidence that the intense disagreement over Iraq between the United States and important members of the EU, especially France and Germany, had any spillover effect in terms of harming the US ability to garner cooperation in WTO negotiations; see Brooks and Wohlforth, *World Out of Balance*, 164.

47. The next three paragraphs draw extensively from ch. 6 of Brooks and Wohlforth, *World Out of Balance*.

48. The best compact constructivist treatment of legitimacy is Ian Hurd, "Legitimacy and Authority in International Politics," *International Organization*, Vol. 53 No. 2 (Spring 1999), pp. 379–408.

49. Bruce Cronin, "The Paradox of Hegemony: America's Ambiguous Relationship with the United Nations," *European Journal of International Relations*, Vol. 7, No. 1 (March 2001), pp. 103–130; Christian Reus-Smit, *American Power and World*

Order (Cambridge, UK: Polity Press, 2004); Richard Ned Lebow, *The Tragic Vision of Politics: Ethics, Interests, and Orders* (Cambridge, UK: Cambridge University Press, 2003).

50. As Bruce Cronin explains, "If the hegemon fails to act within the boundaries established by its role, the credibility of the institutions it helped establish weakens. . . . When these organizations are undermined, the legitimacy of the international order is threatened. If this persists over time, the hegemonic order declines." Cronin, "The Paradox of Hegemony," p. 113.

51. See Brooks and Wohlforth, *World Out of Balance*, pp. 179–193.

CHAPTER 10

1. G. John Ikenberry, *After Victory: Institutions, Strategic Restraint, and the Rebuilding of Order after Major Wars* (Princeton, N.J.: Princeton University Press, 2001); Ikenberry, *Liberal Leviathan: The Origins, Crisis, and Transformation of the American World Order* (Princeton, N.J.: Princeton University Press, 2011); Ikenberry, "Is American Multilateralism in Decline?" *Perspectives on Politics*, Vol. 1 (2003), pp. 533–550; Ikenberry, "State Power and the Institutional Bargain: America's Ambivalent Economic and Security Multilateralism," in Rosemary Foot, S. Neil MacFarlane, and Michael Mastanduno, eds., *US Hegemony and International Organizations: The United States and Multilateral Institutions* (New York: Oxford University Press: 2003), pp. 49–70; Robert Keohane, *Power and Governance in a Partially Globalized World* (London: Routledge, 2002); Keohane, "Hegemony and After: Knowns and Unknowns in the Debate over Decline," *Foreign Affairs*, Vol. 91 (2012), pp. 114–118; Erik Voeten, "Outside Options and the Logic of Security Council Action," *American Political Science Review*, Vol. 95 (2001), pp. 845–858; Voeten, "The Political Origins of the Legitimacy of the United Nations Security Council," *International Organization*, Vol. 59 (2005), pp. 527–557; David Lake, "Leadership, Hegemony, and the International Economy: Naked Emperor or Tattered Monarch with Potential?" *International Studies Quarterly*, Vol. 37 (1993), pp. 459–489; Lake, *Entangling Relations: American Foreign Policy in Its Century* (Princeton, N.J.: Princeton University Press, 1999); Lake, "Making America Safe for the World: Multilateralism and the Rehabilitation of U.S. Authority," *Global Governance*, Vol. 16 (2010), pp. 471–484. For our own previous discussion of this issue, see Stephen Brooks and William Wohlforth, *World Out of Balance: International Relations and the Challenge of American Primacy* (Princeton, N.J.: Princeton University Press), ch. 5.

2. Daniel W. Drezner, *The System Worked: How the World Stopped Another Great Depression* (New York: Oxford University Press, 2014), pp. 119–201.

3. See, for example, Kenneth Scheve and Matthew Slaughter, "A New Deal for Globalization," *Foreign Affairs*, Vol. 86, No. 4 (May/June 2007), pp. 34–47.

4. Chris Rasmussen and Jeffrey Hall, *Jobs Supported by State Exports 2013* (Washington, D.C.: Department of Commerce, International Trade Administration, 2014), available at: http://www.trade.gov/mas/ian/build/groups/public/@tg_ian/documents/webcontent/tg_ian_005380.pdf.

5. Jeremy Quittner, "How U.S. Businesses Benefit When Exports Flourish," *Inc.*, September 3, 2014, available at: http://www.inc.com/jeremy-quittner/department-of-commerce-study-links-export-growth-to-jobs.html.

6. Drezner, *The System Worked*, pp. 124, 118.

7. Ibid., p. 119.

8. William Winecoff, "Structural Power and the Global Financial Crisis: A Network Approach," *Business and Politics*, Vol. 17, No. 3 (2015), p. 519.

9. Thomas Oatley, W. Kindred Winecoff, Andrew Pennock, and Sarah Bauerle Danzman, "The Political Economy of Global Finance: A Network Model," *Perspectives on Politics*, Vol. 11, No. 1 (March 2013), p. 148.

10. For a good overview of the general costs and benefits associated with exposure to global finance, see Geoffrey Garrett, "The Causes of Globalization," *Comparative Political Studies*, Vol. 33, No. 6/7 (August/September 2000), pp. 941–991.

11. Robert Gilpin, *U.S. Power and the Multinational Corporation* (New York: Basic Books, 1975).

12. United Nations Conference on Trade and Development, *World Investment Report 2014* (United Nations, 2014), Geneva, Switzerland, available at: http://unctad.org/en/pages/DIAE/World%20Investment%20Report/Annex-Tables.aspx.

13. Department of Commerce and the President's Council of Economic Advisors, *Foreign Direct Investment in the United States* (Washington, D.C.: White House, 2013), available at http://www.whitehouse.gov/sites/default/files/2013fdi_report_-_final_for_web.pdf.

14. For a more detailed discussion of the points raised in this paragraph, see Stephen Brooks, *Producing Security: Multinational Corporations, Globalization, and the Changing Calculus of Conflict* (Princeton, N.J.: Princeton University Press, 2005), ch. 2.

15. See, for example, Edward S. Steinfeld, *Playing our Game: Why China's Rise Doesn't Threaten the West* (New York, Oxford University Press, 2012), and Organisation for Economic Co-operation and Development, *China in Focus: Lessons and Challenges* (Paris: Organisation for Economic Co-operation and Development, 2012), ch. 5.

16. Carla Norrlof, *America's Global Advantage: US Hegemony and International Cooperation* (Cambridge, UK: Cambridge University Press, 2010), p. 90.

17. Quinlan and Chandler report that by 1998 "the exports of U.S. affiliates totaled $623 billion. That figure not only matched the total value of U.S. goods exports but also easily surpassed the export levels of Germany and Japan." Joseph P. Quinlan and Marc Chandler, "The U.S. Trade Deficit: A Dangerous Obsession," *Foreign Affairs*, Vol. 80, No. 3, May/June 2001, p. 90.

18. Norrlof, *America's Global Advantage*, p. 92.

19. Michael Mastanduno, "System Maker and Privilege Taker: US Power and the International Political Economy," in G. John Ikenberry, Michael Mastanduno, and William C. Wohlforth, eds., *International Relations Theory and the Consequences of Unipolarity* (Cambridge, UK: Cambridge University Press, 2011), p. 148.

20. Recent historical analyses noting this dynamic include Francis J. Gavin, *Gold, Dollars, and Power: The Politics of International Monetary Relations, 1958–1971* (Chapel Hill, N.C.: Duke University Press, 2004); Gavin, "Ideas, Power, and the Politics of America's International Monetary Policy during the 1960s," in Jonathan Kirshner, ed., *Monetary Orders* (Ithaca, N.Y.: Cornell University Press, 2002), pp. 195–217; Hubert Zimmermann, *Money and Security: Troops, Monetary Policy, and West Germany's Relations with the United States and Britain, 1950–1971* (Cambridge, UK: Cambridge University Press, 2002); and Harold James, "The Enduring International Preeminence of the Dollar," in Eric Helleiner and Jonathan Kirshner, eds., *The Future of the Dollar* (Ithaca, N.Y.: Cornell University Press, 2009), pp. 24–44. Prominent discussions by political scientists include Mastanduno, "System Maker and Privilege Taker"; Robert O. Keohane, *After Hegemony: Cooperation and Discord in the World Political Economy* (Princeton, N.J.: Princeton University Press, 1984); G. John Ikenberry, *Liberal Leviathan: The Origins, Crisis, and Transformation of the American World Order* (Princeton, N.J.: Princeton University Press, 2011); and Norrlof, *America's Global Advantage*.

21. Keshav Poddar, "The Price of Fear: Geopolitical Favoritism in U.S. Security Alliances," Honors Thesis, Dartmouth College, 2014, pp. 105–106. See also Thomas Oatley and Jason Yackee, "American Interests and IMF Lending," *International Politics*, Vol. 41 (September 2004), pp. 415–429, who find that the IMF is particularly responsive to American economic interests.

22. C. Randall Henning, *U.S. Interests and the International Monetary Fund*, Peterson Institute for International Economics (PIIE), No. PB09-12 (Washington, D.C.: PIIE, 2009), p. 5.

23. Randall Stone, "The Scope of IMF Conditionality," *International Organization*, Vol. 62, No. 4 (October 2008), p. 594.

24. Norrlof, *America's Global Advantage*, p. 2. As Norrlof reviews, seignorage
    refers to the privilege of creating money, coining, or printing money; or, today, increasing credit on the Federal Reserve's balance sheet, and the profit made by creating money. There are two components to seignorage. On the one hand, the United States receives an interest free loan when people all over the world hold dollars. . . . The dollars abroad are nothing but paper IOUs—i.e. claims on the United States—but, as long as they stay abroad, nothing is being claimed, and the funds can be recycled through the banking sector. The second aspect of seignorage is related to the first. The more dollars in circulation, the more the United States is able to borrow interest-free from foreigners. (pp. 119–120)

For further discussion of the economic benefits of being the primary international currency, see Benjamin Cohen, *Organizing the World's Money: The Political Economy of International Monetary Relations* (New York: Basic Books, 1977); Cohen, "Global Currency Rivalry: Can the Euro Ever Challenge the Dollar?" *Journal of Common Market Studies*, Vol. 41, No. 4 (2003), pp. 575–595; Kathleen McNamara, "A Rivalry in the Making? The Euro and International Monetary Power," *Review of International Political Economy*, Vol. 15, No. 3 (August 2008), pp. 439–459; Carla Norrlof, "Key Currency Competition," *Cooperation and Conflict*, Vol. 44, No. 4 (Winter 2009), pp. 1–23; Norrlof, "Dollar Hegemony: A Power Analysis," *Review of International Political Economy*, Vol. 21, No. 5 (2014), pp. 1042–1070; Jonathan Kirshner, "Dollar Primacy and American Power: What's At Stake?" *Review of International Political Economy*, Vol. 15, No. 3 (August 2008), pp. 418–438; and Eric Helleiner, "Political Determinants of International Currencies: What Future for the US Dollar?" *Review of International Political Economy*, Vol. 15, No. (2008), pp. 352–376.

25. James, "The Enduring International Preeminence of the Dollar," p. 29.
26. Eric Helleiner and Jonathan Kirshner, "Summing Up and Looking Ahead," in Helleiner and Kirshner, *The Future of the Dollar*, p. 219. The most extensive discussion of the geopolitical approach is Norrlof, *America's Global Advantage*; see also the analysis in Helleiner, "Political Determinants of International Currencies: What Future for the US Dollar?"; Cohen, *Organizing the World's Money*; C. Fred Bergsten, *The Dilemmas of the Dollar* (New York: New York University Press); and Robert Mundell, "What the Euro Means for the Dollar and the International Monetary System," *Atlantic Economic Journal*, Vol. 26, No. 3 (1998), pp. 227–237.
27. McNamara, "A Rivalry in the Making?" pp. 446–447.
28. A helpful discussion of this point is Carla Norrlof, "Correspondence: The Profitability of Primacy," *International Security*, Vol. 38, No. 4 (Spring 2014), p. 199.
29. To be clear, the United States is not against regional integration; it is fine with so-called open regionalism that promotes regional economic linkages but does not undermine US access to markets or the current multilateral economic order and its associated institutions. In the post–Cold War period, the proposed Asian regional integration effort the United States saw as most concerning as a threat was the East Asian Economic Caucus (EAEC, also sometimes known as the East Asian Economic Group—or EAEG), which was initiated by President Mahathir Mohammed of Malaysia in 1990. The EAEC aimed to establish a regional free trade agreement including the ASEAN countries (Thailand, Brunei, Malaysia, Philippines, Singapore, and Indonesia) as well as China, South Korea, and Japan. American officials not only saw the EAEC as a threat to American access to these markets but also felt that its success would undermine the prospects for the completion of the Uruguay Round of global trade negotiations. As Poddar ("The Price

of Fear," p. 123) recounts, over the years when the EAEC was actively being considered, various American diplomats were sent to Asia to undermine the proposal,
and they directly employed US security leverage as part of their effort to do so.
Most notable in this regard is when Secretary of State James Baker underscored
in a 1991 meeting with the foreign minister of South Korea that "Malaysia didn't
spill blood for this country, but we did." A participant in the meeting recounts
that after hearing this reproach, the South Korean minister told Baker that his
government would agree to US demands and would oppose the EAEG. Japan also
came to strongly oppose the EAEG in response to continued US diplomatic pressure, which included a public warning from then assistant secretary of defense
Joseph Nye that if the EAEC was adopted, "we would probably withdraw our
security presence." Opposition from Japan and South Korea greatly undermined
the EAEC, and the proposal ultimately fell by the wayside by the mid-1990s.

30. Daisuke Igarashi, "Fred Bergsten: U.S., Japan Made Big Mistake Opposing AIIB,"
Asahi Shimbun, April 7, 2015, available at: http://ajw.asahi.com/article/views/
opinion/AJ201504070098; Jing Ma, "An Influential Voice Slams U.S. Handling
of New China-Led Infrastructure Bank," *Wall Street Journal China Real Time
Report*, March 19, 2015, available at: http://blogs.wsj.com/chinarealtime/2015/
03/19/an-influential-voice-slams-u-s-handling-of-new-china-led-infrastructure-
bank/; Dong Leshuo and Lia Zhu, "US 'Miscalculated' on AIIB: Albright,"
ChinaDaily, April 1, 2015, available at: http://usa.chinadaily.com.cn/world/
2015-04/01/content_19972460.htm; Joseph Nye, "The American Century Will
Survive the Rise of China," *Financial Times*, March 25, 2015, available at: http://
belfercenter.ksg.harvard.edu/publication/25169/american_century_will_sur-
vive_the_rise_of_china.html.

31. Igarashi, "Fred Bergsten: U.S., Japan Made Big Mistake Opposing AIIB."

32. For a further discussion of this point, see Stephen Brooks and William Wohlforth,
"The Once and Future Superpower: Why China Won't Overtake the United
States," *Foreign Affairs*, Vol. 95, No. 3 (May/June 2016), pp. 100-101.

33. C. Fred Bergsten, "The Trans-Pacific Partnership and Japan," *Nikkei Asian
Review*, November 27, 2015, available at: http://asia.nikkei.com/Viewpoints/
Viewpoints/The-Trans-Pacific-Partnership-and-Japan.

34. These interviews are discussed in Stephen Brooks, G. John Ikenberry, and William
Wohlforth, "Don't Come Home, America: The Case Against Retrenchment,"
International Security, Vol. 37, No. 3 (Winter 2012/13), pp. 44–45.

35. We thank Michael Mastanduno for a helpful conversation on this point.

36. Norrlof, *America's Global Advantage*, 29.

37. Analysts who argue that the dollar may decline soon include Miguel Otero-
Iglesias and Federico Steinberg, "Is the Dollar Becoming a Negotiated
Currency? Evidence from the Emerging Markets," *New Political Economy*, Vol.
18, No. 3 (2013), pp. 309–336; Jonathan Kirshner, *American Power after the
Financial Crisis* (Ithaca: Cornell University Press, 2014); and Menzie Chinn

and Jeffrey Frankel, "The Euro May over the Next 15 Years Surpass the Dollar as the Leading International Currency," NBER Working Paper No. 13909, April 2008. Analysts who argue that the dollar is not in decline include Benjamin Cohen and Tabitha Benney, "What Does the International Currency System Really Look Like?" *Review of International Political Economy*, forthcoming; Eric Helleiner, *The Status Quo Crisis: Global Financial Governance After the 2014 Meltdown* (New York: Oxford University Press, 2014); and Norrlof, "Dollar Hegemony."

38. James, "The Enduring International Preeminence of the Dollar," p. 44.

39. Helleiner and Kirshner, *The Future of the Dollar*, p. 17; see also Norrlof, *America's Global Advantage*, especially p. 248.

40. See the interviews discussed in Brooks, Ikenberry, and Wohlforth, "Don't Come Home, America."

41. Brooks, Ikenberry, and Wohlforth, "Don't Come Home, America," pp. 42–45.

42. Daniel Drezner, "Military Primacy Doesn't Pay (Nearly as Much as You Think)," *International Security*, Vol. 38, No. 1 (Summer 2013), p. 65.

43. Drezner is up front that his conclusions about this case are "preliminary" and that "greater and deeper dives into the data must be made"; see Drezner, "Military Primacy Doesn't Pay," p. 78.

44. Focusing exclusively on tariff rates, as Drezner did, is inadequate, since nontariff barriers are the key relevant form of Korean protectionism; see the analysis in Yvan Decreux, Chris Milner, and Nicolas Peridy, *The Economic Impact of the Free Trade Agreement (FTA) between the European Union and Korea*, Report for the European Commission (Brussels: European Commission, May 2010).

45. Poddar, "The Price of Fear," p. 41.

46. These differing terms include: (1) government contracts (KORUS gives US firms an ability to bid on a much wider range of government contracts than is specified in KOREU [South Korean-European Union Free Trade Agreement]); (2) FDI (KORUS includes a separate chapter on FDI which creates an investor-state dispute settlement system, whereas KOREU does not contain this FDI chapter); (3) labor and environmental rules (KORUS provides for labor and environmental disputes to be arbitrated through a dispute settlement system, whereas KOREU contains no such provision); (4) services (KORUS contains a much stronger "most favored nation" clause regarding services than KOREU and also specifies that any new kind of service that emerges in the future will automatically be covered by the agreement, whereas KOREU only promotes liberalization in those services that are explicitly specified in the agreement); and (5) the automobile sector (KORUS grants mutual recognition to US safety standards, contains specific provisions regarding Korea's vehicle taxation system that are not included in KOREU, includes a "snapback" safeguard tariff provision that is not included in KOREU, gives US automakers relatively more lenient treatment on emissions standards, and contains a much more favorable tariff schedule in which the United States is allowed

to maintain its tariff on passenger cars and trucks longer than is the case within KOREU); see Poddar, "The Price of Fear," pp. 43–52.

47. Kozo Kiyota and Robert M. Stern, *Economic Effects of a Korea-U.S. Free Trade Agreement*, Discussion Paper No. 557, Research Seminar in International Economics, Gerald R. Ford School of Public Policy, University of Michigan (Washington, D.C.: The Korea Economic Institute of America, 2007), p. 40.

48. Poddar, "The Price of Fear," pp. 54–55.

49. Ibid., p. 58.

50. See the discussion in Joseph S. Nye Jr., "The Changing Nature of World Power," *Political Science Quarterly*, Vol. 105, No. 2 (Summer 1990), p. 181.

51. Nye as quoted in Anthony Rowley, "US Warns against Its Exclusion from Proposed EAEC," *Business Times*, September 5, 1995

52. For a further discussion of this point, see Brooks and Wohlforth, "The Once and Future Superpower," pp. 99–100.

53. Mastanduno, "System Maker and Privilege Taker," p. 141.

54. See David E. Spiro, *The Hidden Hand of American Hegemony: Petrodollar Recycling and International Markets* (Ithaca, N.Y.: Cornell University Press, 1999), especially pp. 146–149 and 87–93.

55. Spiro, *Hidden Hand of American Hegemony*, p. 148.

56. Gavin, "Ideas, Power, and the Politics of America's International Monetary Policy during the 1960s," especially pp. 196–197, 205, 207, 209, and 215, and Gavin, *Gold, Dollars, and Power*, especially pp. 6, 12, 30–31, 113, 162, 165–166. See also Zimmermann, *Money and Security*, especially pp. 103, 107, 140, and 227.

57. See Keohane, "Hegemony and After," and Brooks, Wohlforth, and Ikenberry, "Don't Come Home, America," pp. 47–48.

58. Eugene Gholz and Daryl G. Press, "The Effects of Wars on Neutral Countries: Why It Doesn't Pay to Preserve the Peace," *Security Studies*, Vol. 10, No. 4 (Summer 2001), pp. 1–57.

59. Ibid., p. 41.

60. Ibid., pp. 12–14.

61. See the discussion in Brooks, *Producing Security*, especially pp. 16–19.

62. Brooks, *Producing Security*, p. 17.

63. Stephen J. Kobrin, "Technological Determinism, Globalization, and the Multinational Firm," unpublished manuscript, Wharton School, University of Pennsylvania, 2003, pp. 7, 11.

64. Keohane, *After Hegemony*, p. 139.

65. Michael Levi, for example, notes: "Since oil prices are set on world markets, we would not be immune from volatility elsewhere—unless the United States decided to wall itself off, an extreme measure that could inflict severe pain on the nation's allies. The United States economy is perpetually at risk because spikes in oil prices can quickly strip consumers of cash at the gas pump. This sudden 'tax' can knock the economy on its back, regardless of where we buy oil." Levi, "The

False Promise of Energy Independence," *New York Times*, December 21, 2012, available at: http://www.nytimes.com/2012/12/21/opinion/the-false-promise-of-energy-independence.html?_r=0.

66. Eugene Gholz and Daryl G. Press, "Protecting 'The Prize': Oil and the U.S. National Interest," *Security Studies*, Vol. 19, No. 3 (August 2010), pp. 453–485

67. Ibid., p. 467.

68. In this respect, economist William Nordhaus concludes in his 2002 analysis: "Concerns about oil markets in the context of war in the Middle East are not idle. Every recession in the last three decades has been associated directly or indirectly with turmoil in oil markets, terrorism, or war. Both of the oil price shocks of the 1970s led to sharp recessions, while the First Persian Gulf War induced a sharp spike in oil prices that contributed to the 1990 recession." William Nordhaus, "The Economic Consequences of a War with Iraq," National Bureau of Economic Research Working Paper No. 9361, p. 26. Other economists who critique this perspective do not doubt the overall relationship, just its strength. In this regard, Barsky and Kilian conclude their analysis by noting:

> It is commonly believed that there is a close link from political events in the Middle East to changes in the price of oil, and in turn from oil price changes to macroeconomic performance in the United States. As to the first belief, we stressed that exogenous political events in the Middle East are but one of several factors driving oil prices. . . . As to the second belief, we showed that the timing of oil price increases and recessions is consistent with the notion that oil price shocks may contribute to recessions without necessarily being pivotal.

Robert Barsky and Lutz Kilian, "Oil and the Macroeconomy since the 1970s," National Bureau of Economic Research Working Paper No. 10885, p. 23.

69. Gholz and Press do recognize the significance of panic and fear about oil prices in the final sentences of their article. Gholz and Press, "Protecting 'The Prize,'" p. 485.

70. Ibid., pp. 476, 481.

Index